Catherine Charlotte Jackson

The Last of the Valois and Accession of Henry of Navarre - 1559-1589

Vol. I

Catherine Charlotte Jackson

The Last of the Valois and Accession of Henry of Navarre - 1559-1589
Vol. I

ISBN/EAN: 9783337110062

Printed in Europe, USA, Canada, Australia, Japan

Cover: Foto ©ninafisch / pixelio.de

More available books at **www.hansebooks.com**

THE LAST OF THE VALOIS,

AND

ACCESSION OF HENRY OF NAVARRE.

1559—1589.

BY

CATHERINE CHARLOTTE, LADY JACKSON,
AUTHOR OF
'OLD PARIS,' 'THE OLD REGIME,' 'COURT OF LOUIS XVI.,' 'COURT
OF THE TUILERIES,' 'COURT OF FRANCE IN THE 16TH
CENTURY,' ETC.

IN TWO VOLUMES.

VOL. I.

LONDON:
RICHARD BENTLEY AND SON,
Publishers in Ordinary to Her Majesty the Queen.
1888.
[*All Rights Reserved.*]

CONTENTS OF VOL. I.

CHAPTER I.

PAGE

INTRODUCTORY - - - - - 1

CHAPTER II.

Accession of Francis II.—The King's 'Uncles.'—Catherine and Diana.—The Keys of the King's Cabinet and the Crown Jewels.—Exchange of Chaumont for Chenonceaux.—Francis II. and Queen Mary.—The 'New Opinions.'—Antony, King of Navarre, and Louis de Condé.—Antony's Journey to Paris.—The Flying Squadron.—Antony threatens to head the 'Malcontents' - - - - - - 5

CHAPTER III.

Coronation Festivities.—Tearful Adieux.—The Bridal Cortége.—Terrible Weather and Terrible Roads.—Philip's Perils by Sea.—His Grand Auto-da-fé.—Jeanne d'Albret and the Bridal Party.—The Ceremony at Roncevaux.—Grand Reception at Madrid.—A Sudden Friendship - - - - 32

CHAPTER IV.

The King's Mysterious Malady.—The 'Wise Men:' their Enchantments.—Magic Scenes at Chaumont.—Ruggieri's Predictions.—Religious Persecution.—Anne Dubourg.—Appeal to the Young King.—The Gracious Concession.—The 'Malcontents.'—The Scotch Reformers: their Example followed - - - 45

CHAPTER V.

The Amboise Conspiracy.—Barry de La Renaudie.—The Six Brothers of the House of Guise.—Antony, King of Navarre.—The Plot revealed.—Condé joins the Court at Amboise.—Nemours' Errand of Mercy.—La Renaudie's Encounter in the Forest of Château-Rénault. — Nemours succeeds in his Mission.—Treachery.—Royal Amusements.—Condé's Challenge to Single Combat - - - - - 59

CHAPTER VI.

The Court leave Amboise.—De L'Hôpital succeeds to the Chancellorship. — The Inquisition opposed by him.—Death of Marie de Guise.—Court Gaieties and Court Intrigues.—The Plan of the Tuileries.—Cellini invited by Catherine to Paris.—Much flattered, but declines to leave Florence.—The Admiral at Fontainebleau.—States-General convoked - - - 87

CHAPTER VII.

The Guises and the Protestant Chiefs.—Arrest and Trial of Condé.—Proposed Assassination of King Antony.—Plot a Failure.—Condé condemned to Death.—Illness of Francis II.—His Death, December 5th, 1560.—Queen-Mother's Arrangement with Antony.—Condé Free.—The Chancellor de L'Hôpital - - 109

CHAPTER VIII.

Accession of Charles IX.—Catherine his Guardian with the Power of Regent.—King of Navarre Lieutenant-General.—Cardinal de Lorraine leaves for Rheims.—States-General abolish many Abuses.—The Parliament oppose the Reforms.—Extinction of Debts of the Crown.—States-General adjourn.—Condé's Innocence publicly proclaimed - - - - - 134

CHAPTER IX.

Catherine's Crooked Policy.—Her 'Flying Squadron.'—Mary Stuart's Mourning.—Sir Nicholas Throckmorton's Letters.—Mary in Lorraine.—Her Brother, the Bishop, and other Advisers.—Her Departure.—Charles's Deep Impressions.—Damville, Brantôme and others accompany her.—Arrival in Scotland.—The Nobles sympathize - - - - - 148

CHAPTER X.

Condé's Return to Court.—Antony roused to Action.—The States of Pontoise.—Colloquy of Poissy.—The Calvinistic Minister, Théodore de Bèze.—Catherine's Letter to Pius IV.—Consternation at the Vatican.—The Legate and the General of the Jesuits.—Edict of Tolerance, January, 1562 - - - - 163

CHAPTER XI.

The Cardinal Ferrara.—Antony's Conversion.—His promised Rewards.—His Treatment of Jeanne d'Albret.—Her Heart henceforth closed to Love.—Guise urged to return to Paris.—Massacre of Vassy.—Catherine and Charles at Monceaux.—Court flying from Château to Château.—Guise enters Paris in great State.—Antony and De Bèze - - - 181

CHAPTER XII.

Catherine perplexed.—Massacre of Sens.—Frightful Retaliation.—Churches sacked.—The Admiral's Wife.—Attack on Rouen.—Antony wounded.—Jeanne d'Albret.—Her Anxiety respecting her Son.—Returns to her own Dominions - - - - 197

CHAPTER XIII.

Battle of Dreux.—Montmorency and Condé Prisoners.—Guise's proposed Attack on Orléans.—His Assassination.—The Peace of Amboise.—Condé and the Flying Squadron.—Princess of Condé dies of Grief.—Mademoiselle de Limeuil.—The Maréchale Saint-André.—Catherine's Reign now begins - - - 220

CHAPTER XIV.

Coligny accused of assassinating Guise.—Siege and Capitulation of Havre.—A Royal Tour in the Provinces.—A Change of Tactics.—Catherine decides for the Catholic Cause.—The First Stone of the Tuileries.—Piety and Pleasure the Order of the Day.—The Queen of Spain at Bayonne.—Grand Festivities.—The Salmon and the Frogs.—Double Marriage proposed · - - - 240

CHAPTER XV.

The Court at Moulins.—The Reconciliation and 'Kiss of Peace.'—The New Year.—Horrors in the Netherlands.—Surprise and Arrest of Condé and Coligny projected.—Hasty Departure of the Court.—Charles in a Rage at flying before his Subjects.—A Long Ride; Charles Weary and Hungry.—Battle of Saint-Denis, November, 1567.—Death of Montmorency - 261

CHAPTER XVI.

Anjou Lieutenant-General.—Siege of Chartres.—Jean Casimer and the German troops. — Catherine's Treachery.—Warned by Tavannes. — Fording the Loire.—Jeanne d'Albret and her Son.—Odet de Châtillon and Elizabeth of England.—De L'Hôpital's Retirement.—Don Carlos and Elizabeth of France - 283

CHAPTER XVII.

Battle of Jarnac.—Death of Condé.—Anjou's Delight ; the Te Deum.—Henry of Navarre ; the Oath and the Medal.—Death of D'Andelot ; Poison suspected. —Fifty Thousand Crowns for Coligny, Dead or Alive. —Victory or Death ; Money or Battle.—Battle of Moncontour.—Coligny wounded.—Peace of Saint-Germain, 8th of August, 1570 - - - 304

CHAPTER XVIII.

Peace disapproved by Philip and Pius V.—Marguerite and Duc de Guise.—Anjou refuses to marry Queen Elizabeth.—Philip's Fourth Wife.—Charles marries Elizabeth of Austria.—Marguerite's Hand refused by Sebastian of Portugal.—The Bourbon Marriage resolved on.—Biron sent to Queen of Navarre to offer Marguerite to Henry.—Coligny invited by Charles IX. to Château de Blois.—Sets out from La Rochelle, against Advice of Friends - - - - 328

CHAPTER XIX.

Coligny's Reception at Blois by Charles IX.—Catherine jealous of Coligny's Influence.—Jeanne d'Albret visits the French Court.—Jeanne's Letter to her Son, Henry of Navarre.—The Court of Catherine de' Medici.—The Pope refuses the Dispensation for the Marriage.—Catherine's Proposals to Queen Elizabeth.—Warlike Preparations: Coligny's Plans.—The Court leaves Blois for Paris.—Death of Jeanne d'Albret.—Poison suspected - - - - - - 345

CHAPTER XX.

Marriage of Marguerite and Henry deferred.—Catherine seeks to thwart Coligny's Plans.—Charles flies from his Counsellors.—Catherine opposed to War with Spain.—Elizabeth again pressed to marry D'Alençon.—Arrival in Paris of Henry of Navarre.—The Betrothal.—The Dispensation dispensed with.—'Les Noces Vermeilles.'—Marguerite declares she never accepted Henry.—The Admiral's fatal Confidence in Charles IX.—A Saturnalia - - - - 363

CHAPTER XXI.

Anjou a Candidate for the Crown of Poland.—The Kiss of Peace twice given.—Attack on the Admiral instigated by the Guises.—The King in a Rage when informed of it.—Charles visits the Admiral, but cannot free himself from his Mother's and Brother's Company.—The Admiral's Private Advice to Charles.—The Massacre arranged.—A Band of Demons.—Charles long withstands his Infamous Mother's Arguments.—'Par la Mort Dieu! give your orders. Let them die! Let none remain to reproach me' - - - - - 377

CHAPTER XXII.

Arranging for the Success of the Massacre.—The Provost of Paris, Le Charron.—Catherine regardless even of her Daughter's Safety.—To the Guises the Honour of beginning the Massacre.—Alert before Dawn.—Guilty Consciences.—The Admiral's Death countermanded : Too late.—Already slain.—His Head sent to Catherine.—Charles like a Madman : 'Kill! kill !'—Catherine and her 'Filles d'Honneur.'—Rejoicings in Rome and Madrid.—Bells, Bonfires, Te Deums and Cannon.—Medals, Pictures and Compliments - - - - - - 391

LIST OF PORTRAITS.

VOL. I.

ANNE DE MONTMORENCY . . . *Frontispiece*
    (*Constable of France*)
CHARLES IX. . . . . . *To face p.* 134
THE CHANCELLOR DE L'HÔPITAL ,, ,, 298
CATHERINE DE' MEDICI . ,, ,, 366

THE LAST OF THE VALOIS.

CHAPTER I.

INTRODUCTORY.

THE death of Henry II. of France—suddenly struck down in the full force of manhood, and in the midst of the brilliant festivities following the Peace of Câteau-Cambrésis and the royal betrothals and marriages, pledges of its 'perpetual endurance'—was regarded by Protestants as a signal mark of Heaven's displeasure on the persecuting king. But while the infamous compact he had entered into with the cruel and fanatical Philip II. of Spain was especially deprecated by the Reformers, Frenchmen generally, whether Catholics or Protestants, who were animated by a spark of patriotism, bowed their heads with shame and deplored the political incapacity of the sovereign who had assented to a treaty so humiliating to France, both as regarded her interests and her honour.

For at the instance of a grasping and unscrupulous favourite (the Constable Anne de Montmorency) Henry had ceded to the Spaniard— whose military resources were at the time far inferior to his own, and his financial difficulties even more pressing—all the Italian conquests of the three preceding reigns. The Italian wars, now ended by the renunciation of all the claims of France on Italy, had continued for upwards of sixty years, causing immense expenditure to the State, and a prodigal waste of human life. But this cessation of foreign warfare was not to ensure the future tranquillity or prosperity of France. War more bitter, more bloody, more savage, was to succeed it, and lay waste and depopulate the country for the next thirty-six years—war whose object was not the conquest of territory, but the extermination of heresy.

For Philip and Henry had bound themselves to aid each other, by rigid and persistent persecution, in suppressing the efforts then making in France and elsewhere to secure liberty of conscience and freedom of religious worship.

An entire change soon ensued in the social relations of the French. Instead of going forth to fight their foes Frenchmen now took up arms to fight among themselves, religious fanaticism as a demon suddenly seeming to possess them. The torch of discord blazed forth; the burning pile was ignited; brothers, parents, children, friends and citizens, armed against each other. The wildest and most inordinate passions inflamed and perverted men's minds. The kingdom was given up a prey to various factions, to spies, assassins, executioners; and religious strife and civil war with their attendant horrors stalked through the land.

Thus did the brilliant sixteenth century, the era of the Renaissance, so resplendent at its dawn, become for the greater part of its latter half occupied with the combat of the spirit of progress against the spirit of death—that 'Demon of the South who would have stifled the independent nationalities under a counterfeit Roman Empire, and suppressed the growth of human intelligence under a counterfeit Gregory VII.' (H. Martin).

During the time that Henry lingered, hovering between life and death, the several parties in the State were actively intriguing, each to secure its succession to, or continuance in power. The monarch's death occurred on the eleventh day—10th July, 1559—after receiving the fatal wound at the tournament. It was the signal for the commencement of those intestine troubles and series of calamities which so long afflicted France under the last of the weak and dissolute Valois kings. Urged to crime by their iniquitous mother, Catherine de' Medici; preyed upon by a host of unworthy favourites—to support whose reckless extravagance the people were oppressed and brought to the very verge of desperation and poverty by heavy and unjust taxation—each of Catherine's unhappy sons pursued his short career of vice and bloodshed while revelling in the profligate pleasures of the depraved Court over which she as queen-mother presided.

CHAPTER II.

Accession of Francis II.—The King's 'Uncles.'—Catherine and Diana.—The Keys of the King's Cabinet and the Crown Jewels.—Exchange of Chaumont for Chenonceaux—Francis II. and Queen Mary.—The 'New Opinions.'—Antony, King of Navarre, and Louis de Condé.—Antony's Journey to Paris. — The Flying Squadron. — Antony threatens to head the ' Malcontents.'

THE unexpected event that placed Francis II.—a sickly youth in his sixteenth year—on the throne of France, also raised the Duc de Guise and his brother, the Cardinal de Lorraine, to that prominent and important position in the State which by their intrigues they had already prepared for themselves in bringing about the marriage of the dauphin with their niece Mary Stuart. This marriage, considered at the time the most favourable event that could happen for furthering the views of France on Scotland and England, and for the interests of the dauphin, became in a great measure the source of most of the troubles that followed the death of Henry, by giving a free course to the ambition of the Guises of Lorraine. That their ambitious views would be so speedily realized was, of course, far from being then foreseen. But Fortune was said to be always on the side of the Guises, playing into their hands by a timely clearing away of the obstacles that stood between them and the wealth and lucrative honours they so eagerly coveted, no matter what means must be employed to obtain them.*

Since the release from captivity and return to Court of Henry's bosom friend and 'good gossip' the Constable Montmorency, the influence of the Guises had greatly waned. Consequently they had held much aloof latterly from affairs of State, retiring to their estates in Lorraine to conceal their dissatisfaction, as well as to watch and wait for an opportunity of thwarting the views and schemes—no less rapacious than their own—of

* The Guises were six brothers, of whom the two eldest, François de Lorraine, Duc de Guise, and Charles de Lorraine, Cardinal and Archbishop of Rheims, played the most conspicuous part in the government of the kingdom. The other brothers were Claude de Lorraine, Duc d'Aumale, Louis de Lorraine, Cardinal de Guise, René de Lorraine, Marquis d'Elbeuf, and François, Grand Prieur de France, the recognised bastard of the House of Guise.

their formidable rival. To supplant him in the confidence and affections of his royal master it would have been vain to attempt. For so entirely was the weak monarch guided and governed by the constable, whose aim was to abase the Guises, as it was theirs to bring discredit on him, that Henry's opinions and decisions on all matters relating to the government of the kingdom were but the reflex of those of his arrogant and self-seeking favourite.

But the Guises, the Bourbons and Montmorencys were not the only aspirants for power who in that intriguing Court hastened to turn to account this critical moment of general confusion and alarm. The long-pent-up hatred of Catherine de' Medici towards the Duchesse de Valentinois— Diana of Poitiers—was now, she believed, to be fully gratified. The vengeance of the slighted wife should be wreaked on the hitherto powerful and haughty favourite, to whom for many years she had been compelled submissively to yield the honours due to herself as queen. Apparently she had borne this humiliation with much meekness, though her assumed air of subjection deceived but few—perhaps not even Diana herself. The time, however, had arrived for casting aside the mask that so long had partly concealed the true feeling and character of this worthy daughter of the Medici.

No sooner did the heavily long-drawn sigh in which Henry II. breathed his last tell to those around him that the spirit had departed, than the anxious, weeping wife, watching beside him for the supreme moment that was to give her power and freedom of action, rose from her kneeling posture. Already a change had come over her. Her usually subdued manners and forced gentleness of expression—little in harmony with her true feeling, as her large, dark, restless, flashing eyes often betrayed—had wholly vanished. She now stood proud and defiant, and, as some thought, seemed to have gained in stature, as, with a queen-like air she had hitherto never dared to assume, she summoned an attendant and despatched an authoritative command to the Duchesse de Valentinois.

Diana had remained in her apartment at the Palais des Tournelles in the hope that her royal lover, who had received what proved his death-blow while wearing her colours and displaying his prowess in her presence, might yet rally, so robust was his constitution. This was not, however, the general expectation. An order to leave the palace and retire to her estates had been sent to her some few days after the tournament. But on ascertaining that it came from Catherine, and that the king still lived, and had partly recovered consciousness, she replied that 'she obeyed no orders but those of her sovereign.' From hour to hour those in her confidence kept her informed of Henry's condition. On the eleventh morning, on being told that Henry was rapidly sinking and could not survive through the day, the duchess, already prepared for a sudden departure, at once left Les Tournelles and retired to her magnificent Château of Anet. Thus she avoided the mortification of being expelled from the palace by the 'banker's daughter' whom she had so long patronized, compelled her husband to tolerate and to refrain from sending back to her Florentine relatives, as both Henry and Francis I. had at times threatened they would do during the first ten years of her marriage.

In compliance with Catherine's demand for the restitution of the Crown jewels and the keys of the king's cabinet, Diana forwarded from Anet the magnificent rings she for years had been accustomed to wear. Also with the keys of the cabinet, some pearls, diamonds, and other jewels which, although the property of the Crown, were not reserved for the adornment of the queens of

France, but from the time of Francis I. had passed, together with the monarch's favour, from mistress to mistress. They were now deposited with Catherine, who, however, was not to have the satisfaction of appearing in them at Court. For the young king, acting on the suggestion of his 'uncles'—the Guises had arrogated to themselves that title—ordered their delivery to the brilliant young Queen Mary.

Francis II., although legally of age, was of course from youth and inexperience wholly incapable of taking any important part in the government of the kingdom. He was, however, so greatly elated at becoming King of France, that his joy entirely overcame any natural grief or regret he might have been supposed to feel or express at the death of his father, or the accident that produced it. His delight was indeed so excessive that the historian Mathieu says 'it had the singular effect of curing him of a fever he was suffering from when Henry died.' The new king's weakly constitution, and, as most contemporary writers assert, deficiency of intelligence, together with the ascendency acquired over him by the wiles of his lively, pleasure-loving, youthful wife, placed him wholly in the power of the Guises, by whom Mary herself was guided and governed.

By flattery they gained his confidence, and having conducted him and his queen from the Palais des Tournelles to the Louvre on the announcement of Henry's death, they there in full council induced him to announce that 'he desired to be assisted in governing his kingdom by the experience and counsels of his "uncles."' He had therefore committed the command of his armies to the Duc de Guise, and the charge of the finances to the Cardinal de Lorraine, Archbishop of Rheims.

The queen-mother soon perceived that she could not reckon on the obedience of a son so completely under the spell of his wife's fascinations. That wife was her own apt pupil. But Catherine detested her; for it was painfully evident to her that as she had bowed to the yoke of the elderly *maîtresse-en-titre*, she must again dissemble for awhile, and submit to that of a wife of seventeen.

On the former she had hoped for the satisfaction of being revenged; but here the Guises once more thwarted her. Originally they had mainly owed their elevation to the Duchesse de Valentinois; but now they were independent of her favour, needing not her good offices, and, but that these six brothers furthered each other's interests in every way, would have cared little how deeply she was humiliated. One of their number, the Duc d'Aumale, had, however, married the duchess's second daughter ; consequently he was one of her heirs. They were unwilling, therefore, that estates, which eventually, in part if not wholly, would come into their family, should be lost to them by confiscation. A prudent attempt at conciliation had also been made by Diana's offer to Catherine of her château and domain of Chenonceaux-sur-Cher, which she had long desired to possess, and had compelled Diana to pay for, having, in her indignation at Henry's disregard of her wishes, instigated a former owner of the estate to contest her free right to it as a royal gift. Diana had greatly embellished the château and grounds, and Catherine gladly consented to accept her offer, but not exactly as a gift. She gave her in exchange for it the Château of Chaumont-sur-Loire, the advantage of the exchange being greatly on Catherine's side.

It is scarcely probable that her revengeful feelings were fully appeased by the possession of Chenonceaux, as she was supposed to have determined not only on the humiliation, but the death of her rival. But the frustration of her hopes of governing the young king and, as a matter of course, his kingdom, deprived her of the power of carrying out designs to which the Guises, in their own interests, gave no countenance. The Duchesse de Valentinois was therefore so leniently dealt with. She made her splendid abode of Anet her habitual residence, and retained her other estates and the immense wealth she possessed wholly unmolested. Occasionally she visited Chaumont, after its legal cession to her in December, 1559. There, architects and other artists were employed in transforming that feudal fortress into a more modern, elegant, and suitable residence for the lady of Anet.

Meanwhile political intrigue for the purpose of undermining the power of the Guises, and transferring it to herself, occupied the time and thoughts of Catherine de' Medici. The duke and the cardinal shared between them the effective power of the kingdom ; but to conciliate Catherine they left her the apparent general superintendence of the Government. She had, in fact, seized on that almost at the very moment of Henry's death.

The Venetian ambassador, Giovanni Michiel, says, 'She had been thought timid because during the king's lifetime she had not dared to meddle in any matter of importance. But no sooner was the breath out of his body than the courage and audacity of her character were fully displayed.

Disregarding the custom of the French Court, requiring a widowed Queen of France to seclude herself for forty days, she gave no time to such useless grief, but dined in public on the morrow of her husband's death, and gave audience to all who sought it. She sent to the chancellor for the great seal used by the sovereign, and began to take in hand the direction of affairs, less like a woman than a man full of courage and well versed in the government of a State. She has not allowed,' he continues, 'her designs to be easily penetrated, for, like Leo X. and all his race, she is a proficient in the art of dissimulation.'

Catherine, however, accompanied the king and queen, the Guises, and the Dukes of Ferrara, Savoy, and Nemours, who attended them, to the Louvre. When about to enter the carriage, as usual, before her daughter-in-law, she suddenly seemed to bethink her that she had descended a step in rank. Drawing hastily back, and turning with a dignified air towards the young queen, she said, 'Madame, it is now your turn to take precedence of me.'*

Besides his high office of Constable of France, Anne de Montmorency held that of grand-master of the household. This enjoined on him the duty

* Mathieu, 'Histoire de France.'

of remaining with the body of the late king until removed from the palace for burial. Excessive grief at the untimely end of the sovereign, who alone of the Court showed him either friendship or affection, also prevented him from following Francis and his 'uncles,' the queen and queen-mother to the Louvre. But ere the preparations for the royal obsequies—'surpassing in solemn splendour any that France had hitherto witnessed'—were quite ended, the constable, accompanied by his sons and nephews, snatched a moment from his duties to repair to the palace to pay his respects to the new king, and to see and advise the queen-mother.

But the Guises had taken advantage of his forced absence from the council to confirm their own power. If they stood not high in the favour of the Court because of their avarice, and still more because of their success in gratifying it, they were at least not abhorred, as was the constable, for brutally insulting manners. On the contrary, they were exceedingly courteous, and were regarded by the younger nobility as models of courtly dignity and high breeding. Their reputation too, especially that of the duke, was great among the people. Had he not saved Metz and retaken Calais, and shed fresh lustre on his arms by his humanity to the suffering soldiers of the defeated armies? Both brothers had also raised their voices in condemnation of Montmorency's ready concession to all the demands of Philip II., when the treaty of Câteau-Cambrésis was signed. Further, zealous Catholics looked to them, as the declared irreconcilable enemies of the 'new opinions,' to put down and effectually stamp out the 'devilish heresy' now troubling the Church, also the righteous spirit of the violent and persecuting pontiff, Paul IV., as well as threatening disaster to the kingdom.

Such indeed was their credit that Catherine—in conversation with Montmorency, while the young king was learning from 'his uncles' how he should receive the constable, and what he should say to him—declared that she thought it more dangerous to irritate than to raise them to power, and that it was on the whole safer to employ them in the great offices of State than to dismiss them from the Court. But the constable, who had hitherto treated Catherine with much superciliousness, was now willing, in order to regain that influential position in the Government which had been so audaciously, as he considered, snatched from him, to ally himself with her and the Bourbon princes for the overthrow of the Guises. He advised her, therefore, not to allow France at the beginning of the new reign to have reason to doubt of its happy and peaceful continuance. 'The ardent love,' he said, 'which the French bore to their princes made them their willingly obedient subjects; but, on the other hand, the domination of foreigners— as were the Guises of Lorraine—was an odious and insupportable yoke to the nation. He urged her, then, to lose no time in summoning the King of Navarre—first prince of the blood—and his brothers to Court; their absence being much to be regretted.

Hitherto the constable had paid assiduous court to Diana, and entered into family connections with her by marrying one of his sons to her granddaughter. Diana's day, however, was ended, and Montmorency, like the Guises, had turned his back on her. But the 'Florentine banker's daughter,' as he as well as Diana had sometimes called her, abhorred both her husband's favourites. She did not forget that the constable had suggested doubts of her fidelity by remarking to the king 'how strange it was that none of his children at all resembled him except his natural daughter, Diana.'

Yet she dissembled as usual, and while affecting to believe, as he assured her, that her own interests were identical with those of Antony of Navarre, resolved to accept with good grace that share in the government of the kingdom which the Guises were willing to allow her—trusting to the future, and no distant one probably, for the fuller realization of her ambitious aims.

But the constable is summoned to the royal presence ; and Catherine, as he takes leave of her, with a deferential and respectful air he had never shown her before, assures him, with a dignity and graciousness that are no less new to him, of the value she sets on his counsels, and of her sincere goodwill towards him. Yet he was no more the dupe of her fair words and specious manners than she of the professed disinterestedness of his advice. They knew each other too well. He had indeed counselled the queen-mother, when Henry's recovery seemed doubtful, to send for the princes of the blood to act as a check on the Guises. But feeling assured that her longing for power would deter her from following his advice, he had taken the precaution, some days before the king's death, of secretly despatching a messenger to King Antony urging him to set out for Paris without delay.

The young king, Francis II., was not yet an adept in the art of dissimulation. He received the constable very coldly, though his words were meant by the Guises to be graciously spoken while implying dismissal from Court. He assured him of his great respect for his father's much-esteemed minister and friend, of his determination to continue to him the pensions and privileges granted by the late king. And while informing him that he had conferred on his ' uncles '—a startling acknowledgment of relationship to Montmorency's ears—the direction of the affairs of his kingdom, ' he would still,' he said, ' should occasion arise, gladly listen to his opinions and advice.' This was more than the constable, whose equanimity was not great, could bear from a boy whom he regarded with some contempt as a tool in the hands of the Guises. In his haughtiest manner, he replied that ' he should esteem it no honour whatever to follow those whom hitherto he had preceded.'

To this Francis was not provided with a reply, and none appears to have suggested itself to him. He remained confused and silent, and took no notice of the younger Montmorencys and Châtillons, who accompanied the constable. The latter, however, announced his retirement to Chantilly, and immediately withdrew with his sons and nephews—the whole party much displeased by the affront which they considered had been offered to the head of their family. On the other hand, the duke and the cardinal were well pleased to be relieved so easily and speedily, by his own self-banishment, of the constable's inconvenient presence in the council and at Court.

For awhile he devoted himself to superintending the embellishments then in progress, and which had long employed numerous artists, at his splendid palaces of Chantilly and Écouen. At the latter, Bernard Palissy was occupied in decorating the façade with slabs and figures of enamelled earthenware, after the manner of the Château de Madrid, executed by Girolamo della Robbia for Francis I. But fiery indignation and thirst for revenge did but smoulder in the breast of the imperious old soldier. Fuel, too, was added to the fire when Catherine united with the Guises in requiring Montmorency to resign his office of grand-master, as incompatible with that of Constable of France. He, however, obeyed. The survivorship had been promised to the constable's eldest son, but the king conferred the post on 'his uncle,' the Duc de Guise, and a marshal's baton was offered to François de Montmorency. The constable's nephew, Admiral de Coligny, was also required to resign his post as Governor of Picardy, as the Guises believed they could not count on his support. On complying with the demand, he requested that the Prince de Condé, who had married his niece, might be appointed to succeed him. But this did not answer their purpose. They were then strengthening their position by appointing as governors of provinces and commandants of strong towns those men only whom they regarded as their devoted partizans.

So nefarious were the means by which the Guise family had become enriched, and heaped up estate upon estate, that they feared to draw public attention on themselves by recommending the king to confiscate (as they were anxious to do) a large part of the constable's equally ill-gotten domains. They were, therefore, content for a time that a demand should be made for the restitution of Henry's gift of the Château of Compiègne, it being a royal fief (such was their pretext) that could not be alienated from the Crown. Montmorency had been accustomed to domineer in the council of the late king with as high a hand as that with which the Guises now ruled his youthful successor and reigned over France in his name. But his haughty spirit, that ill could brook the slightest opposition, was doomed to be yet further tried by his unsuccessful attempt to ally himself, in opposing the

Guises, either with Catherine de' Medici or the King of Navarre.*

Antony was sojourning at Nérac when the constable's missive reached him. Both he and Queen Jeanne were, with much reason, greatly dissatisfied with the constable's utter neglect of their interests when peace was concluded at Câteau-Cambrésis. Upper Navarre had been wrested from the Albret family in the time of Charles V., and some arrangement had been looked for at the general peace, in recognition of the claims of Jeanne of Navarre, and for the restoration of her heritage. But Philip II. had remitted the two millions at first demanded for the constable's ransom, and he who scrupled not to sacrifice the interests of France in order to show his gratitude to the Spanish king, was not likely to make those of the little kingdom of Navarre an obstacle to his views.

But the husband of Jeanne d'Albret, though reputed brave in the field, was wanting in energy of character. Naturally indolent, too, and very vague in his projects, loving his ease, and caring

* Antony derived his title of king from his marriage with Jeanne d'Albret, Queen of Navarre. He was known previously as Antony of Bourbon, Duc de Vendôme, and was one of the three nephews of the famous constable, Charles de Bourbon.

little for any Court but his own, resentment also inclined him to see in the pressing but somewhat ambiguous missive addressed to him nothing more than that his presence in Paris would in some way be advantageous to Montmorency in furthering his own interests or designs. It was, however, the duty of the princes of the blood to attend the sovereign's funeral, and to take their places in the council chamber of his youthful successor. Antony and his brother, Prince Louis of Condé, therefore set out for Paris, the former travelling by such very easy stages that Prince Louis soon determined to pursue his journey alone.

The brothers, both in person and temperament, were the very reverse of each other. Louis was small in stature, and generally of less prepossessing appearance than Antony, who was an exceedingly handsome man, of a commanding presence, and not a little vain of his personal advantages. But the qualities in which he was deficient were possessed by Prince Louis, who was brave, bold, and ambitious, full of energy, and fired by a restless desire for the reinstatement of his family in that high position of wealth and influence they had lost by the unfortunate revolt of Duc Charles de Bourbon, and the confiscations which followed it. Had the Prince de Condé been the elder brother, it was generally felt that the Guises would have found in him the formidable opponent which Antony should have been, but failed to prove himself.

The roads (or, rather, no roads) of that period were not favourable for rapid travelling; but an advance of two or three leagues each day satisfied the king. At night he and his suite took up their quarters in the châteaux of the nobility that lay on their line of route. Though one of the acknowledged, if not the most ardent, of the Calvinist chiefs, the King of Navarre was well received on his journey by 'moderate Catholics' as well as Protestants, and promises to support him in an effort to curb the power of the Guises were freely given. For many of the Catholic nobility began to be alarmed at the assumption of sovereign power by the Duc de Guise; while the persecuting spirit evinced by both duke and cardinal dismayed all but the most rigid and fanatical of their party.

Unduly elated by the sort of popularity that attended him on his journey, the King of Navarre entered Paris with the two or three hundred gentlemen of his retinue, expecting to create a great sensation, and proposing to do great things. But the course to be pursued for the accomplishment of these vague projects he left to the chapter of accidents to determine.

The Court, at this time, was at Saint-Germain. Two gentlemen of King Antony's suite, therefore, rode out to announce his approaching arrival. According to the etiquette of the French Court, a guard of honour, headed by an officer of the highest rank (the Duc de Guise on this occasion), should have been immediately sent forward to welcome the royal visitor and conduct him to the Palace. But the Guises were resolved to retain the power they had grasped, and to share it neither with a Bourbon nor a Montmorency. No escort, then, was sent to the King of Navarre. He was merely informed that King Francis, the Duc de Guise, and the Cardinal de Lorraine awaited his arrival at Saint-Germain to welcome and embrace him.

But when the crestfallen prince arrived, doubts were expressed whether he could be accommodated in the royal residence; yet the principal apartment (after the sovereign's) should have been prepared for him. It was, however, occupied by the haughty duke, who cared not to cede it to him; though King Antony probably would have offered —it being a mark of great honour and favour at that period—to share his couch with him. However, to spare him the mortification of returning to Paris to find a bed at Les Tournelles, or at the

Louvre, an officer of the household gave up his sleeping quarters to him.

The boy-king, Francis, had been taught by his 'uncles,' whom he regarded as nothing less than oracles, 'to beware of the Bourbons'—'crafty princes,' they told him, 'encouragers of heresy, seeking to change the religion of the State, and watching, waiting, intriguing for a possible opportunity of seizing his "sacred person" and laying hands on the Crown of France.' The poor youth in consequence looked with strong suspicion on Antony's frank and friendly manner of addressing him—assumed, it was hinted to him, as a mask to conceal the conspirator.

It was, however, rather to conceal his own mortification at the evidently studied coldness of the young king, and the absence of due respect and consideration with which he was received by the Guises and their partizans. But notwithstanding all that was done to exasperate him, he had not the courage openly to resent it, as the poorest in spirit might be supposed to have done.

The queen-mother was playing the double part so natural to her. Affecting to be ignorant of the affronts offered by the Guises to King Antony, she received him cordially, whilst he (Catherine was quite aware of the weakest points in his generally

weak character) **forgot his** wrongs in **the society
of** that seductive **youthful circle of** facile **Court**
beauties whom, **in imitation of Louise of Savoy,
Catherine already was beginning to gather around
her. So Antony** accompanied **the Court to
Rheims, where Francis II. was crowned on the
18th** September, **and where, as at the funeral of
the late king, the Duc de Guise arrogated to himself precedence in the order of the procession of
three princes of the blood.**

Great was **the indignation of the old nobility at
the** insult offered **to their natural chiefs—'** *les sires
du sang***'**—by those **'**presumptuous **Lorrainers.'
What** did those **acts of** despotism mean by which
they seemed **to tread** contemptuously underfoot
all the ancient families of France? Was their **aim
usurpation, founded on the feeble state of the
young king's health and the tender years of** his
**brothers? On all sides enemies were multiplying
around them, and already they were beginning to**
encounter **the inconveniences as well as to** enjoy
**the advantages of that uncontrolled possession of
power they had so eagerly pursued. There was**
an urgent **demand from all classes for the assembling of the States-General, for the ' free** discussion
of public grievances **and the want of order in** con-
ducting the affairs of the kingdom ; as well as to

devise such remedies for them as should calm the present agitation of the public mind.'

But this did not suit the plans and purposes of the Guises. They told the king that 'such a demand from his subjects was nothing less than high treason. Were it granted, they would proceed to dictate laws to him from whom they should receive them, leaving him the mere title of king, they usurping the power.' The poor languid, suffering youth, whom some historians describe as naturally of a gentle disposition, was greatly alarmed by his 'uncles'' report of his subjects' rebellious projects. Their bad feeling towards him perplexed him. He knew not what he had done to excite it, or, indeed, what his people demanded of him.

'What could he do for their benefit more than he had already done?' At the instance of the duke and that holy prelate, his 'uncle of Lorraine,' he had solemnly announced his unalterable determination of rigorously carrying out his father's compact with Philip II. for the utter extermination of heresy. This, he was told, was his duty as Most Christian King; alike towards the Church, the sovereign pontiff, his father's memory, his promise to his brother-in-law of Spain, the welfare of his subjects, and the prosperity of his kingdom.

Immediately following this announcement many persons, obnoxious to the Guises, were arrested on suspicion of heresy and imprisoned. Others were tortured, and burnt or hanged on the Place de Grève.

The Prince de Condé endeavoured to rouse his brother to take up arms—many besides the Protestants, to whom the oppressive rule of the Guises was hateful, being willing to join him—and to assert his right to the foremost place in the Government. But Antony was not to be moved by the arguments of his more fearless brother to any bolder demonstration than a threat to head the malcontents. Empty as were the threats of the King of Navarre, the Guises determined that both he and the princes of his house should quit the kingdom. The queen-mother—acting in concert with the duke and cardinal, though at the time affecting to favour the Protestants, and to give them hopes of less rigorous treatment—wrote to Philip II., setting forth that King Antony, his brother, and other Bourbon princes, were inciting the people to demand the convocation of the States-General. 'Their aim,' she told her son-in-law, 'was to reduce her to the position of a chambermaid, and to nullify the authority of the king, her son.'*

* Regnier de La Planche, 'La France sous François II.'

Philip replied immediately to Catherine's alarming epistle. He is said to have had at the time neither troops nor money to carry out his own secret schemes of thwarting the projects of the Guises in Scotland and England; yet he declared that 'he had ready 40,000 men, whom he would willingly send to France to support the authority of his brother-in-law and his minister, should anyone have the temerity to dispute it.' It was, however, 'imperative,' he said, 'that those abettors of heresy, the Bourbons, should not be allowed to have any share in the government.'* The King of Navarre was summoned to the council-chamber, and in his presence the Guises had the satisfaction of reading Philip's letter.

Antony trembled. He feared that the brave words he had uttered might be responded to by a Spanish invasion of his wife's possessions in the Pyrenees. But when the Guises graciously relieved him from this embarrassment by offering him the honourable mission of conducting Elizabeth of France, the young Queen of Spain, to the frontier of his kingdom, where the Spanish envoys would be in waiting to receive her, Antony gladly accepted, and withdrew his menace of assuming a

* 'Règne de François II.'

hostile position and disputing with them his right to the possession of power.

The Duc de Guise had already honoured Prince Louis de Condé with the title of ambassador, to ratify at Brussels in the name of Francis II. the Treaty of Câteau-Cambrésis. This annoyed the prince greatly; and a further insult, reminding him of his indigence, was the doling out of a thousand crowns by the Minister of Finance (the cardinal was careful to allow little of the public money to find its way into any pocket but his own) for the expenses of this important embassy. He would have rejected it, could he have roused his brother to energetic action. But in vain for that purpose he delayed his departure. At last, hoping to serve the cause of Reform in the country to which he was accredited, Condé set out on his journey with a retinue and equipage in accordance with the modest sum the cardinal financier awarded him. Thus Catherine and the Guises, now—in appearance at least—acting in perfect accord, were freed for a time from the troublesome presence of the Bourbons at the French Court.

CHAPTER III.

Coronation Festivities.—Tearful Adieux.—The Bridal Cortége.—Terrible Weather and Terrible Roads.—Philip's Perils by Sea.—His Grand Auto-da-fé.—Jeanne d'Albret and the Bridal Party.—The Ceremony at Roncevaux.—Grand Reception at Madrid.—A Sudden Friendship.

FOR some weeks past the Court of France had been the scene of continued revelry; the coronation of Francis II. occasioning these prolonged festivities. But the heroine of the fêtes was the youthful and brilliant Queen Mary, around whom the younger courtiers fluttered, and paid homage as to a divinity. The boy-monarch himself, who was suffering from the effects of a tertian ague, was unable to participate in the gaieties of the Court further than by his presence.

Even this his physicians, with an ominous shake of the head, were unwilling to grant, and urged him to forego. But to gaze entranced on his queen as, brightly smiling, she mingled with all the fervour of youthful spirits with the throng of dancers, or glided before him, uttering as she passed some lively remark that brought momentary animation to his countenance, acted on him as the spell of an enchantress, briefly reviving his languid frame.

Dancing and mirth are, however, soon to be succeeded by tearful adieux and sorrowful partings. The princesses Claude and Elizabeth of France, now so sprightly and happy, are indeed too young to be troubled with forebodings as to what the future may have in store for them. But willingly or not, they must bid farewell to these festive scenes, and at an inclement period of the year set out on long and dreary journeys to the frontiers of the respective countries where envoys are waiting to conduct them to new homes, strange in their customs and language, and to husbands whom they have never seen, but to whom, by proxy, they are married. Claude is the bride of the reigning Duke of Lorraine, the head of the sovereign house with whom the Guises claim kindred. Elizabeth is the third wife of the 'Demon of the South,' Philip II. of Spain.

The Venetian ambassador, Giovanni Cappello, writing to the Senate a few months earlier, says of Catherine de' Medici's young family of four sons and three daughters, they are 'all nice children.' The eldest, Francis, he thinks 'wanting in vigour both of mind and body.' 'He has had excellent preceptors,' he says, 'but shows little inclination for study.' They, however, strove to teach him 'never to refuse anything asked of him, in order that by constant habit he might acquire that lavish liberality deemed indispensable in royal personages.' But he seems to have disappointed his preceptors, and to have adopted a contrary course until 'his uncles' taught him better—at least so far as they were concerned.

In the second son, Charles, afterwards Charles IX., the ambassador appears to have taken great interest. He speaks of his 'very pleasing countenance,' and, as he hears, 'he has a generous heart. For one so young,' he says, 'he shows great talent and fondness for learning, and by-and-by much may be looked for from this young prince, for he is a child of great promise.' The third son, Henry, he mentions as having some defect of speech preventing distinct utterance, and concludes with the remark that all are indeed 'too young to exhibit any certain indications of what their real characters may eventually prove to be.'* Though,

* 'Reports of Venetian Ambassadors.'

with the exception of the two daughters then leaving France, the unfortunate children of Henry II. developed, under the training of their infamous mother, into monsters steeped in blood and crime, yet at the period in question they seem to have been affectionate towards each other, and to have felt their first separation a heavy sorrow.

But to return to King Antony: he with the royal lady committed to his charge, and attended by an imposing retinue, left the gay Court of France towards the end of December. Every arrangement was of course made for the comfort of the young queen. Her litter and those of the ladies accompanying her were luxuriously furnished, and when weary of that mode of travelling, or desiring to contemplate more at ease the beauty of the country they traversed, or to visit other attractions on their route, well-trained *haquenées** were provided, and experienced grooms to attend them. But from the beginning to the end of the journey the royal bridal party encountered the most terrific weather—frightful whirlwinds, intense cold, heavy snowstorms, and torrents of rain. The state of the roads, too, still further impeded their progress. At all times hilly and stony, they were now in

* Mules.

some parts blocked with ice and snow through which paths had to be cut, and over them the queen and her maids of honour conducted on foot, while horses and men with difficulty dragged the litters and the baggage of the whole party after them. Again, they would have to wade through slushy roads along which mountain streams had coursed, and made them like the bed of a rivulet. But at length they reached Bordeaux, where the Queen of Navarre with her son—the future Henry IV., then in his seventh year—had already arrived to greet her god-daughter, and to accompany her on her journey thence to the frontier. But at Bordeaux they rested for awhile, the bad weather continuing.

It seemed as if the Fates had determined to frustrate the intended meeting of the child-bride and her bridegroom. For no less violently than the princess was Philip opposed by the elements on his return by sea from the Netherlands to Spain to celebrate his marriage. The royal galley and nearly the whole of the flotilla convoying it were destroyed in a furious tempest when nearing the Spanish coast. Philip had a narrow escape— one of the small vessels with difficulty managing to aid him and receive him on board, when his own galley, with all the priceless jewels and rare objects of art collected at Brussels by Charles V., and which Philip was transferring to Madrid, was swallowed up by the ocean. His gratitude to God for his rescue from death he displayed on his arrival in his capital by a grand *auto-da-fé*. Nearly a hundred persons, many belonging to the first families in Spain, were then publicly burnt, the Inquisition having found them guilty of favouring the 'new opinions,' and Philip having made oath before that iniquitous tribunal that 'he would not spare even his own son should he find him tainted with heresy'—thus justifying the epithet generally applied to him of 'Demon of the South.'

When news reached Paris of the perils by land encountered by the travellers, and the perils by sea by the voyagers, many superstitious but God-fearing people declared them to be signs of the marked displeasure of Heaven at the sacrifice of the young princess to the gloomy, cruel, fanatical ruler of Spain. Some three years earlier, when the five years' truce was concluded between Henry II. and Charles V., through the intervention of the Constable Montmorency, whose private interests induced him to cling to the Spanish alliance, Elizabeth of France, then ten years of age, was betrothed to Don Carlos, a child of eleven, the grandson of Charles, and son of Philip of Spain and his first wife, Donna Maria of Portugal.

Ere five months had elapsed the five years' truce was broken, and war ensued—the Spanish army invading France and defeating the French at Saint-Quentin. In the following year, September 2, 1558, died Charles V. at his monastery of San Yuste. Two months later the death of Queen Mary of England left Philip II. a second time a widower. Not, however, a disconsolate one, as he immediately became a suitor for the hand of his wife's successor, Queen Elizabeth. The terms of the Treaty of Câteau-Cambrésis were then under consideration, and their discussion greatly prolonged, especially with reference to Calais, by the fluctuations of hope and despair agitating Philip's breast. Would England become a province of Spain, and—happy result—her heresy be trampled out in blood and flames? Elizabeth, also anxious respecting Calais, its temporary loss or eventual restitution, seemed for awhile to waver. But soon she made it unmistakably evident that she had no mind to marry her deceased sister's husband.

Then arose the question whether it would be more desirable to complete the marriage of the affianced young couple, or to set their betrothal aside, and Philip himself take the young princess to wife. Don Carlos was said to have been weak and infirm from his birth. He was now fifteen, and his state of health gave no promise of improvement. A fall in infancy, attributed to careless nursing, was said to have so far injured him as to cause a slight contraction of the sinews of one leg. In view of these discouraging statements, it was thought that the father would be a more eligible husband for a daughter of France than the son. Philip was still in the prime of life—he was but thirty-two. But his temper was gloomy, no smile was ever seen on his countenance; his disposition was cruel, his fanaticism extreme. This, together with the excessive dulness and formality of the Spanish Court, offered but a poor promise of happiness for a lively young princess of fourteen. But, on the other hand, at once she would be elevated to the Spanish throne; while the young prince's reputed infirmities made it very doubtful that she would ever be called on to share the throne with him. This view of the Spanish proposals prevailed, and they were in consequence readily acceded to, much to the satisfaction of the constable. The former betrothal, as so frequently happened with royal betrothals in those times, was declared null, and the new engagement (by proxy) took place with great ceremony in the presence of the king and queen and the Court.

We left the young princess with the King and Queen of Navarre at Bordeaux, whence, after a brief interval of repose, they resumed their journey. While the marriage cortége continued its course on French soil, Jeanne and her husband gave precedence to the bride; but as soon as they entered their own domains they asserted their sovereign supremacy, of which the Queen of Navarre was induced to make a formal act, as a challenge to those who sought to deprive her of it. The Spanish envoys affected to consider the Navarrese frontier reached at Pignon, a small town or village near Saint-Jean-Pied-de-Port, connecting Lower with Upper Navarre, which the spoliation of 1521 had made Spanish.

But the spirited heiress of the House of Albret declined to accept a limit that would have carried with it a recognition of the fact of unjust possession as an acquired right. She drew the frontier of her kingdom at the separating line of Upper Navarre and Castile. However, this was not a convenient time for discussing her claims: so the Spanish authorities yielded, and the bridal party passed on without stopping at Pignon.

But the elements still warred against them, the

tempest so increasing in violence that it compelled them to halt at Roncevaux. In consequence, it was decided that the ceremony of delivering the bride to her husband's ambassador should take place there, at the abbey; the King and Queen of Navarre protesting that only necessity forced them to consent to this, in order to fulfil their mission. At the conclusion of these formalities, when the bride was transferred to the charge of the Duke of Alva, King Antony made a speech, setting forth the many virtues and accomplishments of the princess. The Archbishop of Toledo should have replied to this oration by lauding in glowing terms the transcendent qualities of the royal bridegroom; but he was so highly indignant at the conduct of the Court of France in selecting heretics to take charge of the princess, that for sole reply he turned towards Elizabeth—not deigning to notice Antony—and said, 'Listen, my daughter, to these words, and let them be engraven on thy heart: Forget thine own people and thy father's house;' the Bishop of Burgos adding, 'Then shall the king have pleasure in thy beauty, for he is thy lord.' Whether he finished the Scriptural quotation, 'For he is thy Lord God, and worship thou him,' the chronicle and the letter of the Bishop of Limoges to Francis II., February 23, 1560 (from the latter most of these particulars are derived), do not inform us. But worship of her gracious lord was probably expected of her.

After the grand *auto-da-fé*, which bore witness to Philip's zeal for the glory of God, he set out to receive his bride at a village two leagues distant from Madrid, to which city she was conducted with great pomp. A reception, attended by the grandees and ladies of the Court, was held at the royal palace. All were anxious to see Philip's girl-queen. But the chilling effect of the formal etiquette of the Spanish Court formed so strong a contrast with the freedom and gaiety of the festivities in which she had so lately taken part, that the gravity, pomp, and splendour of her first grand reception seemed rather funereal to this young daughter of France.

A gleam of pleasure, however, lighted up her countenance (noticed with some curiosity by most of the company, but disapprovingly, it is said, by Philip) when Don Carlos was presented to her. It was reported that he had but recently recovered from a fever, and still was weak, but that, at his earnest request, he was allowed to attend the reception to pay his respects to the new queen. And Elizabeth received her former *fiancé* both gracefully and graciously, appearing to take an affectionate interest in him—treatment to which, it is certain, the poor youth was but little accustomed. A sudden liking for each other sprang up between these young people, who naturally looked forward to pleasant companionship in the future. These hopes were, however, destined to be crushed in the bud, as, under the circumstances, it was advisable they should be.

Marriage fêtes on a grand scale followed the bridal reception, and many boleros and fandangos were danced by the people in honour of their Catholic majesties' nuptials. But the programme of the Court festivities, distinguished by pomp and solemnity rather than gaiety, was scarcely half completed when the young queen fell ill—her malady proving to be small-pox. It seems to have been but a slight attack, for her recovery was speedy; her beauty suffered no damage, and the interrupted fêtes were resumed—Spanish etiquette requiring that no part of them should be omitted.

The Bishop of Limoges, who accompanied the young queen, and remained in Spain until after her recovery, when writing to Catherine de' Medici to inform her of her daughter's restoration to health, says that 'during her illness she has grown amazingly;' and, with reference to Don Carlos, he adds, 'the prince had cause to be greatly delighted at her majesty's amiability and friendliness towards him, as, indeed, he has shown, and continues to show, that he was. But his visits to her cannot be frequent, for besides that opportunities for conversation are fewer in this country, and intercourse more reserved than in France, his quartan fever so exhausts him that day by day he grows weaker.'

On leaving Spain, the bishop was the bearer of a letter from the Spanish queen to her mother. Probably it would not, if entrusted to other hands, have reached its destination. Evidently her elevation to the Spanish throne has not brought happiness to the lively and youthful French princess. She is oppressed by the formality and gloomy etiquette of the Spanish Court, and complains of the people about her, especially of her *maître-d'hôtel*, the Condé d'Alista, who seems to have watched her closely. He was a relative of the cruel Duke of Alva. She speaks of him as a 'harsh, meddling, mischief-making man.' Neither of Philip nor Carlos does she venture to speak ; probably she dared not.

CHAPTER IV.

The King's Mysterious Malady.—The 'Wise Men:' their Enchantments.—Magic Scenes at Chaumont.—Ruggieri's Predictions.—Religious Persecution.—Anne Dubourg.—Appeal to the Young King.—The Gracious Concession.—The 'Malcontents.'—The Scotch Reformers: their Example followed.

SCARCELY had the king's physicians pronounced their royal patient free from the quartan fever from which he had lately been suffering, than he was attacked by a mysterious malady, against whose progress all remedies seemingly were unavailing. His complexion became livid; his face disfigured with blotches; his slight frame weaker; his spirits more drooping, and the languor consequent on his physical and mental condition greater than before. It was whispered about that some subtle Italian poison was slowly but surely undermining his constitution and bringing him to an early grave. Some there were—and the historian Mézeray seems to confirm their opinion—who thought the king's malady was leprosy, of which Louis XI. was said to have died.

Catherine de' Medici, whose position was then an exceedingly difficult one, succeeded in having her son removed to Blois, ostensibly to try the effect of change of air, but really for the greater convenience of assembling in daily consultation around the sick youth's bed the numerous soothsayers and astrologers in whose predictions she placed so much confidence. It was rumoured, and the story found credence among the ignorant and superstitious people, that the 'queen-mother's wise men' had ordered as the only sure remedy for the purification of the young king's blood—vitiated from his very birth—daily baths of the blood of healthy infant children.

Though Catherine for the time being had succumbed to the Guises, her craving for power had in no way abated. To obtain it, she was believed to be capable of any crime, while as an intrigante she was regarded with distrust, alike by both the political factions then dividing the Court. From the state of the king's health, it seemed likely that the ambitious hopes of the Guises would ere long be shattered, and the dormant ones of the constable revive; while on Catherine would devolve a much larger share in the government of the kingdom.

It might be almost undivided sway, unless the Bourbons should act with unusual vigour and take charge of the helm of State, as a large party, both Protestant and Catholic, desired, instead of placing it—as a regency seemed imminent—in the hands of a foreigner.

Anxious to dive more deeply into the future, to ascertain whether its aspect were menacing or favourable to her, Catherine hastened from Blois to Chaumont. There, undisturbed, she had witnessed or borne a part in many scenes of magic. There, in the lonely tower she had raised on the summit of a rock, she had often, guided by her favourite astrologer, the Florentine Cosmo Ruggieri, sought in the stars a knowledge of the projects of her enemies, and in the movements of those heavenly bodies the best mode of defeating them.

There, towards the end of December, 1559, the same astrologer awaited her in the spacious apartment or hall communicating with Catherine's private suite of rooms in the tower.* Around the walls of this room were suspended, or placed on brackets, various articles of the most heterogeneous

* This was Catherine's last visit to Chaumont, the transfer of the château to the Duchesse de Valentinois being arranged to take place at the end of the month.

nature—instruments of singular form, suggestive of torture; probably for goading refractory demons into revealing more fully or clearly the hidden events of the future. Also dried plants and seaweed, with numerous specimens of minerals; skins of the lion and panther; stuffed animals and birds—conspicuous amongst the latter, an owl of enormous size, with on either side a vampire bat. On the tables lay parchments, covered with geometrical lines, curves and figures; planispheres; dial-plates; several horoscopes; scientific instruments; divining rods or magic wands; waxen figures transfixed with pins and needles—in a word, all the appliances and appurtenances of the magician and astrologer, whose art was then at the height of its glory and development.

The apartment was but dimly lighted when Catherine entered, and a mistiness at the further end added to the weird solemnity of the scene. Being seated, and having overcome the slight nervous agitation which the usually intrepid Catherine is said to have displayed on this occasion, the astrologer first showed the queen the horoscopes of her four sons, which, in obedience to her commands, he had computed, and whence it appeared that two of them were destined to a violent death. All four were to die young, and without leaving any direct successor; but stranger still, all would wear a royal crown. Apparently much affected, the queen inquired, 'Are they then destined to succeed each other on the throne of France?' to which the astrologer appears to have given no precise reply—' It was not clearly set forth.' The prophecy, indeed, erred in several respects, and probably, like many others, was altered after the events to correspond as nearly as it does with what actually occurred.

Catherine, however, was not quite satisfied. She wished for something more positive; therefore desired to know if magic would confirm the language of the stars and establish their decrees with more certainty. Ruggieri then led the queen in front of a magic mirror, in which she beheld a spacious hall, but expressed her disappointment on perceiving there none of her family. The magician explained that they were about to enter the hall, and that each would reign as many years as the number of times he passed round it. The first to enter was Francis II., the reigning king—sorrowful and dejected—who vanished so speedily that Catherine had scarcely time to recognise him ere he was gone. Her eldest son, then, was to die before a full year had elapsed!

Pale with terror she looked again. The future Charles IX. appeared, and made thirteen turns, vanishing at about the middle of the fourteenth, the enchanted mirror at the same time becoming dimmed by a blood-stained mist. Following him came the Duc d'Anjou (Henry III.), who passed nearly fifteen times round the hall—Henry of Navarre (Henry IV.) suddenly appearing before the last turn was completed. 'The Navarrese prince,' says Nicolas Pasquier, 'began the course with a nimble step and jovial air.' Twenty full turns were made, and the twenty-first was begun, when having completed three-fourths of it he suddenly vanished. The Duc d'Alençon did not figure in this scene of magic; no royal crown, notwithstanding the prediction of the stars, being destined for him. Louis XIII., however, is said to have made his thirty-eight turns before the queen.

But her interest in the enchantment ended with the disappearance of the Duc d'Anjou and his Bourbon successor. By a gesture, for she was too much agitated to speak, she intimated that she cared to see no more. The magic mirror immediately became dim, and the supernatural light in the enchanted hall faded away into darkness.

Several old French writers describe this wonderful exhibition of Ruggieri's phantasmagorial skill; but they differ widely in the details given.* Brantôme ascribes it to the magician Nostradamus, in which he appears to be in error. Others also, instead of a magic mirror, substitute a magic circle, within whose limits the princes ushered in made their several rounds. The Guises, according to some accounts, were also introduced, and by their speedy disappearance the tragic end of Duc Henri de Guise was supposed to be indicated.

It has been asserted that a profound impression was made on Catherine's mind by Ruggieri's prophecy. But although constantly studying the stars herself, and seeking the aid of magicians and astrologers, in order to lift the veil concealing the future, it is certain that she accepted only so much of what she regarded as revealed to her as suited her immediate purposes. For the rest, her skilful Italian perfumers, with their subtle poisonous scents and powders, enabled her by secret means, when public ones were dangerous or impossible, to remove those obnoxious persons who were obstacles to the carrying out of her tortuous policy. Thus she believed that she could thwart

* Brantôme, Nicolas Pasquier, Bayle, Felibien, the historian of Navarre, André Pavin, and others.

or reverse the decrees of Fate when inimical to her, and turn the knowledge she had gained of them to her own advantage.

The queen-mother returned from Chaumont to Paris and Blois to find the public mind greatly agitated by the religious persecution then proceeding by order of the Guises. Not only were Protestants, but all moderate Catholics, horrified by the atrocities inflicted on unoffending persons, for whom snares were laid, and spies employed to discover whether they held what were still called the 'new opinions.' Madonnas were set up at the corners of the streets; images of saints also, crowned with flowers, and those who passed by these idols without saluting or bending the knee before them were beaten with sticks by men set to watch, or dragged off to prison, followed by a jeering, cursing, fanatic mob. Then they were tortured, every refinement of cruelty practised on them; and if that did not subdue them into renouncing their heretical opinions, and confessing that they had sinned against holy Mother Church, they expiated their crime in the flames.

The execution, in December, of the sentence on the Councillor Anne Dubourg excited general indignation. For six months this upright magistrate and distinguished savant had been a close prisoner in the Bastille. He had been accused of holding heretical opinions, and did not care to deny it. His plainness of speech had so much irritated Henry II., that he signified his intention of feasting his eyes on the torture and death agonies of his victim, as soon as the close of the Court festivities gave him leisure. But ere this moment for gratifying his resentment arrived, the hand of Death had beckoned the monarch away. Dubourg, however, was not forgotten; but what with pompous funeral pageants, a coronation, public entries, etc., the duke and the cardinal had been fully occupied. Others, accused of a like crime, less steadfast than Dubourg, had recanted, or pretended to do so, and thus escaped the gallows or the burning pile.

Many of Dubourg's friends were so sanguine as to believe that an appeal to Henry's youthful successor would result in an act of justice, as well as of clemency, wherewith to grace his coronation. But 'the uncles' forbade this. Francis II. was reminded that he had confirmed the contract entered into between his father, the late king, and Philip II. of Spain. He replied that he would carry out his father's wishes to the letter, and thoroughly exterminate heresy from France.

Dubourg's trial was a long one, because of his

several appeals to the Parliament and the various Courts, both secular and ecclesiastical, against the injustice of his sentence. He had no objection to taking that course; indeed, he believed it to be his duty, in order, if possible, to enforce his rightful claim as a magistrate to be tried only by the full assembly of the Parliament, of which he was a member. But the few words, in denial of his faith, which would have saved him, no entreaties of his friends could prevail on him to utter. 'He was a Christian,' he said, 'and was prepared to die as one.' So great was Anne Dubourg's reputation, that persons of every class, not only in France but throughout Europe, were interested in his fate. The Protestant Princes of Germany made a representation in his favour. Plots were organized with the view of effecting his escape from the Bastille, but resulted in nothing but a more rigorous treatment of the prisoner. Catherine de' Medici was implored by some friends to intercede for and save him; others threatened her and the kingdom with disasters innumerable if she did not prevent this martyrdom; while, as an earnest of what would follow, the President Minard, who had first denounced Dubourg as a heretic, was shot dead one evening on leaving the Palais de Justice, the murderer escaping undiscovered.

This circumstance led the Cardinal de Lorraine to urge that the execution of Dubourg's sentence should take place without further unnecessary delay. Another motive for hastening it was the information (privately given) that the Elector Palatine was about to despatch an embassy to France, to ask of the clemency of Francis II. the pardon of Dubourg, whom the elector was desirous of appointing to a professorship in his University of Heidelberg. Dubourg's condemnation to death was, therefore, finally confirmed on the 22nd of December. The next day, on the Place de Grève, the sentence was executed ; one concession being graciously made to the earnest entreaties of friends and relatives—instead of being thrown living into the flames, it was permitted first to strangle him. With calm heroism the Christian martyr met his fate, and in eloquent language that touched all hearts and bedewed all eyes—even those of his craven judges—he bade adieu to both friends and foes. When the elector's ambassador arrived the deed was done, and his majesty and his 'uncles' were spared the pain of refusing the elector's request.

Numerous executions followed that of Dubourg. Those of his friends who had most earnestly interposed to rescue him from death became by that act suspected persons, and the Guises, in their holy zeal, spared none on whom the shadow of suspicion rested. Hitherto the Protestants had borne submissively the yoke of their persecutors. They were now exasperated to the highest pitch by the recent acts of the Guises, and for the first time in France reprisals were contemplated. It was not the Protestants only who were dissatisfied with the rule of the duke and the cardinal. The general name of 'malcontents' included many to whom the question of religion was one in which little interest was felt; but to overthrow those usurpers of the kingly power, those *soi-disant* descendants of Charlemagne, they were willing to join hands and fight for their rights side by side with, or as leaders of, those to whom liberty of conscience and freedom of religious worship were the most absorbing questions.

Those military men, mostly poor gentlemen, whose services after the signing of the Peace of Câteau-Cambrésis were no longer required by the State, had been dismissed without any settlement of the long arrears of pay then owing. Their occupation being gone and great distress ensuing, they became clamorous for the money due to them. The cardinal Minister of Finance was with the Court at Fontainebleau. Thither, in great numbers, these needy soldiers of fortune followed him, some demanding payment, others humbly soliciting pension or place by way of compensation. His eminence was irritated beyond measure at conduct so insolent and rebellious, and to free himself from the importunities of such unwelcome visitors he had gibbets erected before the gates of Fontainebleau (as was then at times the custom, to scare seditious or threatening intruders), and a notice attached that if any of those people who came to solicit favours were found within the precincts of the Palace at the expiration of twenty-four hours they would certainly be hanged. These suppliants for the cardinal's favours at once withdrew, but with the determination that he should hear from them again in another character.

The moment appeared to them exceedingly opportune for the organization of a sort of league for the 'defence of legitimate authority and for the public weal.' The young king, they said, was evidently incapable of governing, and his declared majority a mere fiction. 'It was desirable, therefore, for his and the people's welfare that he should be rescued from the toils of the foreign usurpation.' Indignation at the arrogance of the Guises induced many of the nobility to join this adventurous band, while the recent successes of John

Knox and the Scotch Covenanters against Mary of Guise, though advised and supported by her brothers, inspired the French reformers with courage to rise up against their persecutors in 'defence of their religion.' The introduction of the military element changed the character of the struggle for Reform. There was a vigorous awakening of the Protestants to a sense of their rights, and the doctrine inculcated by Calvin of submission to the powers that be no longer held them in bondage. Thus was prepared that event known as the Conspiracy of Amboise. It was then that the Calvinists, to distinguish them from the Lutherans, were first called Huguenots, a corruption of the German Eidgenossen—allies or confederates

CHAPTER V.

The Amboise Conspiracy.—Barry de La Renaudie.—The Six Brothers of the House of Guise.—Antony, King of Navarre.—The Plot revealed.—Condé joins the Court at Amboise.—Nemours' Errand of Mercy.—La Renaudie's Encounter in the Forest of Château-Rénault.—Nemours succeeds in his Mission.—Treachery.—Royal Amusements.—Condé's Challenge to Single Combat.

THE short reign of Francis II. was one continued period of turmoil and tragic events, of which the 'Conspiracy of Amboise' may be considered the most important. In it the long-pent-up discontent of political and religious factions, which for years past had distracted France, suddenly found development. The tyrannical rule of the Guises had aroused a spirit of resentment which, galling as was the yoke inflicted on the country by such rulers as Francis I. and Henry II., had yet been kept in check by the deep feeling of loyalty cherished by the people towards their rightful sovereigns.

Voltaire's remark that 'the Conspiracy of Amboise was the first conspiracy known in France,' has been repeated by most French writers who since his day have treated of the subject. Numerous instances were, however, already on record of serious Court cabals, political intrigues and plots, as well as menacing risings of the populace, when taxed beyond endurance to supply the needs of prodigal, dissolute kings and their favourites. Yet a conspiracy including amongst its members men of humblest rank and of the lower and upper *bourgeoisie;* the disbanded military, many of the *petite noblesse*, also those of greater distinction (for instance, the Baron de Castelnau, of a very ancient family and of eminent learning and piety), with a prince of the blood for its head, had probably never before been known in France.

A gentleman of Perigord, named Barry de La Renaudie, undertook the organization of the confederates, which was conducted with so much thoroughness and skill, and so much audacity yet secrecy, that in this respect the Amboise Conspiracy has been compared with that of Catilina, and the Ghibelline plot of the Pazzi of Florence. The plan of execution was decided at a general meeting convoked by La Renaudie at Nantes in the early part of February. A body of several hundred Huguenots, unarmed, was to advance on Blois on the 15th of March to present a petition to the king praying for liberty to worship God according to the rites of the reformed religion.

Five hundred cavaliers and a thousand men on foot, commanded by thirty captains, all thoroughly equipped, were to follow the above, who were to open the gates of Blois to them. The Prince de Condé—hitherto, for concealment, designated *le prince muet*—was then to place himself at their head, and arrest the Duc de Guise and the cardinal, who were to be tried and punished according to the laws of the kingdom. The young monarch being thus freed from their usurped domination, a legitimate Government, after a general consultation, was to be established. The leaders of the confederates were in correspondence with Queen Elizabeth through the English ambassador, and were largely subsidized by her 'for the cause of God and religion,' Reformers and dissatisfied politicians alike sharing her bounty. For though all those assembled under the banner of Reform were not Protestants, and probably had other aims than religious ones, yet equally with them they demanded a cessation of persecution and the tolerance of religious differences.

While the preparations for this daring enterprise were still proceeding, the attention of the Guises was in a measure diverted from them by the innumerable pamphlets, menacing, caustic, or derisive, with which they were overwhelmed. For their authors or printers, diligent, though generally fruitless, search was made. The printer of the famous pamphlet, 'Epître au Tigre de la France,' addressed to the cardinal, was, however, discovered and duly hanged on the Place de Grève. The vigorous language of this pamphlet appears to have made the cardinal tremble. He was a terrible coward; but though he had a fertile brain for the concoction of schemes and plans for his own and his family's benefit, he was fearfully alarmed when any serious resistance to them seemed probable, and his personal safety at all endangered. The duke, however, supplied what was needed in boldness and audacity. The six Guise brothers were remarkable in this respect, each possessing in a high degree some quality of mind or natural endowment wanting in the others. No wonder, then, they became so enormously wealthy, so distinguished according to their several or their united attributes, and so dangerous to the State when they began to fix their gaze on the crown, and declare themselves the lineal descendants of Charlemagne. Some intimations of what was going on could, in fact, hardly fail to reach them. They had their spies in the capital and in the provinces, ever on the alert to detect heresy or 'those guilty promoters of it' who failed to denounce suspected friends or relatives. But these occasional warnings of some great movement on foot in the Vendômois (the appanage of Prince Louis de Condé) the Guises appear to have but lightly regarded.

Sir Nicholas Throckmorton, the English ambassador at the French Court, conjointly with special envoys from Elizabeth, had endeavoured to tempt King Antony of Navarre, by promises of money and the secret support of their queen, to head an expedition against the duke and the cardinal,[*] who had sent French troops to Scotland to aid their sister, the Queen Regent Mary of Guise, in putting down the Protestants. For awhile she gained some advantage and seemed on the point of succeeding in her object; but assistance despatched by Elizabeth resulted in the triumph of the Covenanters.

The historian Lingard has said that Elizabeth,

[*] See 'Calendar of Foreign State Papers,' 1560-61.

by encouraging the internal dissensions in France, hoped to regain possession of Calais. It was natural, however, that the English queen should resent the assumption of her title of Sovereign of England and Ireland, and the quartering of her arms, by the youthful pair then on the throne of France; also that she should be willing to assist the Reformers in their attempt to obtain recognition of their right to pray to God after their own manner, as well as to free themselves from the cruel persecution of those ambitious tyrannical men who governed France in the name of its invalid boy-king. But it was soon very clear to Elizabeth's agents that King Antony was wholly unfitted to take the lead in an enterprise requiring in its chief great energy of character, audacity, endurance, and unflinching firmness, with the power of inspiring those under his control with similar courage and daring and perfect confidence in him.

The accounts of the famous Amboise plot contained in the memoirs and journals of contemporary writers are exceedingly numerous; but their discrepancies are so great—written as they are in the spirit of partizanship—that it is difficult to disentangle from them trustworthy materials for a connected narrative. However, before the time for action arrived—said to have been fixed first for the 10th of March, then for the 15th—La Renaudie appears to have crossed the Channel, either to seek an interview with Queen Elizabeth, or to consult with her ministers. He probably received, besides a supply of money, assurances of her goodwill and interest in his hazardous undertaking. Beyond that, and that she was kept well informed of its progress, there would seem to have been neither aid nor interference from that quarter.

The Spanish king, who had his emissaries in every country and Court in Europe, had seen with pleasure the defeat of the Scottish queen-regent and her adherents by the troops of the heretic Elizabeth. It thwarted the plans of the Guises, who desired to unite the kingdoms of France and Scotland—an arrangement entirely opposed to Philip's own views. 'The death of the young Queen Mary at this time would have relieved him,' as he said to his minister Granvelle, 'of much embarrassment and anxiety by depriving her uncles of all influence in Scotland.' But while waiting and hoping for that desired event, he felt bound to support those zealous sons of holy Mother Church in their efforts to exterminate the Reformers and 'free the land from the damnable sin of heresy.'

Two days then before the date fixed for laying the Huguenot petition before the king, the duke and the cardinal were fully informed by a Spanish agent of the serious appearance of the impending storm—he at the same time handing to them a plan of the intended confederate operations. The queen-mother also received information of a like alarming nature from, it is said, one of the confederates named Lignières, whose courage failed him as the moment for action drew near. Another account attributes the failure of this carefully organized and well-combined scheme to the imprudence of Renaudie in imparting it in confidence to a lawyer, with whom he was either on terms of friendship or had monetary transactions which, as some relate, compelled him partly to reveal his secret—the secret without a moment's loss of time being again revealed at Blois.

But whoever may have been the traitor, great was the consternation when the news of a conspiracy (whose object was declared to be the dethronement of the king, the murder of his 'uncles,' and the transfer of the crown to the Prince de Condé) reached the Château de Blois. The amusements of the Court, but recently resumed in consequence of a slight improvement in the young king's health, were at once brought to a close, and general alarm prevailed. The poltroon cardinal quaked in his shoes, lest his worthless body should be roasted alive, as by his intervention the flames had consumed the bodies of so many of his betters—good men and true. So great was his terror, that momentarily it is said to have acted on his brother, the duke, almost paralyzing the indomitable courage of that daring soldier. But speedily recovering himself, he ordered the instant removal of king, queen, and Court to the Château d'Amboise—a fortress of far greater strength than that of Blois—while he hastened secretly to assemble the king's guards, and as large a body of armed men as on the spur of the moment was possible.

At the suggestion of Catherine de' Medici, Admiral de Coligny and his brother d'Andelot were requested immediately to attend the Court, 'their opinion and counsel'—such was the pretext—'being desired by the duke and queen-mother.' They were suspected, wrongly it appears, of being actively concerned in the conspiracy. But without any show of distrust, Coligny and d'Andelot, joined by their brother the Cardinal Odet de Châtillon, at once obeyed the summons. By their presence at Amboise, 'Catherine hoped to perplex the confederates and induce a suspicion that these military chiefs of Reform were as hostile to their project as the religious ones—Calvin, Bèze, and others.' His advice being asked, the admiral frankly declared that to exterminate the Reformers by force was now out of the question; but that if there was to be peace in France, an edict of relaxation of severity with liberty of worship must be granted. The Guises affected partly to yield to this advice, and issued a sort of amnesty, but rendered their concessions null by secret orders forbidding the release of any prisoner detained on account of his religion who was not prepared fully and publicly to recant his errors.

Though the Court was transferred to Amboise, and the conspiracy divulged, it seems that the confederates might yet have attained their object, and by an audacious *coup-de-main* effected an entrance, treachery within the château aiding them. It was, nevertheless, a perilous undertaking. Yet sixty gentlemen offered themselves to accomplish it, or die in the attempt. The Prince de Condé was on his way from Orléans to Blois, when informed that the plot was divulged and the king and Court transferred to Amboise. He, however, had the courage—or exceeding folly, as some of his friends thought—to continue his journey and join the royal party at the château. He was received there with great coldness; but accusation at that moment was considered premature.

La Renaudie being still absent in Paris, the chief command was held by the Baron de Castelnau-Chalone, who occupied the Château de Noizay, belonging to the Sieur de Raunay, one of the confederates. It was situated within two leagues of Amboise, on the right bank of the Loire. Thither the Duke de Guise, uncertain as to the number of the confederates assembled there, would have despatched Marshal Vieilleville with a small party of gentlemen of the king's guard to reconnoitre and to parley with the baron. But Vieilleville, suspecting that treachery was intended, suggested that to inspire confidence in the conspirators a prince of the blood should be entrusted with the message of peace—a request from the king to know what they complained of, and his royal word given that in all security and without any fear for their lives the confederates might approach and lay their griefs at the foot of the throne.

The Duc de Nemours,* who, says Brantôme,

* Jacques de Savoie, the head of the younger branch of the House of Savoy, on whose ancestor Francis I. bestowed the Duchy of Nemours.

was 'the very flower of chivalry,' was induced to accept this mission. Five hundred men were to accompany him; but unless persuasion should utterly fail he was determined not to use force. In the morning the king made oath to pardon the conspirators if they presented themselves respectfully before him, and Nemours in all good faith set out on his errand of mercy.

La Renaudie was then hastening to the relief of Castelnau, a small body of troops following. But when traversing the forest of Château-Renault, he encountered a cavalier (Regnier de La Planche, in his 'Reign of Francis II.,' says he was his cousin), a partizan of the Guises, with one or two attendants. Furiously the cavalier rushed upon him, and took aim with his pistol; but the cumbrous weapon missed fire. La Renaudie, with more effect, replied with his sword; for his adversary at the first thrust fell from his horse, and was killed as he fell by a second blow, the sword passing through his body. The servant of the slain cavalier, who seems, thus far, to have been a quiet spectator of the fight, then dismounted, and passing quickly, it is stated, behind La Renaudie, lodged the charge of his arquebuse in his back. This proved fatal; but the dying man, whose hand still grasped his sword, had yet strength enough left effectually to aim a deadly blow at his second adversary. The men who followed La Renaudie disbanded themselves on learning the death of their chief, and those who did not escape the vigilance of the king's troops, now out in all directions, were cruelly massacred. The bodies of the three combatants were removed—two for 'honourable burial;' that of La Renaudie to swing on a gibbet on the bridge over the Loire, with an inscription above it, ' La Renaudie, Chief of the Rebels.'

When news of this *contretemps* reached the confederates, the men of whom La Renaudie was to have taken the command, and whom he had inspired with courage and a confidence of success similar to his own, were so enraged, that to avenge him they wildly rushed forth, heedless of all attempted restraint, and in open day made a desperate attack on the Château of Amboise. Though the assailants were finally repulsed, dispersed, pursued, and tracked to their hiding-places —where, as the account has it, they were 'cut in pieces'—it yet appears that could they but have subdued the thirst for vengeance until darkness concealed their movements, the attack would have been successful. It, however, caused exceeding terror to Catherine de' Medici, who affected to incline towards the conciliatory policy recommended by the admiral, and supported by the Chancellor Olivier, then at the château. The chancellor was a friend of the Baron de Castelnau, and was also strongly suspected of being 'tainted' (according to the expression then in vogue) with the ' new opinions.'

In spite of the *espionage* both within and without the château, information was conveyed to the king that it was not against him but his ministers, the duke and the cardinal, that the confederates had taken up arms. This he repeated to them, and begged that they would retire from the Court for awhile, that he might ascertain if it were truth, and also inquire what his people really wanted. ' But the Guises,' says La Planche, ' utterly rejected this proposal,' telling the feeble young king that ' should they leave him, neither he nor his brothers could be sure of their lives for one hour—the House of Bourbon being bent on exterminating the royal line of Valois.' And so effectually did they work on his fears, and persuade the weeping youth that their vigilance was necessary for the preservation of his crown and his life, that by a royal declaration of March 17th the Duc de Guise was named Lieutenant-General of the Kingdom, with powers unlimited. It was, in fact, a sort of abdication, conferring on the duke, as a right, that exercise of royal power which hitherto he had usurped.

This was a step entirely opposed to the views of the queen-mother; but to resist it would have been vain. Power seemed always to elude her grasp; but once more the opposition of their enemies had resulted in placing it more securely in the hands of the Guises. For long years Catherine had played the part of watching and waiting, but she now looked forward to a change in her favour, which she believed would at no very distant period occur. Meanwhile, regarding the Huguenots as a salutary restraint on the encroachments of the Guises, she sought to incline the Court to clemency towards them. At the same time she secured for herself a certain measure of popularity amongst those who had adopted the 'new opinions'—popularity which she might turn to account by-and-by. And, in spite of the cardinal, she did succeed in obtaining the liberation of some of the humbler members of the conspiracy, who, lagging behind on foot, had been taken prisoners. They were sent back to their homes with a testoon (5d.) each from Catherine for their journey.

While these things were taking place in the château, the Duc de Nemours had accomplished the object of his mission. Persuasion had succeeded with the Baron de Castelnau; who (according to the historian de Thou) still, in preference to force, favoured the first peaceful demonstration proposed of sending a body of unarmed Huguenots to lay before the king a statement of the grievances, both religious and political, for which redress was sought. Some there were, however, who declared themselves unable to place the same reliance as their leader on the promises of their sovereign, controlled as he was by unscrupulous ministers. Nemours—who, it has been generally considered, had no part in the treachery of the Guises—replied to these objections by engaging his own word, as a man of honour and a prince of the blood, that the king's promises would be religiously performed. His assurances of good faith were accepted. The confederates assembled at Noizay then issued from the château, and, led by their chief, peacefully mingled with the soldiers and gentlemen of the prince's suite, and accompanied them to Amboise. Thus, nothing doubting, were they led as a flock of sheep to the slaughter-house.

The last of the long line of victims had passed the portcullis when the foremost ones began the ascent of the great north tower, in the upper portion of which were the royal apartments, under the guidance of the archers of the guard. Suddenly there arose one long piercing cry of indignation, reaching the ears even of the king and his ministers, when a halt was made by their conductors on the lower landing leading to the dungeons, and the confederates discovered that they had been betrayed. Nemours was still with them. He is said to have been pierced to the very soul with anguish when his eyes met the accusing and contemptuous gaze of Castelnau fixedly bent upon him. Rage in his heart, he rushed to the king's apartment, and reminded his majesty of his promises. The duke being present, he reproached him in bitterest terms, and was laughed at for his credulity in supposing that faith would be kept with rebels and heretics. Indeed, so much were both François de Guise and the cardinal elated by Nemours' success, that they exultingly told him such a triumph was quite unexpected, and scarcely could have been achieved but for the part (the infamous part) assigned him, and which, however unconsciously, he had most adroitly played.*

The Guises being now masters of the position,

* Brantôme represents the Duc de Nemours as a persuasive speaker and 'aussi agréable que brave.'

the slaughter of their prisoners began without loss of time. The cardinal had remarked that the ladies were growing weary of the secluded life they were leading at Amboise, and longing for the signal to return to the livelier pastimes of Blois. Gallantly, therefore, he proposed for their amusement a most unique and enlivening after-dinner recreation. The whole Court attended—the king and his 'uncles,' the queen, the queen-mother with her young sons, Charles and Henry, and the ladies and gentlemen of the household generally. For a whole month they assembled daily at the broad open spaces or grated verandas fronting the castle windows, where they ranged themselves to assist at their ease at—and possibly, as good Catholics, to enjoy—the horrible spectacle of the unfortunate Huguenot prisoners writhing in the agony of a cruel death, or under the infliction of atrocious tortures. Water, fire, and sword were all employed in the perpetration of the unspeakable horrors devised by the ferocious imaginations of the wretches to whom the Guises entrusted the massacre of their victims.

Before the windows of the royal apartment was a broad projecting balcony, and from it a full view of the Loire. The thoughtful cardinal, anxious that his young sovereign should have the satisfaction of watching the death-struggles of a heretic as closely as possible, ordered several, whose limbs had been dislocated on the rack, to be suspended by cords to the rails of the balcony. To add to the attractions of the river scene many of these unfortunates were tied in sacks, others attached, five or six or more together, by long iron poles passed through their bodies, and then thrown into the Loire, there to struggle and gasp out in agony, for the royal party's amusement, their few remaining minutes of life.

Headless bodies (many of the heads being placed on poles on the ramparts of the château) lay weltering in blood on the ground, while flames were consuming the rest. When from any of these poor sufferers, less heroic than others, cries of anguish proceeded, the cardinal, with an air of much satisfaction and a *benignant* smile, would draw the young king's attention to it. But when those from whom no satanic device of their tormentors could extract a word of confession, a groan, or complaint, died with fortitude, then his eminence would approach the king, his countenance full of indignation, and in a trembling agitated voice thus address him: 'Behold, sire, those shameless and enraged ruffians! even the fear of death cannot abate their pride or subdue their treasonable hopes. What, then, would they not do if your majesty were in their power?' Thus the poor youth, whose eyes are said to have been often filled with tears at the spectacle of horrors before him, when those of his young queen were dry, was led to believe that he was abhorred by his subjects, and that he owed his life to the care and vigilance of the Duc de Guise and the cardinal.

But killing and slaying went merrily on day and night both in the château and the town of Amboise—many parties of Huguenots being still at large in the neighbouring woods and villages. Respecting them the orders of the duke (who is said to have been as one drunk with blood) were not to send them to the château, but to shoot them down wherever met; for the dungeons were full, and so many dead bodies still lying about that the air was infected by them. Besides this, 'the ladies were beginning to feel compassion for those rebels, and to plead for mercy.' 'The streets were therefore planted with avenues of gibbets, and dead bodies dangled like tapestry hung up against the walls, while down either side ran a rivulet of blood. But the daily spectacle of death at the château began to pall on the fair occupants of the balconies. The Duchesse de

Guise, daughter of that very rigid Calvinist, the daughter of Louis XII., Renée de France, from the first expressed her repugnance to be present at such scenes. Sickened at the sight, she one day, addressing Catherine de' Medici, exclaimed: 'Ah, Madame, this blood will surely call for blood! May Heaven save your sons and mine!' Her exclamation was indeed prophetic.

The formalities of a trial and judicial sentence had been wholly dispensed with in the case of those of the confederates who were not, as the Guises considered, of a rank in life to give them any future trouble from the vengeance of relatives or friends. But with the gentlemen of noble birth captured at Noizay it was in some respects different, though the sanction of the king to their execution as rebels and heretics might seem to render the farce of a trial unnecessary. However, a tribunal was constituted, composed of the Cardinal de Lorraine, the craven-hearted Chancellor Olivier, and the grand-provost, Du Plessis de Richelieu (an ancestor of the great cardinal).

After a very summary *procès* the chiefs of the 'Tumulte d'Amboise,' as this plot is sometimes called, were condemned to die. Great efforts were made to save the Baron de Castelnau, whose family had given several famous captains to France. His own career also had been one of distinguished loyalty and good service to the Crown. But his opposition to the tyrannical rule of the Guises was an unpardonable crime in the eyes of those despots, who urged or rather commanded the young king to close ears and heart to any appeal for mercy.

Another account* states that the king (we hear nothing of any intercession on the part of his queen) joined the queen-mother in pleading for clemency. One of the Guise brothers, the Duc d'Aumale, also added his supplications to theirs on this occasion. But 'le grand Guise' was inexorable. Any entreaty coming from those three caged 'suspects,' the Châtillons (who were highly indignant at their detention at the château), and the more than suspected Condé, would of course

---

* That of Regnier de La Planche, who, in his record of 'L'État de France sous François II.,' enters more fully into the details of the Amboise massacre than other contemporary writers. He has, however, been accused of some exaggeration. But it is very probable that, having himself openly embraced the Reformed Faith, the tragic result of the plot and the sufferings inflicted on the confederates excited deeper sympathy and greater commiseration in him than in those 'untainted' with heresy. Exaggeration of the horrors that ensued seems scarcely possible, and any attempt to describe their atrocity is likely to fall far short of the actual facts—second in infamy only to the revolting deeds of the St. Bartholomew.

be unheeded. But the presumptuous interference of the former aroused the righteous wrath of that excellent prelate, the Cardinal de Lorraine. Having ensnared his prey, he was now very bold. Forgetting in the heat of his anger the saintliness of his office, he rose from his seat and with great vehemence exclaimed: '*Par le sang Dieu!* that rebel shall die, and not a man in France, whoever he be, shall save him!' But if he would not save his head, he was at least desirous, it appears, of saving his soul by bringing him back to that true faith of which he was himself so shining an example.

The programme of that afternoon's entertainment included the execution of Castelnau; Raunay, the owner of the Château de Noizay; and the Chevalier de Mazères—the two last-named being cruelly tortured before laying their heads on the block. Then followed the decapitation of Calvin's friend, the Sieur de Villemongis. This victim, before resigning himself to his fate, dipped his hands in the blood streaming from the headless bodies of his two companions, and spreading them forth, with eyes raised towards heaven, said: 'Behold, O God! this is the blood of Thy children: Thou wilt avenge it!'

A scaffold was erected, under the windows of

the royal apartment, especially for the execution of these four gentlemen. But the Baron de Castelnau was the last to ascend it. The cardinal had detained him to listen to the pious exhortations that were to effect his conversion. For while condemning him as unfit to live, he still was anxious to dismiss him to another, and haply a better, world certificated by himself that his victim was worthy to find in that the mercy denied him in this. The baron, however, spoke with eloquence and dignity in defence of the faith that was in him, ably refuting the cardinal's arguments. The duke was present, and with singular brutality replied to a casual gesture of appeal from the baron that 'he understood nothing of discussion and argument, his profession being that of cutting off heads, which he understood thoroughly.' This fruitless colloquy ended, de Castelnau ascended the scaffold. As, with unflinching firmness, he laid his head on the block, 'The justice of God,' he said, 'will surely overtake the Guises!'

These predictions and dying appeals to heaven, if they moved not the Guises themselves, yet were heard with fear and trembling by the men employed to execute their barbarities. On two of the council of three chosen to judge and pass sentence on the confederates of higher grade, their appeals, predictions, and reproaches also made a deep impression. The Chancellor Olivier, who had acted a very pusillanimous part, either from complaisance to the Guises, or from fear of compromising his own safety, was so much affected by the taunts of some of his friends and co-religionists, and the censure and upbraidings of others, that, conscience-stricken, he returned to his home, took to his bed, and died. The cardinal visited him when at the point of death, seeking again, excellent prelate, to bring back a wandering sheep to the fold of the faithful. But the chancellor rejected his offer to confess and absolve him. 'Cardinal,' he exclaimed, 'you are bringing us all to perdition.'

Willingly would the Guises have added a few more murders to their already long list of crimes. They thought the air of gloomy quietude assumed towards them by the Châtillons very menacing, but could not find in it a pretext strong enough for immediately arresting them. As regarded the Prince de Condé, the disclosures of several of the confederates while undergoing the torture were so strongly accusatory that an order was issued at the instance of the cardinal for the seizure of his papers. His Château of Vendôme also was thoroughly ransacked; but not a line was found that could in any way be strained into proving his connection with the recent conspiracy.

The fact that he was its destined head was known to many and doubted by few, but the Guises failed to bring it home to him; while he with great courage and audacity demanded of the king the assembling of the princes of the blood, the chevaliers of the orders, the private council and foreign ambassadors then at Amboise, amongst whom was Sir Nicholas Throckmorton. At once they were commanded to repair to the royal audience-chamber. There, in their presence and that of the king, the queen, the queen-mother and her two young sons, the Prince de Condé 'declared that whoever had informed his majesty that he was the chief and leader of a seditious band, said to have conspired against the king and the State, had lied, and most unworthily accused him. On that account, setting aside his rank as prince of the blood, he would make them confess at the point of the sword that they were cowards and scoundrels, seeking themselves the subversion of the State and the Crown, in the maintenance of which it was his duty to assist by a better right than his accusers.' This pointed to the Guises. The prince ended by calling on those present, if among them there was anyone who had accused him and was willing to maintain his accusation, there and then to declare himself.

The Duc de Guise then stepped forward, not, as was expected, to take up the gauntlet, but to announce that if anyone present accepted the prince's challenge, he, as 'his cousin,' claimed the right of acting as his second. Astonishment was general, silence also, no adversary presenting himself. The duke then advanced towards the prince and offered his hand. But the vengeance of the Guises was but deferred. 'They drew back for the present, having failed to prevail on the young king to stab his kinsman with his own hand after the manner of the Italian tyrants.' The prince was therefore allowed to depart. He returned to Béarn to rejoin his brother, but by a very circuitous route, in order to avoid any snares that his enemies might have laid to entrap him on his journey. At the same time the Châtillons also left Amboise, expressing great dissatisfaction at the treatment they had received from the Guises (La Planche and 'Mémoires de Condé').

The Amboise plot had served then, at the sacrifice of so many and valuable lives—variously stated from five to fifteen hundred—but to increase the power of the very men whose persecuting tyranny its aim had been to overthrow; Duc François de

Guise now exercising that unlimited sway in the affairs of the kingdom which in former days was usurped by the mayors of the palace. Yet both duke and cardinal well knew that their enemies were less afraid of than exasperated against them, and that instead of having secured a real victory, they had but entered on a desperate struggle, of which the result was doubtful.

CHAPTER VI.

The Court leave Amboise.—De L'Hôpital succeeds to the Chancellorship.—The Inquisition opposed by him.—Death of Marie de Guise.—Court Gaieties and Court Intrigues.—The Plan of the Tuileries.—Cellini invited by Catherine to Paris.—Much flattered, but declines to leave Florence.—The Admiral at Fontainebleau.—States-General convoked.

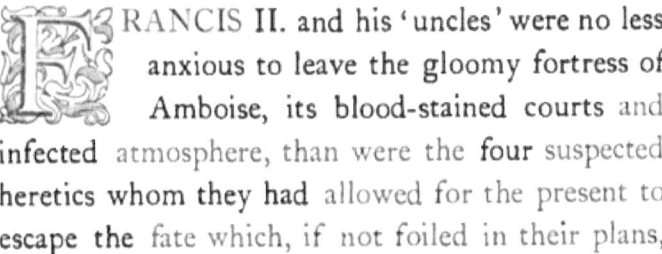RANCIS II. and his 'uncles' were no less anxious to leave the gloomy fortress of Amboise, its blood-stained courts and infected atmosphere, than were the four suspected heretics whom they had allowed for the present to escape the fate which, if not foiled in their plans, the Guises still had in reserve for them.

The young queen and her ladies, the queen-mother, her train of fair damsels, and her two boy princes, were also well pleased when the signal was given for departure. In the brighter abodes of Saint-Germain and Fontainebleau, in mirthful *fêtes champêtres* in their parks and gardens, in the excitement of the royal hunts and the more private Court festivities, which both queen and queen-mother were so fond of—rivalling each other in the lavish expense and *éclat* of their preparation—some perhaps there were who amidst such scenes would soon forget the murderous deeds, the mental agony, the physical suffering they had recently, with but little visible emotion, witnessed.

But if the memory and mental vision of the greater number of the frail fair ones of the demoralized Court of Francis II. and Catherine de' Medici retained but a faint impression of that sanguinary scene, the massacre of the heretics, all, doubtless, at the time would have greatly preferred a more enlivening pastime than that sombre one the cardinal so gaily prepared for them. That zealous prelate may, however, have intended, while amusing the ladies of the household, to convey a needed warning to them. For it had been whispered about that more than one, two, or three of Catherine's *filles d'honneur* had been detected assisting in disguise at 'heretic conventicles,' as the meetings of the Reformers were contemptuously termed. It had even been asserted that the queen-mother herself was not free from a bias towards Reform, though it was a fact patent to all that the party to which she ever inclined was that which for the time being **was in** the ascendant, and **at** that moment the prospects of the Huguenot party had sustained a severe blow.

The Guises mistrusted the queen-mother, **but** as they preferred her alliance **to** her opposition, they yielded to her wish **to** recall Michel **de** L'Hôpital **to** France to succeed Olivier in **the** chancellorship. 'This greatest and one of the most upright of the chancellors of **France,**' as described even by the frivolous and libertine Brantôme, '**was** a man of distinguished literary and judicial capacity. **He was also** an eloquent orator, a great Latinist, the elegance of his Latin verse commanding the admiration of the *savants*, while his just and patriotic views of government and inflexible honesty of purpose secured **the** respect of those who with less disinterested aims were his frequent opponents. His manners were **courteous,** his countenance grave but pleasing, and his general bearing dignified.

De L'Hôpital was at the Court of the Duke **of** Savoy—who had appointed him his chancellor—when recalled to France; having, at the request of the newly-married duchess (Margaret de Valois), who sincerely esteemed him and admired **his** great literary attainments, accompanied **her** and her husband to Nice. Catherine's great acuteness in discerning character, her ability to appreciate such qualities as she perceived in de L'Hôpital, and her desire to elevate such a man to the position of her guide and counsellor, would seem to speak in her favour. But Catherine de' Medici accepted from personal interest those views which in her chancellor were inspired purely by patriotism. 'Strange association!' exclaims a modern historian (H. Martin), 'that of a man so conscientious as de L'Hôpital with a woman so utterly destitute of all moral principle as Catherine de' Medici!'

The chancellor aimed at the pacification of the kingdom by less repressive measures against the Protestants, whom he would have ceased to persecute, and with certain limitations have conceded to them freedom of religious worship. These were the views of the party called 'Les Politiques,' consisting of moderate Catholics, including amongst them many persons of influence and distinction. Catherine also concurred in them so long as she felt persuaded that by peace alone could she reign. But when she was made to believe that the zealots of Catholicism would sacrifice her to their hatred of the Calvinists if the latter were allowed to remain unmolested without further attempt to extirpate them, then the opposing counsels of the chancellor seemed to her fraught with both danger and suspicion.

Throughout the kingdom great agitation prevailed, for the Guises proposed to follow up the defeat of the Amboise conspiracy by establishing the Inquisition in France. To their surprise, the new chancellor firmly opposed it. They knew not his character, and had expected to find in him an intelligent but docile agent to assist in the realization of their plans. He, however, pointed out to them that the result of such a step would be a rising of both Catholics and Protestants against them, and that, as had happened in Naples and Rome, it would be difficult, if not impossible, to pacify the opponents of this measure, to whatever party or faction they belonged. Pens and pamphlets again made war on the duke and the cardinal; the fears of the latter waxing stronger as the menacing language of their foes increased in violence. This led to a royal decree—the Edict of Romorantin—a modification of the first proposal, which henceforth gave the bishops the exclusive right of taking cognizance of the crime of heresy. The Parliament murmured against such a concession to the clergy, and refused to register the edict. Forthwith a royal mandate enforced it.

Working on the fears of the young king, the cardinal obtained from him a further decree, commanding that 'all houses in which heretical conventicles at any time had been held, be razed to the ground and the site never again be built on; and that all persons who had been present at those heretical assemblies be irremissibly put to death.'

The sanguinary deeds which Francis II. had witnessed at Amboise, and the terror he had experienced of the murderous intentions—as he was taught to believe—of his rebellious and heretical subjects, had acted with most unfavourable effect on his fragile frame. Since his return to Saint-Germain, his thoughts had dwelt long and frequently on those things, and again in some mysterious way it had been whispered to him that it was not he who was the object of the people's hatred, but the Guises who were the cause of all the dissensions and troubles of the kingdom. But the poor youth was too fast bound in their coils to be released by any weak efforts of his own. He was surely, if slowly, approaching his end; his quartan fever had returned; the symptoms of his mysterious disease appeared in the blotches on his face and an abscess in his ear. Yet at times the improvement in his condition was so hopeful, that his eventual recovery was **deemed by his** physicians probable.

In the time of Francis I., and to a great extent **during** Henry's reign, Catherine de' Medici had been accustomed to accompany those monarchs, their mistresses, **and their Court from** château to château—Francis I., especially, seeking in **the** excitement of **endless** changes **and** journeys a renewal **of energy if not** of health. **This rambling** life pleased the daughter-in-law **of the** 'chevalier king,' and she seems at that period to have found in the exercise which these continual 'goings and comings,' arrivals and departures, necessitated, **a** means of keeping within reasonable limits that tendency to *embonpoint* which **later on became** excessive.

A removal to **Chambord** for change of air and **scene** was now suggested **by** Catherine and approved by the physicians as likely to benefit the **king, and** cheer the spirits of the young queen—a little saddened at that moment by news of the death **of her mother,** Marie de Guise. This event had also its effect on the influence of the queen-regent's two brothers, by depriving them of what little remaining power they had hitherto contrived to retain in Scotland, and completing the ruin of the Catholic **cause in that country.** The representatives of France were, however, authorized by the duke to treat with Elizabeth and the rebel Scots—the country remaining Protestant and under English influence; its old connection with France being severed, and Mary Stuart its queen but in name.

But whatever the incident that thwarted the plans of one faction, it invariably served to elate the hopes of opposing ones — thus the queen-mother secretly rejoiced, as much as did the Huguenots openly, at the discomfiture of the Guises and the failure of their schemes in Scotland. The duke and cardinal, however, suppressed their resentment, and deferred for awhile taking vengeance on Elizabeth. With a view of regaining the ground they had lately lost and securing popularity, in the event of royal favour failing them on the young king's death, they resolved, as a preliminary to compliance with the wishes of the people for the assembling of the States-General, to convoke an assembly of notables for the 20th of August at Fontainebleau.

The Court then set out for the Château de Chambord—preceded by the whole of the domestic royal household and some hundreds of workmen to prepare for the Court's reception the desolate apartments of that yet far from completed 'wonder of the Renaissance,' and accompanied by a retinue so numerous that, as the Venetian ambassador remarked—with a little exaggeration, perhaps—' it might have been mistaken for the migration of the whole of the inhabitants of some populous city.'

Catherine had always been fond of Chambord. At night, ascending the loftiest of its many pinnacles, surmounted by its gigantic *fleur-de-lys*, she could study the courses of the stars; gleaning from them, as she imagined, that the future would repay her for the neglect and isolation in which her earlier years were passed. By day, accompanying the royal hunt, she would pursue the stag through the intricacies of the extensive forests that for a distance of several miles surrounded the château. Though she was short and her figure the reverse of slim, she was a skilful and daring if not a graceful horsewoman. If we may believe Brantôme, it was she who first attempted to introduce the side-saddle. But it was not so much for the greater ease and convenience she found in it when riding that she invented the mode of putting one leg on the pommel of her saddle, as for the display of the 'fine *tournure* of her ankles, with their perfect-fitting silk stockings, which,' he says, ' she delighted in wearing.'

With the same object Catherine had been fond of joining in the dance. Not the formal passing and repassing, bowing and curtseying, which preceded the more regular and stately Menuet de la Cour, and for which her *embonpoint* unfitted her to take part in with becoming dignity; but the more airy mazes of the dance introduced by the Italians, then so numerous in France, and cordially welcomed at the Court festivities as a new and inspiriting pleasure. Though Queen of France, Catherine de' Medici was then a mere cipher in her own Court. Her personal attractions were few, as generally supposed. But whether she really 'surpassed all the ladies of the Court,' Diana of course included, 'in the fairness of her complexion,' or that 'her complexion was of a dark olive tint;' whether 'her features were of the "finely chiselled" Italian type,' or of 'that grosser one distinctive of the Medici, whose short list of virtues and long one of vices she, as the last of the elder branch of that famous family, fully inherited;' whether she was 'tall and dignified and her figure elegant,' or that 'she was short, stout,' and while still in her prime unwieldy and with no dignity at all—'a dumpy woman,' in fact, such as Byron 'hated,' who shall now declare? For in this varied fashion she has been described by both the pen of the historian and the pencil of the painter.

From the record of her deeds a better judgment may be formed of her character. The habit of reticence and dissimulation acquired in her girlhood concealed abilities and ambitious aspirations, which, from the time of Henry II.'s death, began to be developed in connection with duplicity, depravity, and crime of deepest dye, rendering her at once the evil genius of France and of her own sons and daughters.

The pastimes of royalty had changed but little, if at all, since Francis I. in 1545 held his Court at Chambord. It was the chevalier king's last visit; he was then but a wreck of his former self; old before his time; the result of a career of frenetic dissipation. Like his grandson, Francis II.—a feeble youth but yet on the threshold of life—he went with the hope of obtaining perhaps temporary relief from the agonizing pains of a fearful disease, and to shake off for awhile the melancholy that oppressed him. But both with the young man and the elderly one the hope proved vain. Francis I. survived his last visit to Chambord not quite two years; Francis II. but six months.

There was, however, no relaxation of the customary festivities on the latter occasion. To curtail them would have been like announcing to the king that his doom was sealed. Queen Mary's sorrow, too, proved fleeting as a summer cloud; so the usual round of gaieties went on with so little of variety or novelty that it is surprising the effect was not rather depressing than cheering. The tournament had gone out of favour since Montgomery's encounter with Henry II. proved fatal to that monarch. There remained then little more than the chase, the tennis-court, the dance, and the banquet; in all of which the young king strove to take a part. Perhaps the banquet was the most hurtful to him. For the prodigal expenditure on the royal table during the brief reign of the youthful Francis II. is said to have exceeded in lavishness that of Henry II. to no less an extent than that monarch's surpassed in extravagance the costly banquets of Francis I.

Catherine de' Medici had an enormous appetite, and put no restraint on gratifying it. This propensity for indulging in the so-called 'pleasures of the table,' her sickly son seems to have inherited, and probably it was not the least of the causes of his illness. Indeed the vicious habit of the excessive indulgence of a voracious appetite appears to have been far too general amongst the *grands seigneurs*, and even the *grandes dames* of that day.

But the paucity of amusements may, in some measure, have induced both in sovereign and guests the custom of lingering long at the amply provided State banquets, and in doing something more than justice to the many rather coarse delicacies then in vogue at royal and other tables; for no engagements at concert or play, opera or ball, called them from the festive board, whether assembled at an early dinner or a later, but no less substantial, supper.

There was then no society, in fact, beyond that narrow and dissolute yet exclusive circle called the Court; and dark, dingy, plague-stricken Paris, with its narrow lanes and crooked passages, its mean houses, its pestiferous Palais des Tournelles, had not yet begun to prepare for more social refinement and generally a more genial state of things. It had many years yet to wait for its Place Royale, its Place Dauphine, and other improvements, especially that of the famous Hôtel de Rambouillet, and the opening of the first *salon*—the *salon bleu* of that hôtel, to the *beau monde* of fashion and intellect—and for the *début* of the first queen of society, its celebrated marquise.

While the Court was at Chambord, the queen-mother received from the architects, Philibert Delorme and Jean Bullant, the first designs for the palace of the 'Tuilleries lez Paris.' She proposed to erect this palace for her own residence on ground purchased for a like object by Francis I. forty years before. But that monarch had so many projects of a similar kind in hand, besides many even more expensive fancies to provide for, that there was little or nothing to spare of the vast sums he lavished on his pleasures for the payment of the artists and their assistants employed on those great works. Several were therefore left unfinished, and the projected Tuileries was not in his reign, or that of his two successors, even begun. The unsettled state of the kingdom, and more particularly the emptiness of the public treasury, delayed for yet some years the laying of the first stone of the edifice. Meanwhile an order was given by Catherine for the demolition of that terrible plague-spot, the old Palais des Tournelles. But the work was so slowly accomplished, that several years elapsed ere the ground was cleared and the pestiferous sewer filled up.

There was another expensive project in whose progress she was much interested, and which the sojourn at Chambord and the temporary suspension of open persecution (though secret intrigue was actively at work amongst all parties) gave Catherine an opportunity of attending to. It was the erection of the splendid monument (which has been called 'a lie in marble') to the 'adored memory' of a faithless husband by—if not actually faithless—a more than indifferent wife. She strove to persuade Cellini to leave Florence in order to superintend in Paris the erection of the tomb, and to execute some portion of its sculpture. But Cellini, who in his younger and wilder days abhorred the climate of Paris and France generally —thinking that it damped his spirits and dulled his genius—was now more than ever attached to his native Florence. He had sobered down since the time that he fled so abruptly from France; had married a wife; had sons and daughters growing up around him; was in easy circumstances, and much honoured in his own country. He therefore, though professing himself much flattered by the queen-mother's proposals, yet begged to be permitted to decline them. Germain Pilon, then at the height of his fame, and whom Catherine was then employing in the changes she was making in the sculptured decorations of Chenonceaux, was chosen as Cellini's substitute. The group of the Fates is attributed to him, also that of the Graces bearing an urn, destined to contain the hearts of that devoted pair, Henry II. and Catherine de' Medici.

The month of August was well advanced. On the 20th the 'Notables' were to assemble at Fontainebleau to take into consideration the unsatisfactory state of affairs in France. Being a purely deliberative assembly controlled by no fixed rules, the Guises expected to dominate it entirely. But as it was just possible that the Bourbon princes, together with the constable, his sons and nephews, might unite and thus outweigh the influence of duke and cardinal, and dictate instead of being dictated to, they employed their leisure at Chambord in corrupting the trusted agents of King Antony. Through them false intelligence was conveyed to Nérac, and Antony's fears were once more aroused respecting the safety of his wife's domains. He was very assailable on this point, being fully convinced that Philip would neglect no favourable opportunity of completing the conquest of Navarre. The king and his brother, the Cardinal de Bourbon, therefore determined, most unwisely it was considered, to absent themselves from the Assembly of Notables, merely sending thither an agent to act for them in concert with the constable and the admiral. This agent was arrested by order of the Guises, and of course confessed all he knew, or thought he knew, of the aims and intentions of the Bourbons, and especially of the **Prince de Condé.** The prince was then in the **South** endeavouring **to incite the Protestants of Dauphiny and Provence to further action, with** the view of making a bold attack **on Lyons.**

Greatly **annoyed by the conduct of the** elder Bourbons **in thus giving heed** to timid and treacherous **counsels and their own vague fears, the constable determined to convince the Guises that their manœuvres had failed to disconcert either** him or his family. **On the 20th of** August, **Anne de** Montmorency, accompanied **by his sons and two** nephews, arrived at Fontainebleau, escorted by upwards of eight hundred **cavaliers. The king and queen, the queen-mother** and **the ladies and** gentlemen of **the Court, arrived at the château at** nearly the same hour. **Several of the principal** nobility, very numerously attended, **also entered the town in the course of the day; so that** Fontainebleau, **with its palace, its neighbouring** châteaux, and dwellings of humbler pretensions, found it difficult to accommodate this great **influx** of distinguished visitors.

The Assembly began their deliberations on the following day, and after certain preliminaries had been discussed and settled, adjourned **to the 23rd,** when the young king was to preside. It may be inferred from this that his few weeks' sojourn at Chambord had been at least of some temporary benefit to him. During the second *séance* Admiral de Coligny arrived from Normandy, of which he was governor, bringing with him a petition to the king from the Reformers of that province. In it—after protesting their 'unswerving fidelity to their sovereign, and their condemnation of such enterprises as that of Amboise—they proposed to prove that their doctrine was in strict conformity with the Holy Scriptures and the traditions of the primitive Church. They therefore demanded that liberty of worship with the free exercise of their religion be conceded to them.' On handing the document to the young king, Coligny assured him that 'in Normandy alone there were not fewer than fifty thousand persons ready to place their signatures to it, if they were permitted to assemble for that purpose.'

The Duc de Guise with difficulty commanded his temper while Coligny read this plain-spoken petition, and addressed some favourable comments on it to the king. The Assembly, by many signs of approval and murmurs also of disapproval, testified to the difference of feeling with which they had listened to it. Such, however, was the extreme irritation of the duke and cardinal and other members of their family, on finding that it was not unanimously condemned and rejected, that they would have attempted to close the sittings at once had not the king, who seemed to take much interest in the proceedings, requested all present to express their opinions on the subject. Catherine was present, very anxious as to the result of the discussion, but prepared to support the party, whatever its principles, that should prove itself the strongest.

Two prelates, the Archbishop of Vienne and the Bishop of Valence, declaimed in eloquent terms in favour of tolerance. The latter was influenced by views similar to those of the queen-mother. He thought the Reformers would gain the upper hand, and that speedily. Therefore he loudly condemned the dissolute lives of the Catholic clergy, and approved the austerity of the Huguenots; called on the king to summon a National Council in which the doctrines of the Reformers might be freely and fully discussed; concluding his address by a demand for the immediate assembling of the States-General.* The admiral supported the

* This Bishop of Valence was Jean de Montluc, brother of the famous Captain Blaise de Montluc, distinguished for his bravery as a soldier and his skill as a commander. But his fame was tarnished by his exceeding cruelty, his laurels being always deeply dipped in blood. The bishop was a wily

bishop's demand, and commented on the maladministration of affairs by the Guises. To which the duke replied in very harsh terms that 'All the councils in the world would never prevail on him to abandon the faith of his fathers. And that if fifty thousand Huguenots were ready to sign the petition the admiral was deputed to lay before the king, his majesty could oppose it with more than a million of the true faith.'

The cardinal declared that 'all points of doctrine had been fully discussed and finally settled by former councils. The reform therefore of some abuses, and inquiry into a few instances of laxity of discipline which had lately occurred, could alone justify the assembling of another National Council; but on these grounds he would not oppose it.' He pretended to deplore the little effect the recent 'grievous executions' had produced on the heretics, and suggested that until the

---

and clever diplomatist, often employed by the queen-mother. He was secretly married, and had the Huguenot cause triumphed, as he expected, would have embraced the 're-formed religion.' But it did not, and the excellent bishop had no fancy for becoming a martyr. He therefore turned his back on Calvinism, and that so completely that in 1572 he was one of the most eloquent apologists of the St. Bartholomew massacre. He ended his career a worthy member of the Society of Jesus.

proposed council had concluded its sittings, the punishment of those persons who had strayed from the faith—but had not taken part in acts of sedition—should be suspended. Some of the clergy were not inclined to favour the cardinal's proposal.

However, after further discussion, the Guises yielded to the demand of Catholics and Protestants for the convocation of the States-General. They were to assemble at Meaux on the 10th of December to discuss the long list of grievances which each of the three estates of the realm then proposed to bring forward. The National Council was convened for the 20th of January—their sittings to take place in Paris, where the impossible task was to be attempted of bringing the 'new opinions' into some conformity with the doctrines of the Church of Rome, that Catholics and Protestants might refrain from murdering each other 'for the glory of God,' and dwell together in peace.

'Those Huguenots who would quietly wait the result of the council's deliberations would not in the interval be interfered with.' Such was the promise given by both duke and cardinal; but with no intention of keeping it. It was merely a *ruse* to throw their enemies off their guard. But woe indeed unto those of a more restless spirit, who gave occasion to the myrmidons of the Guises—now more on the alert than ever to entrap them—maliciously to distort incautious words or acts into proofs of seditious intentions, whereon to manufacture false charges against them! The prisons were full of such unwary unfortunates, awaiting in damp, dark cells their miserable doom.*

* See Regnier de La Planche, De Thou, etc. La Planche was a friend and confidant of Marshal de Montmorency. He was well informed of all that was passing relating to the above events. The Guises and Catherine were desirous of enticing him to Court, to extract from him—and they would not have been scrupulous as to the means employed—the secret plans of the Montmorencys and Châtillons. But he seems to have been clever enough to baffle them.

CHAPTER VII.

The Guises and the Protestant Chiefs.—Arrest and Trial of Condé.—Proposed Assassination of King Antony.—Plot a Failure. — Condé condemned to Death. — Illness of Francis II.—His Death, December 5th, 1560.—Queen-Mother's Arrangement with Antony.—Condé Free.—The Chancellor de L'Hôpital.

IT is surprising with what real or apparent zest the Court resumed its customary diversions, while France was agitated to its centre by the violence of political and religious dissension, and Death, in the form of a severe epidemic, was carrying off his now annual tithe of the Parisian population. The most reckless extravagance prevailed in the royal household. To support it the people were bowed down by an intolerable burden of taxation. Steeped in poverty they plotted the overthrow of their tyrants, and, further maddened by the frenzy of religious enthusiasm, both Catholics and Protestants saw in the misery that afflicted the land and the ravages of that fearful scourge, the plague, the hand of an avenging God—the former, on the heretics; the latter, on the idolatrous Church of Rome.

Huguenots and Papists were assembling their forces; waiting but the signal from their respective leaders to fly at each other's throats; to imbue their hands in each other's blood; to march through the land, burning, devastating, laying waste all before them. Plots and counterplots were the order of the day. But the timidity of the King of Navarre again occasioned the failure of a bold and arduous enterprise prepared by the Prince de Condé against the Guises. The latter, having arrested the prince's agents and seized all the documents and private papers which, after a little pressure in the way of torture had been applied, the agents confessed were in their possession, proceeded to concoct an audacious scheme of their own—a tragic plot indeed—whose aim was the destruction of all their enemies at one fell swoop, leaving duke and cardinal masters of the field—omnipotent, in France at least.

Beyond that country the Duke of Savoy and the Italian princes promised, if aided by French troops and money, which last the French clergy were to supply, to exterminate the Vaudois of the valleys of Piedmont, and effectually, once for all, to destroy that hot-bed of heresy, Geneva. Pope Paul IV. had consented to reassemble the Council of Trent, which would interdict the convening of the promised National Council, as well as the discussion of any religious question at the forthcoming meeting of the States-General. The 'Catholic King,' the 'Demon of the South,' must of course have his share in this good work. He proposed to invade Navarre, and to put down any attempt of the heretical subjects of the House of Albret to rise in arms and avenge the assassination of the Bourbon princes.

Catherine de' Medici, as yet, knew not of this murderous scheme. By the advice of her chancellor she held aloof from both parties, and assumed an independent part in view of the increase of power she expected shortly to fall into her hands. Her attitude thus flattered alike the hopes of Huguenots and Catholics, while in the end it disappointed both. The Guises greatly distrusted her; but as the young queen, their niece, was no less *rusée* than the cardinal himself, who had had some part in forming her character, she was entrusted by the brothers to play the spy on the queen-mother. This was by no means an easy task, for Catherine's impenetrability was often the theme and the despair of diplomatists. She was therefore not likely to be thrown off her guard by the wiles of her young daughter-in-law, however well instructed in her part by her uncles, and the less so as Mary Stuart was greatly disliked by the queen-mother.

This feeling was shared by the ladies of the household. It may have been only feigned, as it was their interest to propitiate the queen whose influence was likely the longest to endure, and the days of Queen Mary's authority were already numbered. This they doubtless knew, for those very modest ladies began to accuse her of rarely following their example of wearing a mask. 'She highly esteemed her own beauty,' they said, ' and never failed to avail herself of every opportunity of displaying it.' Even in the religious processions she would appear with an uncovered face ; her palm in her hand, and under an affected air of modesty triumphing in secret joy in eclipsing in magnificence every other toilette, and outshining all beauty by the radiance of her own.'

The courtiers, however, the younger men especially, were less severe in their judgment of Queen Mary. They named her 'Queen of the *beaux esprits*,' admired her singing with the twittering accompaniment of the lute, the facility with which she wrote pleasing verses, and the piquancy of the remarks—slightly satirical—she would sometimes indulge in on the rival Court of the queen-mother and her maids. At a time 'when all the women,' as a French writer says,* 'ate with the appetite of the heroes of the "Iliad,"' and of dishes requiring the digestion of an ostrich, Mary's table, in contrast with the queen-mother's substantial repasts, was served with extremest delicacy. The napkins were perfumed with *sachets* of flowers; the beaks and claws of game and poultry silvered or gilded; pastry, fruits, jellies, and creams arranged in fanciful or artistic forms. No sturgeons, bitterns, and peacocks, or steaming, smoking joints, and similar horrors, requiring the fumes of scented pastilles and a liberal supply of perfumed waters to save the queen and her ladies from fainting. Nothing but *fricassées, fricandeaux, ragoûts, des vols-au-vent*, and similar delicacies; all exquisitely flavoured according to recipes known only to the *chef* of the royal kitchen. The more expensive their preparation, and the greater the difficulty in procuring the ingredients, the better they were relished.

Mary ate but sparingly of these luxuries, and always to the murmur of soft music. She took

* Dargaud, 'Vie de Marie Stuart.'

but little wine, we are told, and that only of the most rare and exquisite kind and highest quality.* To eat or drink at all, it would seem that her appetite needed coaxing and pampering; while the craving one of her royal husband, despite his feeble state of health, must surely have demanded a more substantial *régime*—the delicate kickshaws favoured at Mary's table serving but as a sort of pleasant *entr'acte* to while away the interval between the more solid and serious scenes of his dinner and supper.

The fastidiousness and general extravagance of the queen of 'a poor and barbarous nation,' as the French were apt to term the Scotch, did not escape the severe comment of the 'banker's daughter,' as Mary before Henry's death, following the discourteous example of Diana and her partizans, was wont at times to speak of Catherine. The queen-mother, however, may have expended on the quantity of the viands beneath which her table groaned, as much as her daughter-in-law on the quality of her lighter, appetizing repasts. But it is certain that as regards her toilette she was no less extravagant than the youthful Queen Mary. Before her widowhood she was fond of arraying her bulky figure in the richest-coloured and gold

* Dargaud, 'Vie de Marie Stuart.'

brocades, velvets, and jewelled fabrics that the looms of France and Italy could produce. Now, in imitation of her late husband's mistress, she had resolved to deplore her loss to the end of her days in flowing robes of superb black velvet, damask, or satin, embroidered in seed-pearls, or ornamented with diamonds. She had not the use of the crown jewels, which were not indeed remarkable for either their number or their value, but in both respects were far exceeded by those that were her own private property.

Queen Mary was especially fond of fancy dress, and for every fête was credited with the invention of some startling novelty. Sometimes she would appear in the royal tartan, in which she is said to have looked very charming—*ravissante*, as the courtiers declared. Another time she would appear in the piquant Spanish costume, veiled in the mantilla, and coquettishly fluttering her fan. Again she would charm all hearts draped as a Grecian lady, or wearing some picturesque Italian costume. She is said to have been one of the first to use a real side-saddle, with improvements suggested by Catherine's idea of laying one leg on the pommel to display her silk stockings and the fine *tournure* of her ankles. Those fine silk stockings came from Spain, whence our Queen Elizabeth, who began about this time to wear them, received, as is very well known, her first pair as a present. Doubtless Mary Stuart was not behind the fashion in that respect, though the fact does not appear to have come down to us. Her shoes have been spoken of as wonderfully artistic productions, also her Spanish gloves, richly embroidered, fringed with gold, and adorned with jewelled fastenings.

Alas! Poor Mary! With the period in question—the spring-time of her life—ended, as many have thought and written, all she ever knew of this world's happiness. Perhaps it was so. Yet to be happy would seem impossible for one so young after the deeds of blood she had witnessed, and her knowledge of the cruel persecution going on around her. But from her early training under the watchful superintendence of Catherine de' Medici and that excellent prelate the Cardinal de Lorraine, no wonder that even from her girlish years she should have shown more hardness than tenderness of feeling, and an utter insensibility to the sufferings and sorrows of others. The Guises no doubt expected to find in her a ready and useful tool for the furtherance of their schemes, and the sustaining of their influence over the king, should he at any time display symptoms of a weariness of control. She had shown herself latterly, it was reported, less docile than they expected, and her espionage on the queen-mother does not appear to have been very vigilant or fruitful in its results.

Meanwhile the Guises had spared neither time nor pains to secure the success of the heavy and final blow they were about to deal on the doomed heads of their adversaries. Early in September a royal mandate, issued at the instance of the Guises, had required the attendance of the King of Navarre and the Prince de Condé at Orléans. The king replied that 'if his brother's calumniators were not to be also his judges, he would without delay bring the prince to Court, attended by so small a retinue that his innocence and good intentions would be at once acknowledged.' It was thought advisable to lull rather than excite the fears of the timid King Antony; consequently 'assurances were conveyed to him and the prince on the part of the king, of perfect personal safety, an impartial hearing of the charge against him, and free return.'

Condé would have summoned the people to arms—a summons they were well disposed to obey—and with a sufficient force to defend themselves marched boldly into Orléans. He had not, like Antony, the fear of the 'Demon of the

South' ever before his eyes. Antony, however, was much perplexed. Implicit reliance on the king's promise, or rather that of the Guises, was out of the question. Yet being reassured by his brother, the Cardinal de Bourbon, who was the bearer of the promise, that it was made in good faith, and that the feeling of the queen-mother was favourable to them, Antony determined to set out, and with a very small escort; that, at all events, his own good faith in the matter should be perfectly clear. He had but a vague idea of the course he would take, or the attitude he would assume on arrival, but proposed to discuss the question fully on the journey northward.

Numerous were the letters and messages received *en route*, warning them of the fate awaiting them at Orléans. The Princess de Condé, who—unlike most of the ladies of the Court of that day—adored her husband, implored him to return to Béarn. The absence of one of the brothers, she thought, might be a protection to the other. She knew that against Antony no pretext could be found for a charge of high treason; but she knew not that the Guises found him a stumbling-block to the realization of their plans, and had decided to assassinate him. Her mother, the Dame de Roye —a sister of the Châtillons—added her supplications to her daughter's, **but without avail**. 'The chancellor contrived secretly, by the **agency of** the Duchesse de Montpensier, who stood high in the favour of the queen-mother, but was much attached to the princes and inclined towards the "new opinions," **to urge the** king and **the** prince to change **their route, march south, take up** their quarters in some strong city, **and call on the** ancient allies of France in Germany to **aid** them against the Guises.'

A thousand gentlemen also—well armed **and** equipped—met them as they entered Vienne, and in the name of the Reformers of the South offered to support them with ten thousand combatants **if** they would undertake to carry off the person **of** the king from the Lorrainers. Condé might perhaps have consented. **But** Antony, while thanking **the** gentlemen for **their** offer, forbore to accept it. His scanty *cortége* was reassembled, the journey resumed, and in full reliance on the king's **word** they marched straight into the **arms** of their enemies. Their reception probably **pre**pared them for what was to follow. **No** escort met them outside the town, and on entering the king's apartment he **received** them in that cold and sulky manner that had become almost habitual to him, from the distrust with which he was persuaded to regard all about him except his uncles and protectors, the Guises. But these protectors had so cleverly arranged their plans, that the odium of the treatment they proposed to inflict on the Bourbon princes and their friends should fall alone on the young king. They refrained from being present at his interview with them. Having thoroughly taught him his lesson, they cared not to see it put in practice, withdrawing as soon as the princes entered.

Catherine, however, was present, and bade them welcome in a voice faltering with emotion, and eyes moistened by tears which she seemed scarce able to restrain from streaming forth in a torrent. She would have them infer from that crocodile demonstration that, deceived by the Guises, she had unwittingly aided them in their schemes by her assurance that the King of Navarre and his brother had nothing whatever to fear in repairing to Orléans as Francis requested.

'I have commanded your presence here,' said the young monarch, 'to hear from your own mouth the truth concerning those enterprises imputed to you against the throne and the kingdom.'

Indignantly disclaiming all treasonable acts or intentions, Condé flung back on the Guises the charges brought against himself, at the same time reminding the king that he relied on his promise for his personal safety. For reply the guards entered the royal apartment—a concerted signal being given—and Condé was arrested, and imprisoned in a house that had been fortified and surrounded by cannon expressly for his reception.

The Princess de Condé was permitted to see the king, the Guises affecting to stand aloof as unconcerned spectators of the progress of their own plot, which they were secretly straining every nerve to bring to a desired issue. But in vain the princess knelt at the feet of the royal youth and implored her husband's release. She was harshly repulsed. 'Shall I not be avenged,' he cried, ' on the man who would have deprived me of my crown and my life!' The princess's mother was arrested, and several other persons suspected of favouring the views of the imprisoned prince.

Both the duke and the cardinal had withheld their signatures from the order for Condé's arrest, drawn up in private council and signed by the king and, with the above exception, all present. De L'Hôpital is said to have felt some hesitation at the time of signing it; but his refusal would have involved the resignation of his post, and prevented him from serving the prince more effectually, as he trusted he might be able to do, either during or after his trial.

The King of Navarre, though not placed under arrest with his brother, was treated with the greatest indignity, lodged in a mean house, deprived of the small escort that had accompanied him from Béarn, surrounded by spies, and no further liberty allowed him than to cross over—guards following—from his own lodging to the royal residence, and similarly guarded to return. His complaints of the harshness of his brother's treatment, and his appeals to the king for its relaxation, were received with much haughtiness or with extreme contempt. This course was adopted with the view of betraying him into retorting by menacing or violent language, or some imprudent act. Then, as arranged by the Guises, the king—roused to anger by his vassal's insolence—was to rise from his seat and with his own hand stab him.*

Should strength or courage fail the feeble youth to do the deed, or should King Antony, under his many temptations to resent the insults offered him, still contrive to command his temper, he was to be 'invited to join the royal hunt at Chambord, and an opportunity being arranged to despatch

* Regnier de La Planche.

him by an assassin's hand, his death was to be ascribed to a fatal accident.' The cardinal was exceedingly elated at his own ingenuity in contriving so cleverly for the perfect carrying out of the plot without either he or his brother appearing to raise a finger to help it on. Some qualms respecting the success of their plans—though not qualms of conscience—they, however, did begin to experience. They had cast their net, in the form of a royal mandate, for a large draught, but the fish they wanted were not all disposed to be drawn into it. More than one summons reached the constable. But the arrogant Anne de Montmorency, little accustomed to obey, did not scruple to reply that 'he could not then leave Chantilly;' and, again, 'he was not well enough to take the journey to Orléans.' His eldest son, the marshal, had left for Languedoc, of which province he was governor, and ruled there so royally that he was called its king; tolerating and protecting the Huguenots, though a Catholic himself, but of the moderate or the 'Politique' party. The affairs of his province of course occupied him, and the second son could not do less than remain in filial attendance on his father.

Conjointly with them, the Châtillons were included in the fictitious charge of being associated with the Bourbons in plotting against the State; but the admiral alone obeyed the summons to present himself at Orléans. He knew that the King of Navarre and Prince Louis de Condé were destined by the Guises to die as traitors and heretics, and that on the same scaffold his own head was to fall. His farewell to his wife was therefore, as both believed, a final one. He implored her to adhere with constancy to the true religion, and to suffer death rather than allow her then unborn child to be sullied at its baptism by any of the superstitions of the Papacy. Coligny's two brothers, however, were not so ready as he to lay their heads on the block for the gratification of Monsieur le Duc and his Eminence the cardinal. Odet de Châtillon retired to his episcopate, and D'Andelot at about that time made a rather romantic marriage, so might well excuse himself on the ground that 'he had married a wife, and therefore could not come.'

To the absentees of the family, Coligny owed his life. Such powerful relatives being yet uncaught, the Guises did not venture even closely to imprison him; but allowed him provisionally the same sort of liberty as was permitted to the King of Navarre. Meanwhile, they were hurrying on the condemnation of the Prince de Condé; and at the same time, fearing to lose their prey, were preparing for the assassination of his brother, to whom a royal hunt was announced to take place on the 16th of November, at which he was expected to assist. But on the evening of the 15th King Francis, while attending Vespers, fell into a fainting fit. On reviving, he complained of intense pain from the abscess in the left ear, and passed the night in a feverish condition.

The Guises were in the greatest anxiety respecting the progress of Condé's so-called trial. Many of the usual formalities were omitted, and a novel kind of tribunal was hastily got together, consisting of the Knights of the Order of Saint Michel, two or three members of the king's private council, and the same number of peers of France. To this irregularly constituted assembly the various documents relating to his accusation, and the proofs confirmatory of the charges of high treason brought against him, were submitted; and without further delay sentence of death was pronounced, one only of his judges, the Vicomte de Sancerre, refusing absolutely to sign it. Nevertheless they fixed the day for the prince's execution, the 10th of December, and a priest was sent to him, from whom of course he refused to hear what he termed the 'impieties of the Roman antichrist.' Further, to try whether the natural clinging to life might not operate in bringing about a recantation and his submission to the Guises, one of their gentlemen was sent to ask 'if there were no possible means of effecting a reconciliation between him and his cousins of Guise.' He replied that 'the only way he knew of agreeing with them was at the point of the sword.'

Though sentence of death had been pronounced on Condé, the warrant for its execution had not yet received the necessary signature of the chancellor. He withheld it from day to day, protesting that 'sufficient time had not been given to the examination of the charges brought against the prince. The tribunal commissioned to pass sentence on him had decided too hastily, and should be required to reconsider the matter.' The Guises vainly sought to overcome the chancellor's objections. His object was delay. The famous surgeon, Ambroise Paré, was in attendance on the king, and kept De L'Hôpital daily informed of his condition, which, though fluctuating, gave no sure promise of improvement. He had now taken to his bed, and it was the opinion of Paré and the physicians that he could not survive many days longer.

The Guises are said to have been in a state of extremest agitation. Just as Fortune seemed to have raised them to the very pinnacle of their ambition, and to have brought all their schemes and plans to a nearly successful issue, cruel Fate had chosen that supreme moment to utterly overthrow them. Desperately they now sought the queen-mother, who was so soon to take the place they had usurped in the Government. Earnestly they implored her—of course for her own and the nation's welfare—to consent to the immediate execution of both the King of Navarre and his brother. The chancellor firmly opposed it. He knew that she would not be deterred from consenting because of the criminality of the act; but he pointed out clearly to her that to consent to it would be greatly to her disadvantage.

But the Cardinal de Lorraine placed before her the flattering prospect—the Bourbons being destroyed—of wielding the sceptre of France as queen-regent with undisputed and absolute sway; he and the duke being the most devoted of her humble servants. 'Catherine for a moment stood irresolute between her good and her evil genius.' But the advice of the former prevailed. She thoroughly understood the character of both cardinal and chancellor, and was besides fully aware that in ruling the kingdom she had nothing to fear from the vain, weak, and indolent King of Navarre.

Instead then of being despatched to his doom in the forest of Chambord, or laying his head on the block at Orléans, Antony was summoned to the dying young monarch's bedside, and thence to an interview with the queen-mother in her cabinet. She first reproached him, it appears severely, for troubling the peace of the kingdom by joining in Condé's treasonable enterprises; then required of him the renunciation, in writing, of his claim, as first prince of the blood, to the regency, even should it be conferred on him by the States-General; also a promise of reconciliation with his 'cousins of Guise.' On these conditions she would consent to his holding the first place, after her, in the Government; would appoint him Lieutenant-General of the Kingdom; and, greatest boon of all, would spare his brother's life. The king had been secretly informed that if he declined Catherine's proposals, his own doom as well as his brother's was sealed; so that she did not entirely reject the cardinal's advice, or strictly follow the chancellor's, but used both for her own advantage. The timid Antony promised all that was exacted of him, and embraced, perhaps not very cordially, 'his cousins of Guise,' who on the previous day were plotting to cut his throat.*

The English ambassador, Sir Nicholas Throckmorton, writing to Queen Elizabeth on the 28th of November, says he 'had stayed his despatch of the 23rd because of the king's sickness, that begins now so to succeed that men doubt of his being long lasting.' On the 29th he writes again: 'The constitution of the king's body is such as the physicians do say he cannot be long-lived ; and thereunto he hath by his too timely and inordinate exercise now in his youth added an evil accident. Some say that if he recover this sickness, he cannot live but two years. Therefore there is talk of the French queen's second marriage. Some say the Prince of Spain (Don Carlos) ; some the Duke of Austria (Don John) ; others the Earl of Arran.'

November 30th: 'Great lamentation at Court, the king's recovery being mistrusted.' 'I think it not well,' Sir Nicholas adds, 'to let the Scots know of his danger.' December 1st he writes again: 'Physicians hopeful of the king. Amended ; but so weak that he could not keep the feast of the Golden Fleece on St. Andrew's Day.' December 3rd : 'King's illness supposed to be a device of the Guises, that he may hear no prisoner's

* Henri Martin, 'Histoire de France.'

supplication.' This refers to the Prince de Condé, who, however, did not supplicate; but proudly claimed his privilege as a prince of the blood to be judged only by 'the king and princes, sitting in the Court of the Parliament in Paris—the Chambers also assembled.' The king, whose decrees in private council were absolute, rejected his claim. Two days after he died.

On the 6th, Throckmorton announces the event as follows: 'December 5th king died. Indisposition continued from 17th of November, growing in the end to a fever, together with a catarrh, or rather imposthume in the head, which purged a little by one of his ears. This brought him to a state of extreme weakness, and so spent him that at eleven of the clock in the night of the 5th he departed to God, leaving as heavy and doleful a wife, as of right she had good cause to be, who of long watching with him during his sickness, and painful diligence about him, and specially by the issue thereof, is not in best tune of her body, but without danger. The queen (Elizabeth) has good cause to thank God for so well providing for her surety and quietness by taking away the late king and his father (redoubted of all the world) considering their intentions towards her.'*

* 'Foreign State Papers'—Reign of Elizabeth, 1560.

Though Francis II. was always ailing, his death seems to have come as a surprise on the people; not an unwelcome one certainly, especially to the Huguenots, who hoped that the influence of the chancellor would now supersede that of the Guises. But all the unpopular, arbitrary and cruel acts of the short reign of the feeble youth, who at his death had not by some months completed his seventeenth year, were attributed by 'his uncles' solely to him, they rejecting all responsibility concerning them.

On the morning of the 6th Condé was informed of the king's death, and at the same time a messenger from the queen-mother announced that 'Monsieur le Prince was free.' But the prince refused to receive pardon and to owe his life to 'favour or an act of grace,' without knowing who was his enemy, and by whose order he had been imprisoned. 'It was the act and will of the late king.' No other explanation could he obtain; but he was advised to leave Orléans, and remain in some part of his brother's domains until he received that regular and official justification of what had occurred which his honour, it was pressed on him, exacted. This was a *ruse* of his enemies, to whom his presence in Orléans—where, instead of at Meaux, the States-General were to assemble—

was inconvenient. Condé departed, thus playing unconsciously into the hands of the Guises.

The constable had been kept duly informed of the state of the king's health, and a few days before his death found that he was himself well enough to leave Chantilly for Orléans. With a numerous *cortége* he entered that city, placing his own guards at its gates, and dismissing those posted there by the Duc de Guise, who had assumed the military authority in Orléans, which, as Constable of France, belonged of right to Montmorency, who now asserted it and displaced his adversary. The Guises, however, had determined not to abandon the field to their enemies, or to relinquish an iota of the power they had usurped without a resolute effort to retain it.

The duty, therefore, which devolved on the duke, as Grand-Master of the Household, of remaining by the body of the late king and accompanying it to Saint-Denis, he failed to perform. When the poor youth ceased to live, he was of no further use or interest to his 'uncles,' or apparently to anyone else—the princes, his 'cousins of the blood,' or even to his mother. She, indeed, was suspected of having released him from the prospect of protracted suffering by quietly hastening his departure from this world of sin and sorrow. No one could or would openly accuse her, and it may have been merely suspicion. Such deeds were of everyday occurrence; but it was perfectly well known that Catherine de' Medici, in her thirst for power, would flinch from no crime that enabled her to secure and retain it.

Francis II. was buried without any of the pomp and ceremonial customary at royal funerals; and so hastily also, that the almost humble *cortége*— consisting of two chamberlains, one bishop (the Bishop of Genlis, who was blind), and a score or so of the Scotch guards—reached Saint-Denis as Montmorency entered Orléans, the constable's numerous and imposing retinue passing on the road the young king's funeral carriage and its scanty following.

CHAPTER VIII.

Accession of Charles IX.—Catherine his Guardian with the Power of Regent.—King of Navarre Lieutenant-General. —Cardinal de Lorraine leaves for Rheims.—States-General abolish many Abuses.—The Parliament oppose the Reforms.—Extinction of Debts of the Crown.—States-General adjourn.—Condé's Innocence publicly proclaimed.

'TO an imaginary majority—as contemporary writers have observed—succeeded a real minority.' Charles IX. had not completed his eleventh year at the time of his accession, having been born on the 27th of June, 1550. But so great had long been the general prepossession in his favour that at Henry's death all eyes turned towards him; and had it been possible to set aside the elder brother, Francis, the promising boy of nine would even then have been greatly preferred to the languid youth of fifteen. The death of Francis II. was a welcome event to the nation, putting an end, it was hoped, to the tyrannical rule

of the Guises; while the accession of Charles was greeted with pleasure as the promise to France of a great king. All who had had an opportunity of seeing much of the youthful prince, and forming an opinion of his character at that early age, seem to have been agreed in this expectation.

Giovanni Michiel, writing to the Venetian Senate, says: 'The young king is tall for his age, and slight of figure; he has a pleasing countenance, with very fine eyes, like his father's His movements and manners are easy and graceful, and he is as amiable as any child of his age can be.' Another writer says, 'He is of an irritable temperament, easily agitated, lively enough, but of ardent disposition and fiery imagination—capable, indeed, of much that is good, as he grows up and his fine qualities develop themselves; but also capable of much evil, according to the education he receives, and the examples set before him.' 'He is not robust,' continues Michiel. 'He eats and drinks very little, and it will be necessary to be watchful over him, and restrain the inclination he already exhibits for violent bodily exercise. He is fond of tennis, and of riding and fencing, which doubtless are suitable exercises for a prince; but at present they are beyond his strength, and when he is fatigued long repose is needed, for he enters with so much ardour into every active pursuit, that the fragile frame seems to quiver under the spirit's deep emotions, and his respiration becomes difficult.

'He now takes little interest in study, but resigns himself to it, to give pleasure to his mother. Being, however, but an unwilling student, his progress in learning is not great. War is of all subjects the one most interesting to him. The military, therefore, stand especially high in his good graces. When he was but Duke of Orléans, and the State of Milan was spoken of as his appanage (perhaps to flatter and amuse him), he would listen with the greatest delight, and require the military men about him to promise that they would follow him to his duchy in the next expedition. But since his accession to the throne, one of his ministers, when introducing a Milanais gentleman who came to take leave of him on his departure for the duchy, privately told the youthful monarch that it was advisable to receive this gentleman very graciously, he being a person of considerable influence in Milan. With great animation Charles instantly replied, " I know that well. But as I am now a king, you should understand that I ought not publicly to speak of such matters."

'His natural inclination for warlike themes is fostered and confirmed by his governor, M. de Sipièrre, who talks with him of nothing but battles, conquests, and the organization of armies, as matters alone worthy the attention of a king. So that if inclination did not impel him that way, education would train him.' A device was chosen by the chancellor for this royal youth on whom such flattering hopes were built. It consisted of two pillars with the motto, 'Justice et miséricorde.'

The States-General convoked by the late king— ostensibly for inquiring into the administration of the affairs of France and the suggestion of measures for their more satisfactory conduct in future— assembled at Orléans on the 13th of December. The death of Francis II. had greatly changed the face of things, and the Assembly was otherwise constituted than the Guises had intended, including amongst the deputies of the *noblesse* and the *tiers état* many 'malcontents,' as well as known and suspected heretics. These, the Guises, expecting to dominate the Assembly, had proposed not only to exclude as unduly elected should they refuse to sign a confession of the Catholic faith, but to send to the stake at once, without any pretence of a trial; thus, with little trouble, getting rid of a large batch of their enemies at one blow. This test of fitness to deliberate on affairs of State they still made an effort to enforce; but from the indignation it aroused were unable to do so.

The first session was in consequence opened rather clamorously. The young king was present, also the queen-mother, and the King and Queen of Navarre. The first business of the Assembly was the nomination of a regent; the next, to provide for the payment of the debts of the two preceding reigns, amounting to upwards of forty-three millions —'intrinsic value, 160,000,000 francs, according to the exchange rate of the *marc d'argent* of that day,' (H. Martin)—and to release their youthful successor from poverty and the misery of an empty exchequer. The Chancellor de L'Hôpital opened the proceedings with an address to the three estates. His discourse was 'characterized by noble sentiments, great simplicity, dignity and eloquence.' He spoke in strong terms of deprecation against religious persecution, and exhorted the Assembly to refrain from changing the name of Christians for mere party names and offensive epithets—such as Huguenots, Lutherans, and Papists. He concluded his address by asking 'sympathy for the young king left in so miserable a position financially, with the accumulated debts of his father and brother to discharge, to an amount that probably had never before been laid on any orphan. He trusted that the three estates would assist the king in paying those debts, and promised that the expenses of the State should in future be reduced as much as possible.'

The organization of the Government, as adopted after the death of Francis II., viz., that of the regency of the queen-mother, was approved by the clergy. The *noblesse* and *tiers état* preferred that of the King of Navarre. But Antony put forward no claim, though urged by many of the nobility, and expressly enjoined by Calvin, to demand his rights as prince of the blood, 'the interests of the nation being endangered under the rule of a foreign woman.' But Antony kept his promise to Catherine, less, it was said, from any scruple of breaking it than from his love of indolence. Prince Louis might have stimulated him to take a different course; but he had been cleverly induced to retire to his brother's domains in Picardy, 'to await the explanations his honour demanded respecting his recent imprisonment.'

The regency was, in fact, not given to anyone, so much had faction, at that disastrous period, weakened the political order of the kingdom; but the personal guardianship of the king was conferred on Catherine in her maternal capacity. Having, however, fully satisfied herself that this power could not be taken from her, she feigned to have received it from the young king himself, with the approval of the three estates, on consenting to share the administration of affairs with Antoine de Bourbon, who was accordingly named Lieutenant-General of the Kingdom. A State Council, composed of ten of the principal nobility, was also appointed by the three estates to assist the queen-mother and her lieutenant-general by their advice in the transaction of public business. Catherine, in order to excuse herself to Philip II. for allowing the heretic King of Navarre to share the government of the kingdom with her, made it appear that she acted under restraint. But that she might be fully armed against any insidious attempt to seduce her from the true faith, she prayed her amiable son-in-law to send her a Spanish confessor.

The Duc de Guise retained his post of Grand-Master of the Household. The Cardinal de Lorraine retired to Rheims — his niece, Mary Stuart, it is supposed, accompanying him. He had expected to be the spokesman of the three estates; but the clergy alone accepted him as their orator, the two others rejecting him because of the charges they proposed to bring against him of immorality and of extensive depredations on the public purse during the time he held the office of Controller of the Finances. Greatly offended, he thought it dignified, as well as prudent, to withdraw from the Court for awhile.

Catherine being now the first person in the realm, as well in authority as dignity, attempted to re-establish the royal power without the aid of either Bourbons or Guises. She did not wish that her son should really be king, but that by destroying the chiefs of both parties by means of each other, she might govern alone without opposition or contradiction. In this, in a great measure, she succeeded, displaying much skill in managing affairs of State (the hereditary merit of her family). She made the appointments to offices of State and the principal benefices, dispensed favours, granted pardons, and kept possession of the great seal used by the sovereign. She spoke the last word in the Council of State, in order to give a *résumé* of the opinions of others, on which she replied, either in conformity with the deliberations of the Council or her own views and opinions. The lieutenant-general was a mere cipher on these occasions—' changeable and simple enough' (says Suriano),*

* 'Reports of Venetian Ambassadors.'

'and affecting a great knowledge of affairs, but understanding them little.'

She held the young king entirely under her sway, scarcely ever allowing him for an hour to be absent from her, and permitting none but herself to sleep in his chamber. Very early did this machiavellian princess begin her son's education of corruption. The violent religious and political factions which then agitated the country, made it easy for her to persuade him that all about him were enemies against whom he must ever be on his guard, and that in her alone could he find fidelity. She made him an adept in dissimulation, though nature, as we may glean from contemporary witness, had endowed Charles IX. with all the qualities and even the failings most opposed to that vice. And so securely did she fix her yoke upon him from his early boyhood that, although in after years he often in his transports of rage shuddered under its galling influence, never was he able to free himself from it.

The form of government being settled, Catherine contrived to prevent the public announcement of the King of Navarre's official appointment as Lieutenant-General of the Kingdom, that it might be inferred that everything, as well in the government as in the education of the princes, proceeded on her sole authority. But the attention of the nation was then wholly given to the discussions of the States-General, who propounded many wise regulations for the well-being of the people ; for the prosperity of commerce ; for the improvement of the city of Paris and other large towns. Many reforms, both ecclesiastical and judicial, were proposed, and tolerance of the 'new opinions' and freedom of religious worship also met with a favourable reception and hearing, except from the clergy.

On the 28th of July a royal mandate required the Parliament of Paris to suspend all proceedings having reference to religion, even against persons who with arms in their possession had been present at the religious assemblies, and to set at liberty all who for such causes were then imprisoned. This was followed on the 31st by the famous ' Ordinance of Orléans,' which in the king's name promulgated the greater part of the numerous reforms (in some instances slightly modified) demanded by the representatives of the *tiers état*. The adoption of many of these reforms was due to De L'Hôpital's earnest advocacy of them—especially those which abolished the sale of judicial offices, and forbade the judges to receive pensions, presents, or bribes in any form from accused persons whose guilt or innocence they were called upon to adjudge. The majority of the Parliament strongly resented these acts of the reforming chancellor, as they deprived the magistrates of a large part of their gains. Remonstrances on their part proving ineffectual, they revenged themselves by protesting against the public recognition of two religions in the same State, and refusing to register the decree of the 28th of January, unless a further royal decree were issued, banishing those heretics who, on being released, would not promise to live henceforth as good Catholics.

This was to render the amnesty a mere dead letter, as none of the Reformers would make the required promise. Nevertheless, the demand of the Parliament was privately complied with. Even the 'Grand Ordinance,' as it was termed, if not utterly rejected, seems to have remained entirely inoperative. Yet, with the exception of putting an end to the bribery and venality which had long disgraced the Parliamentary assembly, the chief reforms it enacted had often for years past been declared by the Parliament itself most urgently needed. The main cause of this opposition was, however, attributable less to disapproval of the edicts themselves than to jealousy of the States-General from whom they emanated. The periodical assembling of the three estates was then very generally demanded, which the aristocratic magistracy considered threatening to the importance of the Court of the Parliament of Paris.

The two questions which to the queen-mother were of greatest interest and importance (for to gain her ends she was on all sides lavishing promises in default of money) were the replenishment of the empty exchequer and the payment of the debts of the State. They were not yet disposed of, the deputies being of opinion that the powers confided to them were not ample enough to allow them to consent to the immense sacrifices required of them by the Crown. They desired, therefore, to return to their several provinces to lay before their constituents the reported condition of the State's finances, and to invite discussion upon it. An adjournment in consequence, for some months, took place on the 31st of January.

The attitude assumed by the Parliament with reference to the decree of amnesty greatly exasperated the Huguenots, and in several of the provinces the chiefs of the party had with difficulty restrained their followers from interrupting the services of the Catholic Church, even as they at their prayer-meetings had been interrupted and also ill-treated by the Papists. Conflicts had taken place in which blood had been shed; assassinations were frequent; discord was said to reign at Court hand in hand with depravity. A rupture was also anticipated between the queen-mother and the lieutenant-general, when Prince Louis de Condé should reappear to stimulate the differences known to exist in the royal circle, and to incite the Reformers to more energetic action. In full assembly the little king had declared the prince's innocence of the acts of high treason imputed to him by the Guises, authority being also given him to demand another and more ample declaration thereof in the Court of Parliament. He could not, therefore, be longer excluded from his seat in the king's private council chamber; consequently the next meeting face to face of the intended victim and his would-be murderer was looked forward to by both factions with singular agitation and mingled hopes and fears.

The poltroon cardinal, who on his knees had implored the queen-mother to consent to the prince's execution 'while yet there was time'—in other words, ere the grim tyrant Death, whose uplifted arm was about to descend on the head of her own son, had given the final blow—had fled the Court. At his Palace of Rheims, while his enormous peculations and his grossly immoral life were being exposed before the States-General at Orléans, he was passing his days in the pious duties of his archiepiscopacy; reproving the backslidings of thoughtless young abbés; inflicting penances; exhorting the lukewarm to cultivate a more ardent zeal in the interests of Mother Church, and generally exhibiting an edifying example of the blessedness of serenity of conscience under slanderous accusations and unmerited persecution. Whether the exemplary prelate added to those duties the further one of affording at Rheims a retreat to his niece, the young queen-dowager, during the period of her mourning and retirement from the Court, as some writers relate, seems doubtful.

CHAPTER IX.

Catherine's Crooked Policy. — Her 'Flying Squadron.' — Mary Stuart's Mourning.—Sir Nicholas Throckmorton's Letters.—Mary in Lorraine.—Her Brother, the Bishop, and other Advisers.—Her Departure.—Charles's Deep Impressions.—Damville, Brantôme and others accompany her.—Arrival in Scotland.—The Nobles sympathize.

PART of Catherine de' Medici's wily policy for the attainment of her objects was the culpably seductive influence she brought to bear on some of the chief men of the day. It mattered little whether they were associated with her or not in the Government, if likely by their popularity or position to thwart her views or to further them; or might be turned to account, could she ensure their support, discover their secrets, disarm or render null their resentment, as it chanced at the moment to fall in with her schemes. This she accomplished by means of the fascinations of a troop of young girls, especially trained by her for the services she required of them, in disregard of all moral principles and feminine modesty. Their number eventually reached three hundred, their courtesy title being 'maids of honour,' their familiar sobriquet the 'queen-mother's flying squadron,' as they accompanied her (in detachments probably) on her frequent journeys, and in her endless changes of residence.

They were not, however, at the period in question nearly so numerous a force. Great beauty of face and form, graceful manners, and an air of modesty to mask unblushing vice, good birth, much intelligence, and no troublesome scruples to lie in the way of accomplishing their gracious mistress's behests, were the necessary qualifications for the effectual discharge of their duties. To find them united in the person of one fair form was naturally very rare, so that the formation of the queen-mother's wonderful phalanx of dissolute youth and beauty necessarily demanded time, close observation, and all that keen discernment of character attributed to Catherine de' Medici, in order to discover not merely the requisite personal attractions, but with them the ductility of mind that most readily would yield to the impress of corruption.

It appears that Catherine had made some timid attempts of the kind in the lifetime of Henry II., with the view of detaching him from his allegiance to the ever fair Diana. But her success was not great, the elderly Court beauty reigning supreme to the end.

When, however, the youthful and brilliant Mary Stuart became Queen of France and received the homage of the Court, the courtiers, young and old—to the great scandal of the ladies —ready to fall at her feet in adoration, Catherine perceived that in this young Scotch beauty a more formidable rival than Diana had arisen. She had hastened, on Henry's death, to possess herself of the Great Seal; but the sceptre she had thought to add to it, because of the feebleness of the monarch, was grasped by the Guises, who protected their niece from insidious attempts of the queen-mother to weaken her influence with the young king. Until Francis died, Catherine possessed but the mere shadow of authority. But she availed herself of that shadowy power to intrigue in all directions, to flatter the Huguenots with hopes of better things, and the Catholic 'malcontents' with full redress of their grievances, when she and Charles should reign.

Meanwhile she was planning the increase of her squadron. Secretly also seeking to undermine the favour with which many of the nobility—ladies not excepted—who were previously somewhat prejudiced against the Queen of Scots, had begun to regard her, from her affectionate and constant attendance on the young king in his illness. Catherine is said to have 'mortally hated' Mary Stuart, who doubtless had treated her with unbecoming superciliousness. She had resolved that she should leave France, and having demanded the royal jewels, which were sent immediately by Queen Mary to Charles IX., who gave them into the custody of his mother—Catherine at once made it unmistakably apparent to the young widow that she had little consideration or kindness to expect from her. But that Mary did not accompany her uncle the cardinal, when, a week after the death of Francis, the hostile attitude of the States-General induced him to repair to Rheims, is evident from the reports of Sir Nicholas Throckmorton for the information of Elizabeth and her ministers.*

'On the death of the king,' he writes, 'she immediately changed her lodgings' (apartment in the Louvre), 'withdrew from all company, and became so solitary and exempt of worldliness, that she saw no daylight for forty days. For fifteen days she admitted to come into her chamber none

* See 'Foreign State Papers'—Reign of Elizabeth, 1560, 1561.

save the king, his brethren, the King of Navarre, the constable, and her uncles, and four or five days after some bishops and ancient knights of the Order; but none of the younger, saving Martignes, who having done her good service and married her chief gentlewoman, had so much favour showed him.'

'The ambassadors, lastly, were admitted as they came, and all have been with her to condole, saving I, which I have forborne to do, knowing not the queen's pleasure in that behalf.' The Spanish ambassador was with her longer, Throckmorton thought, than he should have been; 'an hour,' he says, 'being more than necessary for the ceremony of condoling.'

He adds, however, that 'her wisdom and kingly modesty are so great, in that she thinketh herself not too wise, but is content to be ruled by good counsels and wise men; so that by their means she could not well do amiss.'

Elizabeth delayed authorizing her ambassador to offer her condolences to Mary until towards the end of February. She had been much irritated by the obstinate refusal of Francis and Mary to renounce the title of King and Queen of England, when the Guises desired their agents, after their sister's death, to treat with Elizabeth's plenipotentiaries. Generally, Throckmorton wrote very favourably of Queen Mary. 'Her ability,' he says, ' was not perceived while the king lived ; but she now shows great wisdom and modesty and great judgment for her years, with wise handling of herself and matters. Some who then made little account of her, now honour her for her wisdom.'

There was then much speculation concerning the young dowager's second marriage. The Spanish ambassador's breach of etiquette by a too prolonged visit of condolence may have been owing to his availing himself of the opportunity of ascertaining her views respecting the suggested marriage with Don Carlos. For the English minister remarks, ' The House of Guise presently beareth small rule. Their hope is in Spain.' But the reports respecting Don Carlos, who was never likely to be King of Spain, were rather discouraging, and Mary said she ' esteemed more the continuance of her honour and to marry one that may uphold her greatness, than she passeth to please her fancy by taking one that is accompanied by such small benefit or alliance as thereby her estimation and fame is not increased.' This also may have been announced for the purpose of damping the ardour of some members of the *haute noblesse* who were suppliants for her favour.'

Sir Nicholas also reported, she 'desires to return to Scotland, but at the request and suit of her subjects. Also she works that those who shall request her to come home shall promise all obedience, to whom she will assure all good favour that a prince can promise to a subject.'

Notwithstanding the dissensions then disturbing the accustomed round of revelry, the young widowed queen evidently occupied more attention at Court than was pleasing to the queen-mother. Much negotiation between the Princes of Lorraine and Spanish ambassador, French ministers, agents from Scotland, etc., was carried on respecting her; but its precise nature has only been suggested. As Throckmorton remarks in one of his despatches, 'They will have time now to provide that the second marriage of the Queen of Scotland shall do but little harm,' it may be inferred that the Spanish marriage was the subject of their conferences, from which, however, nothing satisfactory resulted.

It is, however, certain that Mary Stuart had not many real friends at the French Court; and when her day of power vanished, rapidly also vanished the crowd of flatterers who erewhile had feigned to almost worship her. Even the Guises—the time of mourning, in conformity with the etiquette of the Court, which Catherine had neglected, being fulfilled—counselled departure. Mary was conducted to Rheims, and afterwards retired for a while to the Convent of Saint-Pierre-les-Dames, of which her aunt, Renée de Lorraine, was abbess.

Mary's mother, who died in Edinburgh on the 11th of June, 1560, had requested on her deathbed that her heart might be sent to Lorraine. It was brought to the convent, enclosed in a silver urn, shortly before Mary's arrival. This event occasioned the renewal of her mourning and her grief. One can, indeed, well understand how forcibly the contemplation of such a relic in the unaccustomed quiet and solitude of convent life must have brought home to her feelings the lonely isolated position she was placed in by the double loss she had sustained within the past few months.

Bidding adieu to her aunt, Mary returned to Rheims, and thence (according to the historian Rapin Thoyras), 'knowing that her mother-in-law did not like her, repaired to Nancy.' She was visited while at Rheims by Martignes, De la Brosse, De L'Oysel, and the Bishop of Amiens. The latter was well acquainted with the affairs of

Scotland, and knowing that she proposed shortly to return thither, thought it his duty to give her some information respecting the country she was going to govern, but of which she knew comparatively nothing, having been sent away to France when but six years old. The bishop and her friends recommended her to secure the friendship and goodwill of her illegitimate brother James Stuart, the Prior of St. Andrew's, attaching him to her by favours and benefits; also the Counts of Argyle and Leddington.' Further, ' they advised her to rely for support rather on the Protestants than the Catholics, the latter being in all respects, they assured her, inferior to the former.'

Lesley (the historian, and Catholic Bishop of Scotland), who was sent to France by some of her Catholic subjects to advise with her, and who met her, it appears, while on her journey to Nancy, counselled her to pursue an entirely different course to that suggested by the Bishop of Amiens. He bade her beware of confiding in the Prior of St. Andrew's; urged her to proceed to Aberdeen, where she could put herself at the head of a body of Catholic troops, and re-establish religion on the same footing as before the recent changes.

On the following day the prior appeared in

person to pay his respects to his royal sister, whom he met at Joinville. He approved her resolve to return to Scotland, and gave her advice far more suitable in the then existing state of affairs than Lesley's. She could reign happily and tranquilly, he told her, only by following the course taken by her predecessors with the assistance of the States. Mary seems to have adopted his views, as she commissioned the prior to return to Scotland and prepare for her reception, and to authorize the States to decree whatever they considered desirable for the welfare of the people and kingdom.* Poor Mary, however, was in no haste to leave the country of her adoption for her native land. Naturally, France was far dearer to her, and the ties of family and affection which further attached her to it were wanting in Scotland. A hundred times rather would she have lived at one of the cities assigned her as dowry—Touraine or Poitou—simply as dowager, than have left the 'plaisant pays de France' to reign over a people destitute, as she believed, of politeness or courtesy —little better, indeed, than savages. From day to day her departure was delayed. Her uncles, the Dukes of Aumale and Elbeuf, advised her to remain; but the cardinal, who from political

* See Durgaud's 'Vie de Marie Stuart.'

motives feared to offend the queen-mother, assumed an air and tone of authority, almost compelling her to leave France.

One principal reason assigned for Catherine's anxiety to hasten Queen Mary's departure was the fear she entertained that the beauty and accomplishments of the young dowager should some day touch the heart of the youthful sovereign. Catherine certainly extended her views very far into the future. Should the presence of this enchantress kindle, as she dreaded, a dangerous flame in Charles's heart, her motherly influence over that precocious and ardent youth would be effaced, and Catherine once more be deposed by the Queen of Scots and the Guises. Unable longer to put off the evil day, Mary returned to Paris to pay her respects to the king, who had been crowned on the 15th of May while Mary was at Nancy. She accompanied him to Saint-Germain, where she took an affectionate leave of the whole Court, who replied to her tender adieux, we are told, with many sighs and tears.

These tender adieux seem to have really made so deep an impression on Charles that he ever after spoke of the Scottish Queen as the most beautiful princess in the world. Some years later he could not look on her portrait in the Louvre without emotion, and, with his eyes fixed upon it, would express his regret that she left France. He for some time indulged in the hope of marrying her, often inquiring whether there would be difficulty in obtaining the needful dispensation from Rome. It was not doubted at Court that had she remained he would have shared his throne with her. The cardinal, becoming aware of this, regretted the unwise haste with which he had urged her departure. His manœuvres, in consequence, gave some uneasiness to the queen-mother. It was, however, too late to retract his rash orders, and Catherine would never have consented to his bringing his niece back to France.

Mary was accompanied by the cardinal, the Ducs de Guise and Nemours, and other princes of their house to Calais, where, on the 15th of August, 1561, she embarked for Scotland. She was escorted by the Grand Prior of France, the Duc d'Elbeuf, and several other noblemen, partizans of the Guises. Amongst others who made the voyage with her was Damville de Montmorency, the constable's eldest son. 'This gave many people much to think of as well as to talk about.' It greatly displeased the King of Navarre, who was said to have desired to repudiate his wife, Jeanne d'Albret, that he might marry Mary Stuart.

Damville had long been deeply in love with the young queen, his attentions, it was remarked, being received with unusual complaisance on her part. This gave rise to much jealousy amongst other adorers who sought her smiles with less success, and it was believed that she had a mind to make Damville her husband. He was, in fact, already married. But his wife had recently afforded him a sufficient pretext for demanding a divorce by embracing the reformed faith. Mary, it has been asserted, suggested a speedier method of removing the obstacle to their union—a groundless charge, doubtless, no incident of her life at that early period warranting such a suspicion.

Besides the revenues of her dowry, which included Epernay, Poitou and Touraine, she received from France a pension of 20,000 livres. Many jewels and other valuable property also belonged to her. These the Cardinal de Lorraine advised her to leave with him for safety, as 'she was about,' he said, 'to make a voyage, as it were, for another world.' She, however, knew him too well to follow his advice, but simply replied that 'as she was about to risk her life by sea, she might well venture to risk her jewels and valuables also.'

Brantôme has left us an interesting account of

her last adieux to that belle France she loved so much, as she sat on the deck of the vessel with strained eyes suffused with tears, striving to catch the latest glimpse of its fast-receding coasts. He also accompanied her on her voyage.* On the 19th of August she landed at Leith unexpectedly, and after reposing for awhile was conducted to Edinburgh and the palace of her ancestors.

There, arrayed in the deep mourning prescribed —according to ancient usage—for the widowed queens of France, Mary Stuart received the submission of the Scottish nobles. Her dress was a robe and train of rich white velvet, with sleeves of silver cloth, fitting the lower part of the arm, but full and puffed at the shoulders. Her chemisette was of fine white lace, and, covering her shoulders, she wore a veil or scarf of silver-tissue and lace. Her hair lay in small frizzy curls over the temples, but was plain at the top, and tied back with white ribands. Her bonnet or cap was also of white velvet, of the pointed shape known as the Mary Stuart cap. It was placed rather backward, so as not to conceal the hair, and was edged with three rows of fine pearls. A necklace also of pearls—three rows of unequal length—encircled her throat.

* See Brantôme's 'Dames illustres—Marie Stuart.'

Suspended from her waist by strings of pearls was a white velvet pocket or pouch, and beside it hung the small gold whistle, which the princesses and ladies of the Court then used to call their attendants or pages. The pocket, as was the fashion of the time, contained the literary novelties of the day—the sonnets of Ronsard, Saint-Gelais, or other celebrity in vogue—splendidly bound, as an ornament of dress.

The interesting appearance of their young queen, her acknowledged beauty, and the perfect confidence she appeared to have in them (the cardinal had ably trained her for this scene), touched the rough Scotch barons. They could not but admire such a vision of loveliness; while by her gentle, courteous manners she succeeded, if but for awhile, in gaining their sympathy, though not exactly, as sometimes stated, 'in uniting the different factions which had divided Scotland during her absence.'

The rough John Knox when referring to the youthful queen, exclaimed: 'She is no woman, but some pagan goddess—a Diana or a Venus.' Her return neither weakened Protestant ascendency in Scotland, nor Elizabeth's influence there.

CHAPTER X.

Condé's Return to Court.—Antony roused to Action.—The States of Pontoise.—Colloquy of Poissy.—The Calvinistic Minister, Théodore de Bèze. — Catherine's Letter to Pius IV.—Consternation at the Vatican.—The Legate and the General of the Jesuits.—Edict of Tolerance, January, 1562.

THE return of **Prince Louis de Condé to the Court of France was speedily** followed **by open** rupture between **the King of** Navarre **and the Guises. For the first time the weak and vain Antony of Bourbon was made to recognise the fact that both** he **and his** brother had escaped, **as** it were by a miracle only, the death and **dishonour to which** the duke **and** the cardinal had doomed them. **In a spirit of** unwonted audacity, kindled at last **by a sense of** his own and the prince's wrongs, he attempted— in virtue of his position of Lieutenant-General— **to** dispossess the duke of his office **of Grand-Master of the Household, and succeeded in** depriving him of the insignia of that post—the golden keys of the palace.

Either he or Guise, he declared, must quit the Court. Catherine opposed; unwilling to place herself unreservedly in the hands of either party. Immediately the Bourbon princes invited their friends and partizans to follow them to Paris, there to proclaim King Antony regent of the kingdom. But just as he and Condé were about to set foot in the stirrup, the constable, his sons and nephews, and several hundred noblemen and gentlemen also proposing to mount and accompany them, the old Cardinal de Tournon urged Catherine, who affected to be in despair, to require without delay, and in the young king's name, Montmorency's immediate presence in the king's private cabinet.

As Francis II. was instructed by the Guises to dismiss 'his father's friend' from the Court, when his presence was inconvenient to them, so now the boy Charles was taught by his mother to whine out a prayer that 'his father's friend' would not forsake him, as he, at his tender age, needed his counsels, therefore desired him to remain near his royal person. 'Montmorency—who had no real sympathy with the views of the heretical Bourbons, Châtillons and his moderate Catholic sons, and only on account of his feud with the Guises and the influence of his nephews, had been drawn into seeming unity with this reforming party—was glad to profess himself bound to obey his sovereign's commands.'*

This defection deprived the Bourbons of their chief authority for the step they were taking, and Antony's courage grew rapidly lukewarm. As was foreseen, he declined, in spite of Condé's remonstrances, to pursue his project further until supported by the constable. His constant terror of rousing the ire of Philip of Spain, and of a Spanish invasion of Navarre, also damped his ardour—Jeanne, the more able ruler of her little kingdom, being then also in France. Yet the *noblesse* and *tiers état* (the States-General having reassembled) were clamorous for the regency of the King of Navarre, threatening to withhold the promised subsidies if his election was opposed and the Guises retained a voice in the royal councils.

Also they approved and adopted his audacious and, as they considered, patriotic proposal to pay

* This is said to have been a concocted scheme between the queen-mother, the constable, and the persecuting old Cardinal de Tournon, the young king being taken into their confidence as a lesson for him in kingcraft.

the debts of the Crown by means of the State's resumption of the extensive domains—comprising nearly a third of the kingdom—which, together with extravagant pensions for which no services had been rendered, and the creation of useless offices for sale to the highest bidder, had been lavished with so prodigal a hand on favourites by the late king and his father. This measure, without consultation with Catherine, had been boldly suggested by Antony, spurred on by his brother. It was especially aimed at the Guises; but it touched the constable so closely that it contributed further to alienate him from the reforming party, whose aims and heretical principles he already abhorred.

Marshal Saint-André was another of those favourites, who, by flattering the monarch and paying court to the all-powerful Diana, had obtained the grant of nearly half a province, with governorships and other lucrative posts. The Duchesse de Valentinois herself was menaced with a demand for the restitution of those wide domains that formed a chief part of her enormous wealth, and of which the Guises looked to inherit a considerable portion.

This assumption of independent power on the part of the King of Navarre, and the support he met with from the States-General, alarmed the queen-mother. At first she thought by supercilious treatment to drive him from the Court, but was dissuaded by De L'Hôpital, lest the Huguenots, who were committing sad outrages in the provinces, should resent the affront by further acts of violence. 'Sentence of death was suspended over the heads of all who assembled to pray or to preach according to the forms of the "new religion."' But the Huguenots, setting these decrees of the Parliament at defiance, now assembled openly. Persecution had not thinned their numbers, but added to them daily. This emboldened them, in those towns where they found themselves in sufficient force, to establish their prayer-meetings in some of the churches; after having broken or cleared away the 'images and idols of pagan Rome' and destroyed the altars. They even disturbed the Catholic services, ridiculed the processions, and with so much impunity—though in some towns the Catholics retaliated furiously—that it seemed as if Calvin was about to triumph over Rome.

The King of Navarre took courage, and announced that 'within a year he would cause the Gospel to be proclaimed throughout the kingdom.' But the Spanish ambassador (according to Bouillé, 'Histoire des Guises'), requiring of Antony confirmation or denial of this announcement, which was made, it appears, to the Danish ambassador, he privately explained it as meaning that 'within a year there should be neither preaching nor prayer-meetings throughout the country.' Both services were, however, then daily and publicly celebrated, with all Calvinistic rites, in the apartments of the Prince de Condé and the admiral.

The nobles of the Court looked on such Calvinistic innovations as the abolition of the confessional and the suppression of abstinence in Lent with much approval. The queen-mother herself momentarily seemed disposed to follow the stream in the direction of heresy—eating meat without restraint on the fast-days, and apparently without any qualms of conscience—for which she was unsparingly attacked in many of the Catholic pulpits of Paris. Notwithstanding, the Bishop of Valence (Montluc) was permitted to preach at Fontainebleau before the queen, the king, and the whole Court, on the necessity of praying to God and singing psalms in French, and having the Scriptures translated into that language that the people might read and understand them. Some indirect allusions also he ventured to make to the undue authority usurped by the pope, and concluded his sermon, as he began it, without an invocation to any saint. One at least among the congregation was scandalized beyond measure, and hesitated not to express in the rough and arrogant manner habitual to him 'his horror that doctrines so subversive of all authority should have been uttered in the presence of the youthful monarch. For himself, he had had more than enough of the preaching of Bishop Montluc, whom he hoped never again to see or to hear.'

This indignant personage was the Constable de Montmorency, and mainly from the effect produced on him by the bishop's sermon resulted the political alliance of the constable, the Duc de Guise, and the Marshal Saint-André, named by their adversaries the 'Triumvirate.' But Montmorency did not readily join them. His resentment towards the Duc de Guise was too strong to be easily surmounted. It required the most earnest entreaties and persuasions of political partizans; many appeals to his loyalty; his fidelity to the royal house; and lastly, but by no means the least effective, the prayers of his ancient friend Diana and his fanatical Catholic wife, to overcome his reluctance and the efforts of his nephews and sons to retain him on the

Bourbon side. But conquered at last, the triumviri sealed and sanctified their pact by receiving the communion together at the chapel of the lower court of Fontainebleau on Easter Sunday.

This alliance was displeasing to Catherine, who, to make the balance of power more equal, ranged herself once more on the side of the Bourbons and Châtillons. She had completely won over the weak and vacillating King of Navarre; first by granting the royal letters she had hitherto withheld, proclaiming him Lieutenant-General of the Kingdom, which office he contentedly accepted in lieu of the regency. The perfect intelligence existing between the queen-mother and the Bourbons was also publicly announced. But to retain the ever-fluctuating Antony in close allegiance to her — the 'Triumvirate' desiring to seduce him from her by means similar to her own—Catherine selected one of the most fascinating of her swarm of beauties, a Mademoiselle Du Rouet, who soon obtained complete ascendency over him.

The efforts of the Chancellor de L'Hôpital to modify the severe and cruel edicts of the Parliament against the Protestants, before their final registration, were incessant. His constant advocacy of tolerance and conciliatory measures probably had some effect in bending the queen-mother's views in the same merciful direction, especially as both she and her agent, the Bishop of Valence, believed for awhile that Reform was destined to triumph. But with what object, it may be asked (for it can scarcely be supposed that so accomplished an *intrigante* questioned without an object), did she inquire of the Duc de Guise, when Charles was crowned at Rheims, ' whether if she and the king should embrace the new religion '—which she was careful to add they had no intention of doing—he and his party would refuse obedience to them. The duke curtly replied ' Yes.'*

The wiles of the 'flying squadron' would scarcely have harmonized with Calvinistic austerity. But if Protestantism had been destined to obtain the upper hand and become the religion of the State, she would doubtless then have readily adopted the 'new opinions' to retain, if possible, her position. The queen's letter to the pope (Pius IV.) would seem to be intended as the first step towards it. This 'semi-Protestant epistle,' said to have been the joint production of Catherine and Bishop Montluc, was despatched to Rome some two or three weeks before the assembling of the Catholic clergy and Protestant ministers to take part in the

---

* See Bouillé's ' Histoire des Guises.'

religious discussion known as the 'Colloquy of Poissy.'

With reference to this colloquy, previously announced as a national council, Catherine informs his holiness that 'the dissentients have become so formidable both by their numbers and their power and influence that it is no longer possible to exterminate them. The friends of Catholic unity,' she goes on to state, 'would wish that those among them who are not Anabaptists or persons of dissolute life, should be received into the communion of the Church, or at least, with that end in view, should on points of difference be argued with in a conciliatory spirit. That the occasion would seem to be opportune, in order to prevent further defections amongst the faithful, to remove the images from the altars and the sanctuary; to abolish the ceremonial added to the sacrament of baptism; to re-establish the collective communion, in both kinds, with the abolition of private masses.' The suppression of the '*fête* of the Saint-Sacrament' she also recommends, and suggests the desirability of 'singing the psalms in French.' The reading of this missive stirred the Vatican to its centre. 'Heresy!' was the general exclamation. Nor was consternation at all abated by the queen-mother's assurances that 'no attack on the holy father's authority or any change of doctrine should be permitted at the projected colloquy.'

In the interval that occurred between the despatch of the above letter to the pope and the assembling of the ecclesiastics at Poissy, a section of the States-General—the States of Pontoise— commenced their sittings at Saint-Germain, where the Court was then residing. Amongst the deputies of the *noblesse* and the *tiers état* were many political 'malcontents' and many ardent Protestants, all apparently animated by violent hostility to the Guises, the pope, and the Spanish king. Towards the queen-mother also they assumed an attitude rather alarming—calling upon her to resign the regency in favour of the King of Navarre, of whom, with the rest of the princes of the blood, they were staunch partizans, in opposition to 'the foreign princes—the Lorrainers.' So determined were they to have King Antony to reign over them, that only at his own entreaty, conjointly with that of Coligny, were they prevailed on to allow the arrangement already agreed on respecting his share in the government to continue unaltered. 'There was,' says the historian, H. Martin, 'an audacious grandeur in the views of the *tiers état*, of the States of Pontoise, in which the *noblesse* largely participated.'

The deputies of the clergy did not attend—being wholly opposed to the reform of the abuses insisted on by the two lay orders, whose propositions seem to have been no less judicious than patriotic. The 'Grand Ordinance of Orléans,' which all the efforts of De L'Hôpital had failed to induce the Parliament of Paris to register, the king's private council, at the demand of the States, now imperatively required that assembly duly to record and give effect to. The debts of the State were provided for, without too heavily bearing on the people—the clergy, *noblesse*, and *tiers état* contributing in due proportion. Very numerous were the reforms proposed, both in favour of toleration of religious differences and freedom of worship, as well as the more impartial administration of the law, the abolition of many undue privileges of the clergy, and generally for the welfare of the kingdom and all classes of the king's subjects.

The two cardinals—Tournon and Lorraine—should have been present during the sittings of the States. But when about to take their seats, finding they were placed below the princes of the blood, they left the assembly in great indignation, in order 'that the red hat might not humble itself before the fleurs-de-lys.' As though divining the troubles likely to ensue, should the frail health of Catherine's three sons place the legitimate succession to the throne in jeopardy, the States passed an edict confirming the Salic law.

Great was the terror of the clergy when it was announced that the Colloquy of Poissy, whose professed object was to reconcile theological differences, if possible, and bring the two religions into accord, would open its proceedings on the 9th of September. All was agitation amongst the doctors of the Sorbonne, who implored the queen 'not to expose the youthful ears of the king to the taint and poison of heresy.' Trepidation prevailed at the Vatican, at the Escurial, and amongst the holy brethren of the Inquisition. To invite the Huguenot preachers of heresy to discuss their profane doctrines in all security with the bishops of the Church was so monstrous a scandal, that unless proposed as a snare, with the view of destroying them all at one fell swoop, Rome and Spain, by a united effort, must at once put an end to it.

Catherine's heretical letter had raised exasperation against her to its highest pitch. An energetic part was attributed to her in this supposed concerted plan to favour the 'new religion' and its introduction at Court, in opposition to the Church.

To counteract this, a double embassy arrived in Paris—the pope's legate being Cardinal Ferrara (a son of Lucretia Borgia), charged by his holiness to oppose the opening of the colloquy, and, further, with the secret mission of inducing the King of Navarre to return to the fold of the faithful. The Spanish envoy—Iago Lainez, the general of the Jesuits, and successor of Ignacio y Loyola—was a far less insinuating and courtly personage. They found Catherine and the youthful monarch at Saint-Germain, in the midst of a Court mainly composed of heretics. The Calvinistic form of worship was also established in full freedom in the royal château—Condé and the King and Queen of Navarre being resident there.

The reception accorded to the envoys was rather discouraging than cordial, and the legate and the inquisitor soon discovered that the edict of July, enacting banishment or death to all Huguenots who did not live after the manner of good Catholics, was not only condemned at Court, but everywhere was practically null. The legate, when he appeared in public, was compelled to dispense with the attendance of his cross-bearer, being followed by a mocking crowd of people—servants, for the most part, of the Huguenot courtiers—

whenever he ventured to show himself with the insignia of his dignity borne before him.

The Duc de Guise was absent, but the Cardinal de Lorraine had encouraged rather than opposed the opening of the colloquy. Two discussions had already taken place when the envoys arrived. This surprised both the legate and Lainez. It seemed to throw some doubt even on the cardinal's orthodoxy. His motive, however, was to take advantage of the widening of the breach which he foresaw would ensue from this theological discussion, and the intestine feuds it would lead to—making it necessary to call in the aid of Spain, with whose troops, and if possible the funds also of the 'Demon of the South,' he hoped to stamp out and exterminate this 'evergrowing and damnable heresy.' So, on the date fixed, the famous conference was opened in the grand refectory of the Benedictine Monastery of Poissy—a short address being spoken in a feeble childish voice by the young king.

Besides the king, Catherine brought with her her second son, the Duke of Orléans (Henry III.). The King and Queen of Navarre, the Bourbon princes, and the members of the private council were also present. The chancellor explained the object of the conference, and in impressive and eloquent terms 'exhorted the assembly to conduct the discussion in a serious but conciliatory spirit ;' at the same time enjoining the cardinals, archbishops, bishops, doctors of the Sorbonne, and delegates from various chapters, to the number of a hundred or more, to welcome the ministers of the 'new religion with gentleness and cordiality, as baptized Christians like themselves.' Even this short address excited some irritation, as suspiciously favourable to the heretics.

There were present many who trembled with rage when the learned and eloquent Théodore de Bèze rose to address the assembly, as the spokesman of his co-religionists. He was considered, after Calvin, the head of the 'new religion,' and was usually referred to as 'Calvin's lieutenant.' But indignation, which at the first prevailed mainly because this chief of the heretics had been received with favour at Court, and was the guest of King Antony, soon subsided into approval as he proceeded with calmness, eloquence, moderation, and courtesy, to explain the points of difference and agreement between the Catholics and Reformers.

So ably did he tone down the repellent severity of Calvin's extreme doctrines, that he was listened to with quiet attention until he came to speak of the Eucharist. He then emphatically declared that 'far as highest heaven was separated from earth, so far was Jesus Christ corporally separated from the consecrated elements of bread and wine; His body and blood being spiritually and by faith alone partaken of.' Then were heard murmurs loud and deep, and the old Cardinal de Tournon, turning towards the royal party, his feeble, tottering frame quivering with passionate anger, said, that, 'saving his majesty's presence, he and his colleagues would have risen to put an end to the abominable language and horrible blasphemies which had just been uttered.' Amidst great confusion and excitement the assembly at once broke up.

The old cardinal advised that the colloquy should there and then come to an end. The Cardinal de Lorraine desired to prolong it. He had not yet confuted Théodore de Bèze, and was anxious to show his ability in making the worse appear the better cause. It was arranged, therefore, that he should reply on two points—the authority of the Church, and the Eucharist. After much discussion and much subtle argument on both sides in defence of their several opinions and articles of faith, the dispute ended, as foreseen, in the aggravation of hostile feelings and the widening of the breach already existing between the two religions. After a few more sittings the colloquy was eventually brought to a close—first, by the Cardinal de Tournon's exhortation to the young king to believe no other doctrine than that he had heard from the lips of the Cardinal de Lorraine, and to immediately purge his kingdom of all those persons who refused to subscribe to it; secondly, by a vituperative address of the Jesuit general, in which he spoke of the Reformers as 'serpents, foxes, wolves, and monkeys, who aped Rome at Geneva.' The question in discussion, he said, concerned neither women, children, nor military men, and should be referred to the Council of Trent.

But Catherine and her chancellor, who still inclined her—perplexed though she was—to a policy of peace and tolerance, requested Théodore de Bèze, Pierre Martyr (Pietro Vermiglio), and other 'gospel ministers,' to remain in France for awhile. If it was not possible to bring the two religions into any sort of agreement, it might be practicable, they thought, so to frame an edict of pacification sufficiently satisfactory to both parties to enable the two religions to exist peaceably side by side. The beneficent efforts of De L'Hôpital resulted in the issue of the Edict of Tolerance of January, 1562, approved by the Government, and allowing the Huguenots to assemble for worship with their families privately in their own houses, and publicly outside the walls of towns. The Calvinist ministers readily accepted it, promising for their people strict compliance with all its conditions. But the fanatical priests by their ravings in the pulpit roused the people to frenzy, and the edict, intended as a message of peace, proved but the signal for bloodshed.

CHAPTER XI.

The Cardinal Ferrara.—Antony's Conversion.—His promised Rewards.—His Treatment of Jeanne d'Albret.—Her Heart henceforth closed to Love.— Guise urged to return to Paris.—Massacre of Vassy.—Catherine and Charles at Monceaux.—Court flying from Château to Château.—Guise enters Paris in great State.—Antony and De Bèze.

THE wily Cardinal Ferrara had abstained from taking any part in the colloquy of Poissy, of which he well knew the futility. As suggested by Pius IV., he strove to do the Church more effective service by depriving the Huguenot cause of one who in name at least was its principal leader. The vain, imprudent, and inconstant Antony of Bourbon was not, in a religious point of view, a conquest that so accomplished an intriguer as the grandson of Alexander VI. would have been proud of. But Antony being the representative of 'an heretical faction which it was desirable for the peace of the world to exterminate,' his defection, it was believed, would deal it a crushing blow which, if it did not slay, at least for a time would paralyze, while sterner measures for finally stamping it out were preparing.

But (as Giovanni Michiel reports) the King of Navarre was not a man on whom the Huguenots greatly relied. He had accepted all the rites of the Reformers of Geneva, but more with a view, as was generally surmised, of being chief of a party, than from zeal for the 'new religion.' 'He discourses well,' continues the ambassador, 'is courteous to all, without ceremony or affectation. His manners are frank and thoroughly French; his liberality so great that he is always in debt, and by those two qualities—affability and open-handedness—he has gained the general good opinion; of the nobility especially, who, for the most part, greatly like him. He is very willing to undertake any proposed great enterprises, but is considered wanting in firmness and strength of principle to carry them out.'

The Italian cardinal was too wary to startle the King of Navarre by any reference to a change of religion until he had won his confidence. He was insinuating and deferential, which Antony in his vanity regarded as a tribute this distinguished prelate was anxious to pay to his loftiness of character and general merits. By degrees the cardinal's well-timed allusions to the Prince de Condé's ability and activity, and his apparent influence with his party, excited Antony's jealousy and produced a coldness between the brothers.

The Cardinal de Lorraine now came to the legate's assistance, and Antony was reminded, rather reproachfully, that but for the difference in religion, how much more prominent, how much more suited to his rank than that of the leader of a band of heretics, was the position he might have held—of course as a defender of the venerable pontiff and Holy Mother Church, who desired only the peaceful return of her erring children, whom she longed once more to gather into her maternal bosom. He had, they told him, but to leave the paths of error, into which a too easy compliance with the mistaken views of his wife had seduced him. They even promised, as an inducement to recant and to forsake his party, absolution without the infliction of any penance, and, as a further reward, the hand of the young Queen of Scotland. Her beauty and seductive graces of mind and person they greatly vaunted, in order more closely to ensnare poor Antony, whose weaknesses they knew, and who, they perceived, was lending a willing ear to their solicitations.

Besides sharing the Scottish throne with Mary, they hinted at the probability of the crown of France, at no distant period, descending to him, Catherine's sons being all of sickly constitution. While he, robust of frame and in the prime of life, having thrown aside his 'new opinions,' might govern France for many years. There was even a third crown they could venture to promise him— that of England. The Cardinal de Ferrara, being the holy father's legate, could in the name of his holiness assure him of his willingness to fulminate a bull of excommunication against the heretic Elizabeth, and to adjudge her kingdom to Mary Stuart and the King of Navarre after their marriage.

To the luxurious, ease-loving Antony of Bourbon this was a very pleasing prospect; yet he was inclined to think it too far away in the distance to be realized within a reasonable time. Something nearer at hand, it was perceived, would fascinate him still more. It was now the Jesuit's turn to speak. He was able to promise that Philip II., in exchange for Lower Navarre, would consent to cede to him the island of Sardinia. A glowing description was given of the beauties of this island

—'it was a perfect scene of enchantment.' Antony was in ecstasies. What a dream of love and idleness his imagination conjured up! Shared, too, not with Mary of Scotland or the heretic Queen Jeanne, but one of Catherine's captivating belles.

The enchanting isle possessed the further advantage of nearness to the continent of Africa, where, it was suggested, 'should ambition prompt him to extend his views of territorial acquisition beyond his isle of beauty, he might found an empire no less vast than flourishing.' But, said his tempters, 'Your majesty must reflect on the advantages offered, and compare them with the disadvantages resigned. Above all, let not Queen Jeanne know anything of this project, which assuredly she would oppose.'

But when Antony reflected that the first step towards the realization of the flattering proposals laid before him was his repudiation of Jeanne, he hesitated. The more he contemplated this act, the more his conscience pricked him. Jeanne d'Albret had been a devoted wife, and, as was not often the case in royal marriages, when giving him her hand, and with it a share in the government of her little kingdom, she gave him also her heart. He knew her worth, and had not ceased to admire her, though he had yielded to the fascinations of the facile beauties thrown in his way.* At all events, Antony would try to bring Jeanne over to his views, and to persuade her to enter with him into the fold of the Shepherd of Rome.

As a precaution, probably, against any wavering on his own part, when he came to discuss with Jeanne their renunciation of the 'new opinions,' he privately despatched a member of his household to make his submission to Pius IV. A messenger was also sent off to the Duc de Guise, recommending his speedy return to Paris—the moment, it appears, being favourable for the adoption of any measures for the putting down of heresy that he (the duke) might suggest, and which the now Catholic lieutenant-general would deem it his duty to enforce.

The duke on a recent occasion replied to an appeal to spare the life of a pious, learned, and eloquent man, but a heretic, 'that his trade was cutting off heads, not arguing' (to which he might well have added, ' heads far worthier to remain on their shoulders than was his own'). He had quitted Paris in disgust on the issuing of the

---

* Calvin had recently written a very severe letter to the King of Navarre, in which, while disapproving of much of his conduct at the French Court, he especially reproved him for his 'folles amours' (H. Martin).

Edict of Tolerance of the 3rd of January, leaving his brother the cardinal, whose trade was arguing and discussing, to aid in the conversion of the King of Navarre. The queen-mother, with her children and the Court, had also fled from the capital to seek refuge at her country house of Monceaux from the storm impending over her. The chancellor accompanied, if not in disgust, yet in despair, that the work of peace in which he had induced the queen to concur, had but hastened the catastrophe it was his aim to avert—organized civil war.

From every Catholic pulpit in the kingdom, with but two or three rare and honourable exceptions, the priests, disgracing the name of Christians, appealed to the people in language the most violent to aid in the extermination of the heretics. Not alone on the heads of the Reformers did they invoke fearful curses and calamities, but on those Catholics also who, if any of 'the accursed sect' fell in their way, should listen to the inner voice of humanity pleading for mercy, or sparing from death man, woman, or child.

Would they secure the favour of God? (What profanation of that great name! Should not they rather have said Satan?) They must denounce, betray, hand over to the executioner (even those nearest and dearest to them, would they not risk their own souls), and, if need be, do a murderous deed themselves—' a deed so pleasing in the sight of heaven that absolution was not needed.'

Not all the authority, influence, and entreaties of Théodore de Bèze, Pierre Martyr, and other chief Protestant ministers—who still, at the request of the queen-mother and the chancellor, deferred for awhile their departure from Paris—could wholly restrain the Huguenot people from attempting to retaliate by interrupting the service of the mass, as their own services were daily interrupted. For when exercising their newly-acquired right of assembling together for prayer and preaching, their opponents were in the habit of bursting in upon them, with yells, hootings, and throwing of stones, compelling the breaking up of the meeting.

Calvin's doctrine was to offer no resistance to the authority of the powers that be. But passive obedience to it could not long be yielded by ardent men under such unceasing persecution. A deep and terrible vengeance was near at hand, and surely the blood of its victims should be on those who provoked it. This, then, was the favourable moment for the 'Grand Guise' to resume his congenial calling—so, at least, thought the contemptible King of Navarre.

Antony's efforts to win over Jeanne to follow his example and renounce her religion were doomed to utter failure. She expressed herself astonished at his culpable duplicity, knowing that his opinions had undergone no real change. She reproached him for his unworthy conduct towards his brother and his friends the Châtillons, as well as for his newly-formed alliance with his own and their great enemies. (Antony would have arrested Coligny and his brother, had Catherine been willing; but his zeal in the new cause he had embraced was checked by the chancellor, rather than encouraged by Catherine). Greatly irritated at hearing from Jeanne what he knew to be the truth respecting himself, he complained to the Cardinal de Lorraine of her obstinate adherence to her heretical opinions. The worthy prelate advised him to arrest his wife in the very midst of the Court.

But Antony recoiled from so bold a step. Jeanne was a queen in her own right, and besides, had not obtruded her opinions on the Court. He was aware, also, that she was greatly respected for her modesty, and many virtues then rare in the Court of France, and that any violence of the kind proposed would bring forward many friends to resist it.

He preferred, therefore, to resort to stratagem. He would order her to leave the Court and repair to his Duchy of Vendôme, despatching an agent to arrest her on her journey. He refused her the companionship of her son, then in his ninth year, as he intended, he said, to bring him up in the true religion.* But Jeanne, before her departure, availed herself of an opportunity of conversing seriously with the youthful Henry of Navarre. She urged on him, as her most earnest wish, never to attend mass, assuring him that if he obeyed not that wish she would disinherit him, and never allow him to regard her as his mother.

Friends had not failed privately to inform Jeanne of her husband's base intentions. Consequently, soon after leaving Paris, she changed her route, and while Antony's and the cardinal's myrmidons thought to surprise her at Vendôme, she entered Châtelrault, where she was received with all honour by the Marquis de Caumont de la Force. There she was taken ill, having greatly suffered in mind from the excitement of the journey, the feeling of danger barely escaped, and the shock she experienced on discovering how mean and base was the man she had been accustomed to confide in. Yet courage did not fail her, and after

* Mathieu's 'Histoire de France.'

some few days of rest she was able to continue her journey to Nérac, where she had a very fine château. She was accompanied by her little daughter Catherine, then in her third year.

On leaving her host of Châtelrault, she said : ' I have closed my heart to the love I once felt for my husband, to open it henceforth wholly to my duty to my people and the affairs, civil and religious, of my domains.' * A certain severity of character not hitherto remarked in Jeanne d'Albret is said to have developed itself from the time of this separation from her husband, and her loss of respect for, and confidence in, him. She and Antony met no more. Yet troubles and persecution were still reserved for her. Antony, however, was quite consoled for the loss of his wife in the society of the fascinating Mademoiselle Du Rouet de la Baraudière—*en attendant*, their departure for the enchanting Isle of Sardinia.

François de Guise was in Alsace when King Antony's message reached him. He was visiting the Duke of Wurtemberg who was connected with his family by marriage, and through whose influence he hoped to prevent the German Protestant princes from affording aid to the French

* Mathieu's ' Histoire de France,' and Mademoiselle Vauvillier's ' Vie de Jeanne d'Albret.'

Reformers in the civil war now imminent. To secure his aims he, and, at an earlier period, the cardinal also, had not scrupled to declare that they approved the Lutheran doctrines and shared in the duke's belief in them. 'Never,' François de Guise assured him, 'had he caused any man to be put to death for his religious opinions. Those who had suffered—calling themselves Reformers—were but dangerous political intriguers who had used the "new religion" as a cloak for their schemes.'

With but little delay the Duc de Guise responded in person to the lieutenant-general's message. On his way to Paris, however, he had the satisfaction of achieving a triumph over the 'accursed Huguenot,' as well as of showing his contempt for the Edict of Tolerance, issued by the authority of the queen-mother and the Chancellor of France.

As he and his troop of horsemen were entering Vassy—a small town in the province of Champagne—the Huguenot population happened to be assembled for worship outside the walls—according to the terms of the edict. Their modest temple was a barn, and they were singing psalms—in French, too, to add to the heinousness of their crime. These unwelcome sounds startled the pious ears of the duke, who, galloping forward with his armed escort, attacked the worshippers in the barn. They naturally endeavoured to defend themselves, and strove to barricade the entrance. But unprepared for attack, and much less for an armed one, their efforts at resistance proved powerless. Thus (on the authority of De Bèze) between two and three hundred men, women, and children were either mercilessly slaughtered or badly wounded; victims to the savage fury of the 'Grand Guise' and his infamous myrmidons. The life of the Protestant minister was spared, but for a time only; he and the provost of the town—guilty of obeying the injunctions of the royal edict—were carried prisoners to Paris as trophies to grace the hero's triumph. The carnage is said to have lasted more than an hour—'in the barn, on the roof, and in the street.'

The queen-mother, being informed that Antony had sent for Guise to Paris, was advised to summon the latter in the king's name to repair to her Court at Monceaux. This was in order to avert the conflict likely to ensue there between the duke and the Prince de Condé, who, at the head of an armed band, was protecting the Protestants of the capital from annoyance or attack when assembled for prayer. But Guise, who had set at naught the royal edict, now treated the royal summons with similar disrespect, and a few days after entered Paris with all the pomp and circumstance of a monarch returning to his kingdom with laurel-bound brows to receive the homage of his subjects. Besides his own retinue of several hundred footmen and horsemen, he was accompanied by the constable and Saint-André, and a squadron of cavalry. At the gate of Saint-Denis the provost and officers of the municipality waited in grand state to receive him, and he was joined on entering Paris by the King of Navarre and the Spanish ambassador, 'suitably attended.' The Catholic people, urged on by their priests, by whom the massacre of Vassy was applauded with savage joy, welcomed him with frantic cries of 'Vive Guise!' the messenger 'sent of God for the destruction of the heretics and the glory of His name.'

Very different was the feeling of the Protestants towards this heaven-sent murderer. Scarcely could they be restrained from laying violent hands on him, while 'the Prince de Condé, Théodore de Bèze, and other Protestant chiefs sought the king and queen-mother at Mélun, whither they had fled in alarm from Monceaux.' The ministers demanded justice on the violators of the Edict of January; and in the name of the Reformers generally, Condé supported the demand by offering the queen a force of fifty thousand men. The King of Navarre, however, in the excess of his new-found zeal, inveighed against the action of his brother, and declared that 'whoever touched the tip of the finger of his " brother of Guise " would touch the whole of his body.'

Very rough indeed was his treatment of his former friend, De Bèze, whose proceedings 'in furthering the spread of heresy' he strongly condemned. De Bèze's reply to this foolish prince is well known. 'Sire,' he said, after quietly listening to Antony's angry reproofs and his justification of the murderous zeal displayed by Guise and his companions—attacked, as he asserted, by the Protestants—'Sire, it is true that the part of the Church of God is to endure blows rather than to inflict them ; but you must remember that it is an anvil that has already worn out many hammers.'

CHAPTER XII.

Catherine perplexed.—Massacre of Sens.—Frightful Retaliation.—Churches sacked.—The Admiral's Wife.—Attack on Rouen.—Antony wounded.—Jeanne d'Albret.—Her Anxiety respecting her Son.—Returns to her own Dominions.

ERHAPS at no period of the reigns of her three sons, during which she held the helm of Government, was Catherine de' Medici more perplexed what course to pursue than at the present critical conjuncture. The uncontrolled authority she so much coveted, and looked to possess on Charles's accesssion, still eluded her grasp. Influenced by De L'Hôpital, so far since her possession of power, she seems to have really endeavoured to secure peace, and to have supported the Reformers; but only because being herself troubled by no scruples, religious or moral, they appeared to her likely to become a great power in the State. But now, through the audacity of the Duc de Guise and his colleagues in the '"Triumvirate,' conjointly with their new friend—the convert Antony—a real Catholic Government was constituted in Paris, outside the royal one.

Antony was very anxious to parade his zeal—walking proudly beside his 'brother of Guise' in the procession of the 'Pâques fleuries' (Palm Sunday), a sort of solemn review of the whole Catholic party then in the capital. The *débutant* was also supported by the Spanish ambassador, who addressed him respectfully as King of Navarre—a title that Philip II. had hitherto persistently refused him. He had now no claim to it whatever. The Navarrese, on hearing of his treatment of their queen, to whom they were loyally devoted, had declared that 'henceforth they would neither acknowledge him as their sovereign, nor pay him any obedience.' The Spaniard, then, should rather have addressed him as his Majesty of Sardinia.

The queen-mother's anxiety daily increasing, she fled from Monceaux to Mélun, that she might be within reach of Orléans, whither the Bishop of Valence and other friends of Reform urged her with her sons to seek refuge. The chancellor also advised her—seeing that war was inevitable—to write to the Prince de Condé, placing herself and her children under his protection. This she did, at the same time authorizing him to take up arms. Scarcely, however, had she arrived at Mélun, than a deputation from Paris, headed by the provost, was announced, praying her to return thither with the king. Her answer probably was evasive ; for as soon as the Parisians left she departed from Mélun for Fontainebleau, there to await the arrival of Condé.

But the prince, who from inferiority of numbers was unable to hold Paris against the forces of the 'Triumvirate,' was yet unwilling to abandon the city to his enemies. This occasioned delay. However, his brother, the Cardinal de Bourbon—lately appointed by the queen provisional Governor of Paris—consented, though by no means sharing the prince's opinions, to order both him and the Duc de Guise, with their followers, to quit the capital. Condé, breaking up his camp, obeyed ; but the duke, while affecting to obey, contrived to be compelled to disobey. The military pomp he displayed in preparing for his pretended departure attracted a large number of the excited populace, who 'would not'—as they loudly vociferated—'let their "Grand Guise" leave them.' Condé, who, it appears, was expected to proceed immediately to Fontainebleau 'to protect the sons and their mother,' merely despatched thither one of his gentlemen to inquire what were the queen-mother's wishes. As possession of the king would have fully compensated for the evacuation of the capital, Condé is supposed to have thus neglected a great opportunity of increasing the prestige of his party, of which his enemies failed not to take advantage.

For while the prince was pursuing his journey with all speed to Meaux, where the Protestant nobility were assembled, the King of Navarre—grown very bold since serving under the orders of the 'Triumvirate'—made his appearance at Fontainebleau. He was accompanied by his colleagues, who put him forward as spokesman, they remaining with their troops in the vicinity of the château; his part in the Government being to make promises and proposals for which the 'Triumvirate' cared not to be responsible. The renegade lieutenant-general urged the queen and her sons to accompany him at once to Paris to avoid the dangers that would surely ensue from their falling into the hands of the rebel Huguenots. Undismayed by his representations, and encouraged by the chancellor, she resisted for several days.

An alarming report of Condé's movements

reaching them, determined Guise and the constable to waste no more time in persuasion, and Antony accordingly informed the queen (who seems to have omitted at this crisis to call in the aid of her invincible 'flying squadron') that 'he and his friends had resolved on removing the king and his brothers from Fontainebleau, to prevent their being kidnapped. With her liberty, however, they would not presume to interfere. She might accompany them or remain at Fontainebleau, or elsewhere, as she pleased.' Catherine de' Medici, as usual, bowed before the breeze. The Court returned to Mélun. On the following day they moved on to Vincennes, and thence once more to the Louvre—a strong-armed escort closely surrounding them. The youthful Charles IX., alarmed by these rapid changes, hurried journeys, the serious countenances of those about him, and the closeness with which he was guarded, wept bitterly, and refused to be comforted; being under the impression that the King of Navarre and the Duc de Guise were carrying him off to prison.

A report that 'the sons and their mother' had been forcibly brought from Fontainebleau, and were held captive at the Louvre by the chiefs of the Catholic faction, was quickly spread through the country. Practically, it was so; but a proclamation, purporting to be issued by royal command, speedily contradicted it.

To Coligny's unwillingness to strike the first blow in this civil war, which he foresaw would be long and terrible, the delay in Condé's movements has been attributed. The admiral was a man of far more serious character than the prince. Brantôme says of the latter, 'He was more ambitious than religious, and more a man of pleasure than an ambitious one.' Whether it was so or not, he was undoubtedly a man of great courage; zealous for reform, and true to the cause he had espoused. The admiral was not less zealous, but more prudent and cautious. He perceived the disadvantages the Reformers would be under from their want of means, and the smallness of their forces for carrying on war successfully. The calamity this rising in arms would bring on his family, his friends, and the country, filled him with agony. He had also honourable and patriotic scruples to the Reformers being the first to call foreign soldiers into France to aid them. He therefore retired to his château of Châtillon-sur-Loing, and would probably have wholly refrained from joining the Huguenot army, but for his wife's reproaches and entreaties.

Her zeal bordered on fanaticism. 'The blood

of those,' she said, 'whom he had made no effort to save from death, would be on his head;' and when he proposed a short delay for reflection on her part of what she and her family would have to suffer, she exclaimed that she would be a witness against him at the Judgment of God, if he allowed the further guilt of causing the death of those who were slain in the interval to rest upon him. He had absolutely refused to yield to the solicitations of his brothers. But his wife's earnest appeals conquered. His resolve was taken, his preparations speedily made, and bidding adieu to the 'valiant Charlotte Laval,' mounted his horse, and at the head of two thousand noble cavaliers rapidly joined the prince at Meaux, then in the possession of the Protestants.

In deference to Coligny, it was determined that the pacificatory mediation of the German princes should alone be sought, and the Swiss Protestant cantons requested to prevent the Catholic ones from sending soldiers to the 'usurpers of royal power,' unless similar aid was granted to the Protestant churches of France. The assistance of Elizabeth of England was desired rather in money than in men. But her ambassador, Throckmorton, took a very busy if a secret part in these religious troubles; and if Elizabeth seemed at times to grow lukewarm, Sir Nicholas did not fail to make it his business to infuse a little more ardour into her sentiments, and to urge her to more active sympathy.

The Protestant chiefs formed themselves into an association under Condé, swearing 'before God and His holy angels' to remain united until the king attained his majority. To make it evident that they were friends of the Crown, they adopted as a rallying sign, after the manner of the old French loyalists, the white scarf, which, from the time of Charles VII., had been the royal colour of France. The Catholic chiefs, by a similar association, followed their example; but instead of the white scarf, they assumed the red one of Spain, with which they decorated the young king and his brothers. Many of the Catholic nobility took great objection to this investiture of the king and princes with what they termed the 'insignia of the vassalage of France to Spain,' as determined by the Treaty of Câteau-Cambrésis. So serious was the displeasure they evinced, that the red scarf was modified by an embroidered white cross.

The smouldering flames of civil war, so long with difficulty repressed from bursting forth with full fury, at last resisted all further efforts to stifle them. A massacre, more atrocious than even that

of Vassy, excited the Huguenot people to the
highest pitch of frenzy. Scenes of carnage too
horrible to depict had taken place at Sens, the
archbishopric of Cardinal de Guise, a younger
brother of the duke. Again an unoffending
people assembled for worship were set upon by
a mob of howling demons, and a hundred or more
of men, women, and children savagely murdered,
and their bodies thrown into the Yonne.

Hitherto, the Huguenots, though committing
some inexcusable (as well as excusable) ravages, by
way of revenging the persistent persecution with
which their enemies pursued them, had generally
displayed a spirit of moderation compared with
the Catholics. It has been remarked that while
the rage of the latter was usually shown in savage
and atrocious murder, that of the former was far
less implacable towards men than against things—
statues, images of saints, and the monuments, as
they termed them, of idolatry.

It was important to the cause of Reform that its
leaders should restrain their people within the
bounds of legitimate defence. But on the present
occasion they were powerless. The people were
bent on 'avenging God and annihilating all traces
of the idolatrous worship of the Papists.' The
Huguenots were masters of Orléans, and Catholics

and Protestants had mutually consented to refrain from interfering with each other's mode of worship. But now in their mad fury the Huguenots, heedless of their promise, burst into the cathedral, destroyed the altars, broke the statues, burnt the finely-carved woodwork of the screen and pulpits; tore down the pictures, profaned the tombs, and thoroughly sacked the fine old edifice, growing, as it seemed, drunk with the delirium of their own excesses. Entreaties, commands, on the part of Coligny, De Bèze, and Condé, were alike futile to stay the hands of the devastators.

Nor were the cathedral and churches of Orléans the only sacred buildings desecrated by the infuriated Huguenots. It seemed as though 'the blast of some infernal trumpet had sounded through the land and awakened the spirit of destruction.' The work of hundreds of years was destroyed in the space of a day—sometimes in a few hours. The towns which had fallen into the hands of the Huguenots—Rouen, Poitiers, Clery, Caen, Lyons, Bourges—suffered equally with Orléans in the destruction of all they possessed of the more or less splendid products of human genius. Calvin wrote to De Bèze to express his indignation at what he perhaps too mildly designated the 'indiscreet zeal' of the

Reformers. But especially he condemned those Calvinist ministers who at Lyons had 'allowed themselves to be drawn into taking part, and even directing the fanatical people, in this work of destruction.'

The splendid choir in the church of Saint-Jean de Lyons was utterly demolished. It appears to have been a most superb work of the Middle Ages, constructed of marble, with columns of jasper and porphyry, and decorated with groups of figures representing scenes from the historical books of the Old Testament. The tombs of kings, queens, saints, and other celebrated personages were rifled, and their remains treated with the utmost indignity, burnt, or thrown into the rivers. Some had rested in their graves undisturbed for hundreds of years—William the Conqueror and his queen Matilda, for instance, in the two churches they built at Caen ; Richard Cœur de Lion at Rouen, and that of Rollon the pirate king, and first Duke of Normandy, A.D. 931.

At Clery they destroyed the copper statue of Louis XI., dragged him from his tomb, and burnt his bones with those of his daughter Jeanne. At Orléans they even threw down and battered the statue of Joan of Arc ; burnt the heart of their last youthful sovereign, Francis II., and destroyed the silver urn in which it was deposited in the cathedral of the town in which he died. Before one name only—the revered one of Cardinal Georges d'Amboise, Louis XII.'s great minister— did they pause in their sacrilegious work of destruction. He who had enriched Rouen—his archbishopric—with so many *chefs-d'œuvre* of architecture, had generally improved the town with a view to the greater comfort and well-being of the people, and had been munificent in acts of charity, might well command their respect. It could hardly be admiration of his magnificent tomb that made them stop short in their ferocious acts of vandalism. Yet in the midst of the desolation around it, the cardinal's mausoleum remained untouched, as also some other fine specimens of the sculptor's art especially associated with his name.

This furious iconoclastic onslaught had a most unfavourable effect on the cause of Reform. Many friends were lost to it, while the Catholic people athirst for blood cried aloud for vengeance. At the call of the Parliament the peasantry rose *en masse*; the women like furies marching with the men 'to murder the destroyers of their churches.' Fearful massacres ensued, and tortures the most horrible were inflicted to prolong the sufferings of their victims. Three men, rivals in their unpitying cruelty, Marshal Tavannes, Blaise de Montluc, and the Duc de Montpensier, were scouring the country, 'butchering whole garrisons, filling the wells with the bodies of the slain, and turning the trees into gibbets.'

The Protestant chief, the Baron des Adretz, was as merciless as his adversaries, and as cruel in his reprisals when opportunity offered. These atrocities continued for months, varied by frequent skirmishes. Every town became a stronghold, and its streets fields of battle.

But both Protestant and Catholic chiefs were preparing for more regular warfare. The Triumvirate had not scrupled to seek the aid of foreign troops, and Philip II.—hoping to succeed where his father had failed, in getting possession of Burgundy or other province of France—promised a *corps d'armée* of 36,000 men. Catherine, who had recovered a part of her influence in the Government, was alarmed at her son-in-law's liberality. The nobility and the *bourgeoisie* being also opposed to this Spanish invasion, the Catholic king was immediately informed that money was more needed than soldiers. He therefore reduced the 36,000 to 3,000; but no money was forthcoming—Philip's coffers, notwithstanding his many wide domains, being as empty as those of France. The German Protestant princes, in spite of the Guises' professed Lutheran proclivities, sent troops to the assistance of the French Reformers; while Elizabeth, driving a hard bargain with Condé for the possession of Havre (which the pressing needs of the moment eventually compelled him to accept), promised 3,000 men and 100,000 gold crowns.

The two opposing armies, headed by the two brothers—Coligny serving under Condé—took the field in June. The 'Triumvirate' accompanied King Antony, but to him the chief command was assigned. Taking advantage of the share in the Government which Guise and his colleagues, accused of usurping royal authority, were compelled to yield the queen-mother, she once more assumed the part of mediatrix. Hastening to the Catholic camp at Beaugency, she proposed, as suggested by the chancellor, to grant an amnesty, with liberty of conscience, but not of worship; the King of Navarre insisting—Catherine, it is supposed, being unable to act in opposition to him—that 'the toleration' of two religions in the same State was too monstrous a proposal for the Government to lend an ear to.

Another attempt at negotiation also failed, the advantages offered being rendered almost null by the stringent conditions attached to them. The King of Navarre, 'who had neither heart nor head,' is said to have shown exceeding harshness and want of feeling when discussing his proposals with the friends and nearest relative, with whom, until very recently, he was united in amity and affection, and was the acknowledged leader of their party and their cause. These fruitless negotiations were followed by a raid on the Protestants who still remained in Paris. Some sixty or seventy of them, together with a few persons who were guilty of the humanity of sheltering or not denouncing them, were slaughtered, and their bodies thrown into that bloodstained river, the Seine.

The Protestant army marched towards Normandy, where many reverses were sustained, and several towns lost. Condé, fearing that Rouen also would fall into the enemy's hands, determined—Coligny consenting, though with heartfelt sorrow—to accept Elizabeth's offer. The treaty was signed at Hampton Court on the 20th of September. The 3,000 soldiers who were to form the English garrison of Havre were the first despatched by the prudent Elizabeth. The second 3,000 were delayed by contrary winds and boisterous weather. Before their arrival, Rouen was besieged by the Catholic, lately become the Royal, army—the young king and the queen-mother having been brought to the camp to give authority by their presence to the proceedings of the 'Triumvirate.'

The convent of Mont-Sainte-Catherine was taken by surprise, and two murderous assaults on the 13th and 14th of October sufficed to make a breach in the ancient walls of Rouen. Some few days after, in spite of the vigorous resistance of the Protestant citizens, to the number of 4,000, together with 1,000 soldiers, the Catholics forcibly entered, and the wealthy city of Rouen, then the second in the kingdom, was given up to sack and pillage. To save the lives of the people, and also to save the city, De L'Hôpital induced Guise to propose an amnesty and other conciliatory measures. They were at once rejected. No promises of Guise or the queen-mother could be relied on. Horrors unspeakable ensued, and amongst the heaps of slain lay the bodies of many women who had fallen with arms in their hands.

On the morning of the second attack a ball from an arquebuse wounded the King of Navarre in the shoulder. As the surgeons did not succeed in extracting it, inflammation soon set in, and rapidly increased. But Antony, who did not consider himself in danger, expressed a wish to enter Rouen by the breach, carried in his bed by Swiss soldiers, and preceded by drums and trumpets. His wound, however, proved fatal, and three weeks after the taking of Rouen he died, aged forty-two. Nearly the whole of that time he passed in arranging with Mademoiselle Du Rouet their mode of life in their bower of bliss at Sardinia; the planting of their orange and myrtle groves; their sails on summer seas, and their rambles on the banks of crystal-clear rivers flowing over golden sands.

Catherine de' Medici, on hearing that the King of Navarre was not likely to recover, went to visit him.

'How do you pass your time?' she inquired. 'Have you no one to read good books to you?'

'Madame,' he replied, 'the greater part of the people about me are Huguenots.'

'They are none the less your servants,' she answered.

As soon as Catherine took leave of him, he ordered his attendant to place him on a small low bed near the fireplace, and to tell the Huguenot minister, Bézières, to come to him. On entering the king's chamber, he was told to take the Bible and read the Book of Job. The king listened attentively, his hands clasped, his eyes raised towards heaven. Several Catholics were present.

'I know,' he said, 'you will publish it about that the King of Navarre repented, and died a Huguenot. But do not trouble yourselves about what I am. Be content with knowing that I die in the faith of the Confession of Augsbourg. But should I perchance recover, I will cause the gospel to be again preached throughout France.'

Antony appears to have been regretted by none but the wife he was so unjustly anxious to repudiate. Jeanne alone said a prayer for him. Catholics and Protestants alike rejected him. When he found that life was indeed fast ebbing away, he dictated a very touching letter to Jeanne, concluding with much good advice, and many wise counsels, which he should rather have taken to heart and observed as a rule of life himself.[*] Jeanne's anxiety was now the education of her son. She thought with the great Huguenot captain, La Noue, that 'it was impossible a man should be crowned with honour in his latter years if he had not been taught in the springtime of life to walk in the paths of virtue.'

To shield him from the baneful influence of a shameless Court, where the grossest debauchery

[*] Mathieu's 'Histoire de France.'

incurred no ignominy, and treason and perfidy no dishonour, she desired, and earnestly impressed it on his preceptors, that he should be brought up in the practice of piety ; that he should be made acquainted with the duties of his station, and regard it as rigorously incumbent on him to fulfil them ; that he should be sincere and truthful, and the enemy of all dissimulation and craft (*feintise et cautèle*). It was her wish that he should be forewarned against all that could give him false ideas of men, of things, and his times ; that the great models of antiquity should be constantly placed before his mind, in order to kindle in him a noble emulation, and to preserve him from pride. Finally, this noble Calvinist lady concluded the scheme she drew up for the education of young Henry of Navarre, with the recommendation to his preceptor not to neglect the arts that give pleasure and variety to life, which she would have his pupil cultivate in leisure hours.

Jeanne was not, however, so sanguine as to believe that her son would be trained up in the way he should go under the eye of Catherine de' Medici, who gave no heed to the morals and conduct of her own children. Besides, a prediction of the time assigned the Crown of France to the youthful Béarnais. This might prove a source of danger to him. The Queen of Navarre therefore repaired to Paris as soon as a temporary suspension of arms permitted ; for Jeanne had given shelter and support to the Huguenots to the full extent of her power. Very courteously she requested young Charles, whose majority (thirteen years and a day) had been recently proclaimed at Rouen, to allow her son to return with her to Béarn. He immediately assented, and Jeanne—fearing that the queen-mother, who, it appears, was not consulted by the precocious young sovereign, would find some pretext for detaining Prince Henry, and bringing him up at the French Court as the betrothed of Marguerite de Valois—at once prepared for her departure.

Serious troubles had arisen in her absence, from the acts and intrigues of Philip II., who, as she learned on leaving Paris, had publicly protested against her suppression of Catholicism in Béarn, and the support she gave to the enemies of Rome. By bribes and promises he had seduced from their allegiance many of her subjects in Lower Navarre. The object of Philip and his allies, the Guises, was, through the treachery of trusted dependents, to get possession of Jeanne and her children ; to deliver over the former to the tender mercies of the Spanish Inquisition ; to shut up Henry and

Catherine in separate fortresses ; to invade Navarre, and to offer Béarn to Charles IX. for annexation to France. Preparations were rapidly going forward for carrying out this scheme when, it is said, the young Queen of Spain became Jeanne's protectress.* ('Vie de Catherine de Bourbon' —Mdme. d'Armaëlle.)

The valiant Queen of Navarre was, however, nothing daunted. Instead of seeking refuge, as advised, at Nérac, she adopted defensive measures, visited the fortresses of Béarn, and, with her accustomed firmness when danger threatened, carried the inspection of her frontiers to the very borders of Spain. She then leisurely retreated to the Château-fort of Navarre, with her ladies and her children, prepared to stand a siege. She also wrote to the Court of France, requiring that justice be done to her. The wily Catherine de' Medici, however, was too much intent on recovering the position in the Government, of which recent events had in a great measure deprived her, to trouble herself about justice, and, besides, far too prudent to quarrel with her son-

---

* This is perhaps doubtful, as Philip was not accustomed to be moved to show mercy to heretics from whatever quarter the appeal might come, and in the instance in question even less so than usual.

in-law of Spain for the sake of the Queen of Navarre.

The plot being discovered, and the plotters supposed to be baffled, danger apparently ceased to exist. But the pious zeal of the Court of Rome and the 'Demon of the South' was not so readily baffled, and an unusual and striking act of authority was resolved on. Eight or ten French prelates, convicted or suspected of heresy, were, together with the Queen of Navarre, cited to appear at Rome before the supreme tribunal of the Holy Inquisition, within six months from the 20th of September, 1563. Failing to do so, Jeanne d'Albret would forfeit her kingdom with any other possessions she laid claim to; and this without prejudice to other and graver punishments, which by her heretical acts she may have incurred. The stake awaited poor Jeanne. Once more she appealed to Charles IX. and the queen-mother. This produced a vigorous protestation from the Court of France to Pius IV. in the name of the royal dignity, the Gallican liberties, and the king's suzerainty over the domains of the House of Albret. As it did not suit the Pope's interests to oppose at that moment the views of the Court of France, he quietly allowed the proceedings against Jeanne and the prelates to drop without further notice.

Jeanne, with her little Court, then left the gloomy walls of the sombre old fortress to resume her usually calm and quiet course of life at Nérac, and to devote herself to the superintendence of Catherine's education. The Baronne de Trignonville was the little princess's head governess—a Protestant lady of great learning and severely moral life. But Catherine was not brought up in solitude. Jeanne thought it too dreary, and a check on the natural flow of youthful spirits. The baronne's daughter and other children of the Navarrese nobility were therefore the companions of Catherine's studies and amusements.

CHAPTER XIII.

Battle of Dreux.—Montmorency and Condé Prisoners.—Guise's proposed Attack on Orléans.—His Assassination.—The Peace of Amboise.—Condé and the Flying Squadron.—Princess of Condé dies of Grief.—Mademoiselle de Limeuil.—The Maréchale Saint-André.—Catherine's Reign now begins.

THE fall of Rouen was followed by the submission of Caen, Dieppe, and nearly the whole of Normandy. But again the hopes of the Protestants revived when D'Andelot reached Orléans with 3,000 German cavalry, a corps of 4,000 infantry, and promises of further aid. Though ill, and suffering from a quartan fever, which compelled him to use a litter, he safely conducted these men from the banks of the Rhine—very ably avoiding an encounter with a body of Catholic troops sent to oppose his passage. Thus reinforced, Condé and Coligny left Orléans and encamped under the walls of Paris. This audacity created great alarm in the capital, and a good deal of brisk skirmishing ensued before the boulevards of the Faubourg Saint-Victor. The Protestant chiefs, however, had no expectation of becoming masters of Paris. They had merely replied by an act of defiance to a decree of the Parliament condemning to death 'Coligny and his associates.'

Ten days after they decamped, and marched towards Normandy to effect a junction with the English troops, and to receive the promised gold florins. Their German auxiliaries were already demanding their pay, and, as was customary with them, threatening to desert when their services were most needed. No time was lost by the 'Triumvirate' in following up the Huguenot army, which they overtook at Dreux, where was fought the first regular battle of the first religious war. The Constable Montmorency, who held the chief command of the Catholic army, was wounded and taken prisoner. A reserve under the command of the Duc de Guise then attacked the corps headed by the Prince de Condé, who, with desperate but imprudent valour mingling with his men in the fight, fell into the enemy's hands, his horse being shot under him.

Of the two small armies opposed to each other (18,000 Catholics, and about 16,000 Protestants), between six and seven thousand were left dead or wounded on the field. Coligny's corps retreated in good order, Guise being unable to pursue; yet the Catholics claimed the victory. It was indeed a very barren one, though the Huguenot chief was captured; as the constable was also a prisoner, his youngest son and Saint-André, his second in command, killed, and nearly the whole of their cavalry destroyed. Some fugitives from the Catholic army reported the Huguenots victorious, and both Montmorency and Saint-André slain. This was welcome news to the queen-mother, who on hearing it quietly remarked, 'We must now pray to God in French.' But when a more correct report arrived, she, with equal composure, ordered bonfires to be lighted, and a Te Deum to be sung in the churches.

Though Condé and Guise were mortal enemies, yet the duke did not omit that singular customary act of courtesy towards the captive prince, of inviting him to share his couch. The constable was conducted with a strong escort to Orléans, the Protestant headquarters, where he was received and treated with all due graciousness by the Princesse de Condé, who was his niece. But the absence of the prince, of course, prevented that chiefest mark of distinction—the offer of half a bed—being conferred on him. On the day after the battle Queen Elizabeth's ambassador, Sir Nicholas Throckmorton, was taken prisoner while following the retreating Protestant army. Luckily, he did not carry the gold florins with him. They would have been as acceptable to the needy Catholics to pay their Spanish and Swiss allies, as to the Protestants to satisfy their clamorous German friends.

The Duc de Guise, having received from the queen-mother letters patent appointing him commandant-general of the king's forces during the absence of the constable, at once entered upon the realization of an extensive plan he had conceived for the termination of the civil war. The first act of the sanguinary drama was an immediate attack on Orléans, and a massacre of course to follow. The prince and the admiral being absent, terror reigned in the city; for it was generally reported that Guise, in rivalry of Montluc, had 'determined to slay not only every man, woman, and child, but to extend his murderous onslaught even to the animals, to raze the city to the ground, and sow salt on its ruins.'

The Huguenot infantry was lodged in the faubourg of Portereau, and there Guise began his attack. French and Germans, commanded by

D'Andelot, made a valorous resistance; but their German allies (great cowards those mercenary soldiers appear to have been in those days) abandoned them, and fled for refuge to the city. Eight or nine hundred men were slain, taken prisoners, tortured, or drowned. This satisfied the bloodthirsty Guise for a first attempt.

Hatred the most intense, a burning desire for vengeance, had glowed fiercely in many Huguenot hearts since the massacre of Vassy. Even the detested cardinal, 'the tiger of France,' seemed to be less an object of their implacable hate than the tyrant duke, the instigator of that butchery. Many projects were suggested for 'ridding the earth of this tyrant. Death, anywhere and by any means; but death on the battle-field was too honourable an end for him.'

A young gentleman of Angoumois, Poltrot de Méré, a relative of that Renaudie who took so prominent a part in the Amboise plot, and whose dead body was gibbeted by the duke's orders, had sworn that 'the tyrant should die by no other hand than his.' He was believed to be rather boastful than zealous. Coligny employed him as a spy, in which capacity he had already served the Protestant commander at Lyons. Availing himself of a certain facility this gave him for accomplishing his purpose, Poltrot sought the Catholic camp. Representing himself as a repentant rebel, as several others who had treacherously deserted the Protestant cause had done, he was well received by Guise.

The duke was hastening on his preparations for attacking Orléans from the isles of the Loire, and expecting an easy conquest. For not only were the Huguenots feeble in forces to resist him, but a terrible epidemic was raging, and had already taken off from eight to ten thousand of the inhabitants. Poltrot, when about to do the dastardly deed he had resolved on, seems to have been assailed by doubts of its righteousness in the sight of heaven, or, perhaps, by fears of the consequences of it to himself. But the favourable moment had arrived. It was the 18th of February, and the attack from the isles was to begin on the morrow. The duke, accompanied by two gentlemen only, had ridden out to inspect the advanced posts. In the brief dusky twilight of a February evening he was returning to the Château de Corney to welcome his wife, whom an unwonted anxiety had brought thither to be near the scene of his defeat or victory.

Poltrot, meanwhile, alighting from his horse, and throwing himself on his knees, fervently supplicated God to turn his mind from doing this deed, if it were displeasing in His sight. If not, then he implored Him for strength, courage, and constancy to carry out his purpose to the end. No change of mind coming over him, Poltrot believed himself acting under Divine inspiration, and stealthily following his victim until within six or seven paces of him, he took aim with his pistol, the cumbrous weapon being charged with three balls. The whole charge lodged in the duke's armpit, and he fell forward on his horse's neck, while his assassin, putting spurs to his horse, fled with all speed across the woods and marshes of La Sologne.

The duke was conveyed to the Château de Corney. The surgeons were speedily in attendance ; but the famous Ambroise Paré, the most skilful surgeon of the time, was not so successful in his present operation for the extraction of the balls, as some years before he had been with that terrible wound in the face that had gained the duke the sobriquet of ' Le Balafré.' As Catherine hastened with the young king to the camp on hearing that Guise was assassinated, it may be inferred that it was she who proposed, when his case was declared to be beyond surgical aid, that the methods of the occult sciences should be resorted to, and the cure of his wounds be attempted by incantations and charms. The duke, however, 'objected to recourse being had to enchantments which God had forbidden.'

'Le Grand Guise,' as he was then called, ended his blood-stained career on Ash Wednesday, the 24th of February, aged forty-four. He was a dauntless soldier and an able general; but he was cruel and rapacious in the extreme, a persecutor of the Reformers, and oppressor of the people generally. He and his brother, the infamous Cardinal de Lorraine, by their joint depredations on the public purse, had brought the kingdom to the very verge of ruin. Of course his end was edifyingly pious and Christian-like. He exculpated himself from any blameworthy share in the massacre of Vassy, to the satisfaction of, at least, the courtly priest who confessed and absolved him.* He advised Catherine to make peace, which hitherto he had done all in his power to oppose and prevent. He gave excellent counsels to his eldest son, suggesting moderation in his views, disregard of the world's pleasures, and generally urged him to follow a course of life of which he had failed to set him any example.

Catherine de' Medici, though affecting grief, and shedding an abundance of those crocodile tears

* 'Mémoires de Castelnau.'

she had always near her eyes ready to flow forth as occasion required, as also she had the name of God always on her lips, yet rejoiced greatly in heart at this unexpected breaking up of the 'Triumvirate.' Now she was about to reign—to reign uncontrolled. But a few days since, that devoutly wished-for consummation of her hopes seemed further away than ever. The stars in their courses must surely have fought for her, when 'le Grand Guise,' the great obstacle in her path to power, was suddenly removed. This Poltrot de Méré, against whom her anger seemed boundless, and on whom every species of horrible torture was to be inflicted, she would have willingly set on a pedestal and worshipped for his deed of noble daring, and the immense service he had done her.

In the fulness of her heart she promised all sympathy, consideration, and ample provision for the widow and sons of the man who had been heaping up wealth, and appropriating estate upon estate, with or without the consent of his sovereign, for the last twenty years. At the moment the hand of a fanatic laid him low, a decisive victory over the fever-stricken Orléanists would have thrown into his hands power great as that formerly wielded by the ancient mayors of the palace. Catherine would have received the law from him, and he would have governed the king and reigned in his stead in spite of her. She knew that, and in heartfelt thankfulness for his removal she decreed him an almost royal funeral. In military pomp, perhaps, more than royal—for Guise was very popular with the army; which had sacked, and pillaged, and, sanctioned by their brilliant leader, committed every possible enormity. Naturally, then, those soldier savages regretted 'the Grand Guise,' and followed him to his grave with bowed heads and saddened hearts.

The unfortunate Poltrot de Méré, having lost his way in the woods in attempting to regain the Huguenot camp during the night, concealed himself in the daytime in a farmhouse, where he was discovered and arrested. Under the horrible torture of portions of his flesh being nipped off with red-hot pincers, he confessed to anything and everything his tormentors suggested or desired. He accused first the admiral of having for months incited him to assassinate Guise and other chiefs of the Catholic party. He then said that Théodore de Bèze and D'Andelot had urged him to do the deed, a varying statement being elicited each time the torture was applied to the wretched man. His agonizing slow death was at last accomplished by quartering and burning. Such horrors make the blood run cold and deaden one's sympathies, whether practised by Catholics or Protestants.

Coligny, De Bèze, and other officers and ministers accused by De Méré, absolutely denied, in a memoir addressed to the queen-mother, all complicity in the assassin's deed. But Coligny acknowledged that the death of Guise appeared to him to be the most fortunate event that could have happened for France, for the churches of God, and for himself and his party. 'He had many times,' he said, 'informed the Cardinal de Lorraine and the Duchesse de Guise that plots were on foot to take the duke's life. But since it had come to his knowledge on trustworthy authority that the duke himself had planned the assassination of the Prince de Condé, and of himself and his brother D'Andelot, he frankly avowed, while declaring on his word of honour that he had never counselled or incited anyone to take the duke's life, he yet had not thought it his duty to dissuade any person from doing so. Coligny recommended the queen to keep Poltrot in prison until peace was signed, when he might be confronted with those whom he accused. But Catherine preferred to put him out of the way at once, that an accusation which could neither be proved nor refuted might rest on Coligny to his disadvantage.

Catherine now became anxious to negotiate a peace, Coligny—whose influence with his party she imagined would suffer from her attempt to disparage him as a man of honour—having left Orléans and succeeded in rapidly re-establishing, to her great chagrin, the Huguenot cause in Normandy. The 300,000 gold florins had safely reached him, and with them he had completely reorganized and reinforced his army. The Catholic and Protestant chiefs being both prisoners, a preliminary conference took place between the queen and the Princesse de Condé, and France seemed threatened with another 'Ladies' Peace.' For when Condé and Montmorency were conducted to one of the isles of the Loire to continue the discussion opened by the ladies, the old constable displayed such extreme irritation, obstinacy, and even more than his usual brutality of speech and manners, that Condé's indignation was greatly aroused, and a *duel-à-mort* seemed a more likely result of their conference than a treaty of peace.

De L'Hôpital was then directed to draw up the terms of pacification she was disposed to offer the prince, while privately she informed Montmorency that peace *must* be concluded, and that there need be but little scrutiny of the terms, as it could be broken whenever occasion required. Montmorency, having given full vent to his spleen, became more tractable. He was very weary, too, of his imprisonment; more so, probably, than Condé— the *ennui* of captivity in the prince's case having been rendered more supportable by the amiability of the queen-mother in assigning him a companion —one of the fascinating belles of the 'flying squadron.' By this sort of diplomacy Catherine for awhile subdued Prince Louis, not sinking him to quite so low a level as his brother, King Antony, but sufficiently deep and long enough to suit her temporary projects.

Setting aside the advice of the Protestant military chiefs, and disregarding the remonstrances of the ministers of religion, he signed the Treaty of Amboise without waiting for the approval of the admiral, who, on returning to Orléans four days after, joined his associates in the camp and the pastors of the church in most thoroughly condemning it. Condé was especially blamed, and Calvin in his indignation did not scruple to apply some very harsh and uncomplimentary epithets to him. Liberty of conscience was generally granted by this treaty; and freedom of worship was conceded to the *noblesse*, but in their own dwellings, and for their families only. To the *bourgeoisie* that privilege was forbidden; but in certain towns in their possession they were allowed to continue the form of worship 'called reformed,' while the poorer class could only meet for prayer at certain intervals, and under still more stringent restrictions.

A sort of amnesty was granted, and Condé and his followers were declared 'the king's good and loyal subjects; his majesty accounting them to have acted for good ends, and with the intention of doing him service.' The treaty was published in the form of an edict. The refractory Parliament, as usual, refused to register it. The chancellor in the king's name insisted, and after some further delay his command was obeyed, the whole of the members appearing in mourning robes. Zealous Catholics refused to recognize a peace with the Huguenots who had slain 'the Grand Guise,' on any conditions, and resisted the order to disarm— the Protestants of course also declining—unless the Catholics set the example. It soon became evident that this peace which the chancellor—and the chancellor only—was so sanguine as to believe would prove the foundation of a system of tolerance was destined to be really nothing more than a short truce.

The Duchesse de Guise with her four sons, all in deepest mourning, appeared continually in Paris, agitating and exciting the people by their unceasing demand for vengeance on Coligny, whom they denounced as the murderer of the head of the House of Guise. The duchess had probably forgotten her own prophetic words at Amboise, when, sick with the sight of blood flowing in torrents by command of the sanguinary monster whose death she now deplored and sought to have avenged, 'Madame,' she exclaimed, turning towards the queen-mother, 'this blood will surely call for blood. May heaven spare your sons and mine!' The just judgment of God which she then invoked and, by her words, seemed to foresee, had, in strict retributive justice, first fallen on the chief promoter of that terribly tragic scene.

The Peace of Amboise was, however, celebrated by Catherine de' Medici by one of those brilliant *fêtes* she was fond of giving at Chenonceaux for the purposes of seduction, and to which she invited those whom she was most desirous of chaining to the car of her ambition. There, she exhibited before her dazzled guests her whole swarm of corrupt loveliness, who, arrayed in scanty drapery of transparent gossamer, and with their hair falling loosely around them, served at table, in the presence of the youthful king and his young brothers—'displaying their charms with more art and complaisance than the most severe modesty took pains to conceal them.'

By these lascivious means the queen-mother often succeeded in dominating for awhile those who had most defied and laughed at her efforts; by the same arts she had been working on Condé, and hoped to succeed with him as she had succeeded with Antony. Her object was to read his mind and thoughts, and to seduce him from the Protestant cause by promises of place and power. Condé ventured to put in a claim to succeed the King of Navarre in the Lieutenant-Generalship of the Kingdom. But Catherine had no intention of giving herself another master; she therefore merely reminded him that he had an elder brother, the Cardinal de Bourbon.

The beauty of Isabelle de Limeuil seemed greatly to attract the prince's notice. Catherine observing this—though aware of the Princess de Condé's devoted attachment to her husband, and that she was then suffering in health from the fatigue, anxiety, and excitement she had undergone in accompanying the Huguenot army—forthwith instructed De Limeuil in the course she was to pursue in order to captivate the prince and extract from him a statement of his secret intentions respecting his party; Coligny and Condé being at that moment less cordial in their relations than usual, with regard to their difference of opinion concerning the Treaty of Amboise. Isabelle, constantly thrown in his way, became the frequent companion of those hours of idleness enforced on him by his captivity.

But this captivity ended, Condé showed no eagerness for quitting the Court and rejoining his party. Mademoiselle de Limeuil had not only kindled a flame almost as ardent in the breast of Condé as that Mademoiselle Du Rouet had excited in the susceptible bosom of the King of Navarre; but, unlike that more prudent damsel, she had allowed her own heart to be taken captive. Catherine de' Medici by no means contemplated such a result to the intrigue she herself had originated and encouraged. She was, or feigned to be, exceedingly irritated, the 'invincible flying squadron' being trained to subdue, not to be subdued. Worse than all, this erring member of the queen-mother's forces had discovered no secrets. Condé had made no political statement, and mademoiselle apparently had sought none. Neither had she urged on him the advantage he would find in a change of religion. Without delay the queen-mother ignominiously expelled her from Court, and shut her up in a convent in Burgundy, 'there,' as Catherine remarked, 'to bury her grief and her shame.'

Condé's infidelity so deeply distressed his wife, and so seriously increased her illness, that she shortly after died. Catherine then lost no time in suggesting as her successor the widow of Marshal Saint-André, whose husband was killed at the Battle of Dreux; not exactly perhaps by Condé's own hand, but at all events by the troop he commanded after the marshal was taken prisoner. He, however, had no mind to marry her, though the immense wealth left by Saint-André made his widow and daughter two of the richest matches in France. The daughter was betrothed to the young Duc Henri de Guise. But the widow, in order to dazzle Condé by the vastness of the riches a marriage with her would place at his command, scrupled not to poison her daughter; such, at least, was the popular cry. She offered him as a present her estate of Saint-Valery, and was prepared to make the entire sacrifice of her wealth to him. He, however, remained inflexible.

The deceased marshal was a man to whom vice and crime were unstintingly attributed, and it would seem that he had a wife quite worthy of him; but her wealth, and her crime to increase it, failed to secure a prince of the blood for her second husband.

Neither pencil nor pen has depicted Prince Louis de Condé as a handsome or fascinating man. Yet it was his misfortune to be much pursued by the ladies. Of wealth he possessed very little; but he was a prince of the blood; it was just possible that he might one day wear the crown, at which he was already supposed to aim; and if he was not overburdened with prudence, he was certainly full of courage, and by far the most estimable of the three brothers.

When Isabelle de la Touche de Limeuil heard that the prince was a widower, she too cherished hopes of becoming his wife; for she was of a distinguished family, distantly related to the younger branch of the Bourbons. Doubtless convent life, if not very strict in those days, was a dull affair to a young lady partly brought up at the voluptuous Court of Catherine de' Medici. Her unhappiness and her penitence were brought under the notice of the queen by friends and relatives, who earnestly entreated her restoration to favour. After some real or affected hesitation on Catherine's part, the fair Isabelle was permitted to leave her convent. But not that she might marry

Condé. A husband was provided for her—an Italian gentleman of the queen's suite. Should she refuse him, the only alternative was her return to the convent.

The proposed marriage was utterly repugnant to the feelings of the fair penitent; but when she reflected on the matter, convent life seemed more so. She therefore yielded with the best grace she could under the circumstances. She, however, did not allow the husband she was compelled to accept to forget that she was of higher lineage than he. This he seems generally to have meekly acknowledged. But one day when more forcibly than usual she was impressing on him her great condescension in marrying him, he replied: 'Really, madame, I think I have made a greater sacrifice in this matter than you have.' She was startled at his presumption. 'Have not I,' he said, 'sacrificed my honour to enable you to retain yours?' (Mathieu, 'Histoire de France.')

CHAPTER XIV.

Coligny accused of assassinating Guise.—Siege and Capitulation of Havre.—A Royal Tour in the Provinces.--A Change of Tactics.—Catherine decides for the Catholic Cause.—The First Stone of the Tuileries.—Piety and Pleasure the Order of the Day.—The Queen of Spain at Bayonne.—Grand Festivities.—The Salmon and the Frogs. —Double Marriage proposed.

VERY embarrassing to Catherine de' Medici and her counsellors were the consequences of the death of the Duc de Guise and the trial of Poltrot de Méré; the barbarous punishment of that obscure fanatic not satisfying the duke's family. Popular excitement was kept alive by their frequent mourning processions in Paris, and their unceasing demand for justice on the man (Coligny being understood but never named) who had caused the murder of the hero of their house. To increase the agitation and general bad feeling existing between Catholics and Protestants, the latter were loud in praise of the deed which the Guise family sought to avenge —exalting the assassin as the 'liberator of the people of God, to whom, for his righteous zeal, the martyr's crown was due.'

After the signing of the treaty of Amboise, Coligny retired to Châtillon-sur-Loing to pass some time with his family. He then announced to the queen his intention to repair in the course of a week to Saint-Germain, where the Court was residing. The Guises and their partizans determined to give him battle, even if it were in the grounds of the château. The admiral was already well on his way, escorted by five hundred gentlemen. Catherine—greatly alarmed at the prospect of an encounter which, from the exasperation of feeling on both sides, would probably have been a very sanguinary affray—entreated Condé to set out with all speed to meet the admiral and request him to defer his visit to the Court for awhile.

The prince obeyed. The next day he returned, accompanied by D'Andelot. The private council being assembled, the prince then declared that 'notwithstanding that the edict of peace should cover all acts committed during the continuance of hostilities, the admiral would yet consent to the course demanded—the trial taking place before impartial judges; and provided also that his adversaries would consent to the same judicial measures being taken in respect to the criminal attempts imputed to them.' The prince added that, apart from these judicial proceedings, he should consider any attacks on the admiral as directed towards himself. Marshal de Montmorency, in his own and his father's name, made a similar declaration.

The constable was by no means better disposed towards the cause of Reform. But he had listened to overtures of reconciliation with his nephews because of the extreme resentment he felt towards the queen-mother. To quiet the Guises, Catherine had promised that the young Duke Henry should succeed to his father's post of Grand-Master of the Household, instead of restoring it to the constable, as he had expected, 'the late king having unjustly taken it from him to confer it on his uncle.' To appease his wrath, Catherine now gave him the Duchy of Châtelrault. The private council then forbade both parties to offer any sort of offence towards each other, and deferred the judicial proceedings until they had obeyed the royal command to lay down their arms.

As the late peace seemed to have irritated men's minds, and created new troubles, rather than to have smoothed away differences and restored contentment, it occurred to De L'Hôpital, who was so sincerely anxious to secure tolerance for the Huguenots, and a true religious peace for France, that the recovery of Havre offered a favourable means of drawing Catholics and Protestants together in friendly union in furtherance of the same patriotic aim. He therefore suggested the siege of that town by the troops of both parties, united under the command of the constable, and urged Catherine to make an appeal to the patriotism of both the Catholic and Protestant chiefs. In moving terms, and with tear-suffused eyes, 'she prayed them to set aside their quarrels, at least so long as the foreigner held a footing in the land.' Condé and a large part of the Huguenot army at once hastened to join the constable's forces, while to inspire the waverers with a spirit of loyalty, the queen-mother, with the king, the young princes, and the ladies and gentlemen of the Court, took up her residence at Fécamp.

There were, however, many who steadfastly adhered to their English ally, and even fought in the ranks of the English troops. Coligny refrained from taking any part in the siege. He had at the outset of the civil war been utterly opposed to seeking foreign aid, and bringing foreign troops into France. But as it had eventually been done, their opponents setting them the example, and the aid then asked been granted, he thought it neither right nor politic to break engagements which, he too plainly foresaw, must at no distant period be renewed.

Havre was, however, soon restored to the French. A long resistance had been looked for after Elizabeth's refusal to receive in exchange for it the money she had advanced to Condé and a renewal of the Treaty of 1559, promising the restitution of Calais to the English in 1569. There was a garrison of between six and seven hundred men in Havre under the orders of the Earl of Warwick, who offered but a feeble resistance to the assailants. For a terrible epidemic prevailed amongst the troops, and there was a want of provisions and pure water—the French having succeeded in cutting off the sources whence supplies were obtained. The siege, or merely the preparations for a siege, were scarcely completed when the English commander capitulated (28th of July. The next day a large fleet, bringing a reinforcement of troops and a supply of provisions, anchored in the roadstead. But this relief came too late, and a few days after the fleet returned to

England with the remnant of the fever-stricken garrison which had escaped death. War had been declared on the part of France; but Elizabeth forbore to continue it. Peace was proclaimed in the following year, 120,000 gold crowns being paid for Calais, though 500,000 was the sum stipulated by treaty in case of the failure of the French to restore it to England.

General rejoicing, bonfires, Te Deums, and the queen-mother's usual sybaritic entertainments followed the exit of the foreigner. De L'Hôpital, and possibly Catherine, believed that the flames of discord, if not utterly extinguished between Catholic and Protestant by their combined feat of arms, were stifled, at least for a time. The Court was at Meulan, where the young king hunted daily, Catherine and the Court accompanying him. Charles IX. already began to display those strange outbursts of apparently motiveless anger, and that inclination—as if seeking by such means to suppress it—for violent bodily exertion, which so sorely tried and so early exhausted his naturally delicate frame. Except the queen-mother, who liked the wild sport—as her efforts to keep the king always in sight necessitated great exertion, which she fancied kept down her ever-increasing obesity—few really cared to join in what seemed to be a mere wild-goose chase in pursuit of the flying, frantic young king. Happily, probably, would it have been for him and for France had he, after his majority was declared, possessed the moral courage to shake off by degrees that horrible mother's galling yoke, which even from childhood, when he came to the throne, seemed so heavily to oppress him, and transformed him, as he grew up, from a youth of great promise to a madman and a murderer.

In the midst of these courtly rejoicings there arrived at Meulan a solemn procession requiring an audience of the king. It consisted of the mother, the widow, the four sons, and the four brothers of the late Duc de Guise. A very numerous *cortége* accompanied them, all wearing deepest mourning. 'They desired the king's permission to proceed at once with the inquiry into that most treacherous and inhuman murder of the head of their house.' Of the Châtillon brothers, Odet, the cardinal, only was with the Court. Coligny again was not directly charged by name, though indirectly the crime was attributed to him alone. The cardinal therefore suggested, and Catherine consented, that the Grand Council, instead of the Parliament of Paris, should be required to take cognizance of the proceedings, as more likely to give an unbiassed judgment than that assembly of magistrates, so strongly prejudiced against the Huguenots and Reform.

The Guise family rejected as partial, or incompetent, more than half the members of the Grand Council, and Coligny objected to nearly all the rest. There remained, therefore, but the king and one or two of the councillors to decide the important question of Coligny's guilt or innocence. The decision, however, really rested with the queen-mother, who determined on letting it remain for the present undecided—an edict of January, 1564, announcing that judgment was deferred for three years, in order that a moment more opportune than the present might occur for inquiry into the facts of the case.

No sooner was one dispute settled in those troublous times than another arose, bringing with it further dissension, persecution, and hostile feelings. A grand embassy, comprising representatives from the pope, the King of Spain, the German Emperor, and the Duke of Savoy, arrived in Paris at the time of the issuing of the above edict. The object was to prevail on the king to accept and to enforce in France the decrees of the Council of Trent. This council, after eighteen years of existence, had brought its proceedings to a close by a series of anathemas on the opinions of the Huguenots relative to the existence of purgatory; the setting up of images; the worship of saints; of the Sacrament of the Lord's Supper; of divorce; the marriage of priests, and many other matters, all of which they solemnly cursed, and declared contrary to the doctrines of the Roman Catholic Church, and punishable by death. Other questions, more immediately concerning the Catholics, were introduced into the list of decrees, and an exhortation added, urging on the king the revocation of the absolution (or amnesty) granted to the heretics by the Treaty of Amboise—also the speedy punishment of the well-known murderer of the Duc de Guise.

The boy-king, who, under the able tutelage of the queen-mother, was growing up an adept in the art of dissembling, gave the evasive reply—neither consenting nor refusing—as Catherine had taught him. But privately, the Cardinal de Lorraine—who had returned with the embassy from Rome—urged her most earnestly to command the acceptance of the decrees of the council. As earnestly De L'Hôpital opposed it: thus drawing on himself the anger of the cardinal, who accused him of holding heretical opinions, and of ingratitude to the House of Guise (his father had been secretary to the cardinal's grandmother); but the chancellor replied that debts of gratitude were not to be repaid at the expense of the king and the State. The Parliament of Paris agreed with the chancellor, which was a rather unusual event, and refused to register the decrees. They considered several of them as 'a derogation of the king's rights, and of the liberties of the Gallican Church.' They, however, yielded with regard to the revocation of the amnesty or 'absolution,' which greatly exasperated the Huguenots, but was received with much favour by the Catholics.

Meanwhile, the cardinal attempted a reconciliation between the Prince de Condé and the Guise family, in order to detach him if possible from Coligny and the Protestant cause. Mary of Scotland was again the bribe offered for the renunciation of heresy, and, as in the case of the King of Navarre, the dazzling prospect of three crowns was dangled temptingly before him. But they were temptations that had lost the charm of novelty, and their possible realization had become more distant than ever. Condé, like his brother Antony, preferred to amuse himself amongst the queen's bevy of beauties; but unlike him, he forsook not the Huguenot faith or party.

In the midst of all the troubles and intrigues,

political and religious, that afflicted France, the chancellor was unwearying in his efforts for the encouragement of commerce, and the repression of that ruinously lavish expenditure and luxury which prevailed in the royal household, and had thoroughly exhausted the resources of the State. He had successfully introduced several judicial reforms, and he was now of opinion that the young king should visit the several provinces of his kingdom, believing that it would be productive of much benefit both to the youthful sovereign and to his people. He therefore suggested such a course to the queen, and persuaded himself that the sight of those terrible results of civil war—the ravages that had been committed in various towns and cities—would impress Charles with a desire to preserve peace and unity amongst all classes of his subjects.

Catherine appeared to enter very readily into the chancellor's views. She was exceedingly fond of change of place and scene, and perhaps an interval of comparative quiet after the strife and turmoil amidst which she had so long lived was a pleasant prospect to her. For political objects she was also desirous of seeing her daughter, the Queen of Spain, and of consulting the Duke of Alva, Philip's confidant. The proposed journey from province to province would afford her the opportunity of a meeting at Bayonne, and would also enable her to see and judge for herself in what force the Protestants really were in the various provinces of the kingdom. Doubtless in Catherine's brain there then floated some project, as yet immature, of a Huguenot extermination; not, at that time, by violent or sudden means, but, as she flattered herself, by more subtle arts and gradual extinction.

Towards the end of March the Court left Fontainebleau to make the tour of France, a numerous *cortége* and large detachment of the 'flying squadron' accompanying. Previous to her departure, the queen-mother laid the first stone of her palace of the Tuileries; the building of which was begun in the month of May following, after the plans (preserved by Ducerceau) of Philibert Delorme and Jean Bullant.

According to the programme arranged for the due ordering of the royal progress, the tour was to be accomplished by very short journeys of from two to six leagues.* Long intervals of rest were to follow, to be spent in feasting and fêtes, sanctified by religious ceremonies and prayers. The religious part of the programme was added because

* See Abel Jouan's 'Voyage de Charles IX.,' etc.

of Catherine's recent determination, after much wavering, to place herself and her sons at the head of the Catholic party. She now felt convinced that the Catholics were destined to be triumphant, the peasantry and the mass of the people in the towns being with them. A change in the education of her sons was therefore imperative, and was observed by the Huguenots with some alarm.

Hitherto, the royal children, wholly unchecked, had sung the Huguenot psalms and hymns, to the great scandal of the Catholics. At the dissolute revels at Chenonceaux they had masqueraded in priests' vestments; tossed their rosaries and Catholic books of devotion into the fire; spoken contemptuously of the 'papists;' and eaten freely of meat in Lent and on the customary fast-days. The Court had followed their and the queen-mother's example as she seemed to desire, while many believed that no fasting, no confession, and the singing of psalms and hymns in French were the chief doctrines of 'the people of the religion,' as the Reformers were frequently called. But a change of tactics was now needed, and henceforth the king and the rest of her children were to omit none of the external practices of devotion—the same indifference to principles and absence of moral training still continuing. For the same reason, before setting out on the projected tour, 'Catherine required that the ladies and gentlemen of the Court—under penalty of being expelled for disobedience—should confess, and receive the Sacrament at Easter.'

Escorted by ten companies of infantry, commanded by Marshal Strozzi, the royal travellers first halted at Champagne, passing on thence to Troyes, where they remained a month. The inhabitants were all very eager to see the youthful monarch, the rest of the young royal family, and their gracious Florentine mother — a further interest being given to this visit by the signing at Troyes, on the 12th of April, of a peace between the Queen of England and the King of France. Continuing their journey, Charles and his mother visited the Duchesse de Lorraine, Catherine's eldest daughter ; Charles acting as sponsor to his sister's infant son.

On their road to Lyons they were met at the gates of Dijon by Catherine's formerly devoted friend, Marshal Gaspard de Tavannes—a brave and able general, a most zealous Catholic and cruel persecutor of the Huguenots. On accosting the king he laid his hand on his heart and said, ' This is yours ;' then placing it on his sword, he continued, ' and with this I am able to serve you.'

At Lyons, at Orléans, and other towns which had been the Huguenots' principal cities of refuge, Catherine ordered the construction of strong citadels; appointing as governors men opposed to the cause of Reform. An edict was also issued forbidding the Reformers the exercise of religious worship in any city or town where the king might be sojourning. Pius IV., to whom Catherine communicated her plan for the gradual extinction of Calvinism, by a temporizing system which she explained to him, is said to have been far from disapproving it, though he would have preferred some scheme more swift and sure in its operation.

The winter of 1564 and 1565 was one of unusual severity throughout France. 'So intense was its rigour that it was considered one of the chief calamities of the epoch.' The sufferings of the people were very great; but neither this widespread misery nor the political and religious contests, resulting in frequent assassinations, general disquiet, and the prospect of fresh hostilities, interrupted the round of fêtes, banquets, and balls with which the 'good towns' welcomed their young sovereign, and the *élite* were in return entertained. Charles seems to have been more than once indisposed from excessive feasting and fêting. Into all those 'good towns' he made his public entry with the queen-mother. Generally he was saluted with frantic cries of 'Vive la messe!' The city guilds passed in procession before him. Children were named after the king, queen, and madame. Te Deums were sung from morn till eve, and piety and pleasure marched on hand-in-hand.

But Catherine had expressed a desire to see her daughter, the Queen of Spain. Her son-in-law, the king, she would have preferred to see, alone, but hoped that at all events he would accompany the queen. He did not, but consented that Isabelle (as Elizabeth was called in Spain) should visit her mother, accompanied and guarded by his second self, the Duke of Alva, and other Spanish grandees, as spies on the young queen. Elizabeth was well trained before leaving Spain by Philip himself in the part she was to play; and she seems to have done her best, as attested by Alva, to secure the approval of her amiable lord and master. On the 12th of June, 1565, Charles IX., Catherine de' Medici, and the Court arrived at Saint-Jean-de-Luz, and left the next day to receive the Queen of Spain on the extreme frontier of France, near Fontarabia. The young king was escorted by the detachment of troops under Strozzi, and a company of light cavalry.

A bower, or tent of foliage, was erected in a field on the banks of the river Bidassoa, and a splendid collation of ' Mayonnaise hams, beeves' tongues, Bologna sausages, pâtés, fruit, salads, preserves, and a large supply of good wine awaited there her majesty's arrival.' She, however, dined at Irun, and after dinner descended the mountain, escorted to the river's brink by 300 mounted archers of the Spanish king's guard and an ensign's company of infantry. The queen-mother then crossed the river on a bridge of boats and embraced her daughter, afterwards conducting her to the king, who, with his Court, was waiting to receive her in a boat moored in mid-stream, as he might not set foot on Spanish ground. Having landed on the French bank of the river, the royal party entered the verdant bower to refresh themselves. 'They remained there an hour—trumpets, hautbois, and tambourines joyously celebrating the happy event of the queen's arrival.'

On the journey to Bayonne the Queen of Spain rode between her mother and brothers. On the 15th of June she and her retinue, and Charles IX. and his Court and military escort—forming a grand procession—made their public entry into Bayonne in the evening, by torchlight. During the seventeen days the young queen remained at Bayonne, fêtes, tournaments, jousts, combats of three hours' **duration, plays, balls,** banquets, succeeded each other in one **unceasing round**; while bonfires and illuminations **lighted up the** town during the semi-darkness of the short midsummer nights.*

Notwithstanding that 'the **hopes of Christendom** ran **high concerning** the **result of the Spanish visit**,' the **great circumspection observed on both** sides **not to commit** themselves to the **adoption of** any suggestion in particular, together with **their** mutual distrust, prevented **any definite** scheme for the wholesale extermination **of heresy being positively** agreed to. To seize the **leaders of the faction** and cut off their heads seemed **to be the method** that found most favour. '**The head of one salmon is** worth more than **the heads of** ten **thousand frogs**,' said the **Duke of** Alva, rather **impatiently, in reply to the** queen-mother's plan of gradual **extinction**.

A boy of eleven was amusing himself within **hearing. He was struck by the duke's** remark on **the relative value of the heads of salmon and frogs, and** repeated **it to** his mother. **The boy was** Henry of Navarre. **Jeanne d'Albret with her children had** joined the Court at **Bayonne ; for the**

* Abel Jouan's 'Voyage de Charles IX.'

Spanish interview concerned her also. Unwisely following the example of more powerful sovereigns who had refused liberty of worship to the Reformers, she, *en revanche*, had forbidden the Catholic form of worship in her domains. She now consented to remove that prohibition; the peace of her little kingdom being threatened, and Spanish interference certain.

Whether from fear of her cruel, fanatical husband, or that from her residence in the gloomy, formal, and priest-ridden Court of Spain, Elizabeth had really adopted the bigoted views of Philip and the people about her, she supported the proposals which Alva made in the king's name with a sort of feverish energy, and joined him in urging on her mother the immediate dismissal of De L'Hôpital, 'the abettor and protector of evil-doers.' But Catherine absolutely refused; though she had secretly abandoned the chancellor's policy, while leaving him at full liberty to effect judicial and civil reforms. On the whole, nothing was concluded at Bayonne. Each party desired to deceive the other—Philip and Catherine having secret and separate aims which neither he nor she cared to disclose.

A double marriage was proposed by the queen-mother between her daughter Marguerite and Don

Carlos; and the Duc d'Anjou (Henry III.) and the Princess of Portugal, or other relative of the King of Spain. The young queen replied that the Catholic king was not then disposed to marry his son. In Alva's account of these interviews, he refers with praise to the 'great earnestness and consummate prudence' displayed by the young queen in her replies to her mother in support of Philip's views. The queen-mother herself was surprised at her daughter's warm advocacy of them; but she was generally supposed to be under the influence of fear of failure in the part imposed on her.

On the departure of the Spanish Queen, Charles made her a present of a white mule, on whose trappings, ornamented with gold and precious stones, he is said to have spent 400,000 ducats —disregarding the ruined state of the finances and the poverty of the people; from whose pockets were extracted all the cost of that vain pageantry which preceded and followed, for another seventeen days, the Spaniards' departure. Catherine crossed the river with her daughter and slept at Irun. Elizabeth desired to recross it in the morning with her mother; but Spanish etiquette forbade it. Before leaving Bayonne a hundred or more people, who had journeyed long distances for the purpose of being thus cured of their maladies, were touched by Charles for the king's evil (Abel Jouan).

The royal party then re-entered the interior of Gascony, passing through the domains of Jeanne d'Albret, who accompanied the Court on their leisurely journey towards the Loire. Along this route the fearful ravages of the civil war were but too plainly visible—devastated churches, ruined convents, broken statues, open tombs. The young king, scarcely controlling his rage, pointed out to Jeanne d'Albret this fearful desecration of sacred things—his gestures, his exclamations, showing the deep hatred then kindled in him towards the Huguenots; a feeling very different from that with which De L'Hôpital hoped they would impress him.

This tour of the French provinces had taken, so far, nearly two years to accomplish, ending in the month of December with the arrival of the Court at Moulins, where the princes of the blood, the knights of the Order, dignitaries of the Church, and other great personages were, by command of the king, to assemble in council early in January, 1566.

CHAPTER XV.

The Court at Moulins.—The Reconciliation and 'Kiss of Peace.'—The New Year.—Horrors in the Netherlands. —Surprise and Arrest of Condé and Coligny projected.— Hasty Departure of the Court.—Charles in a Rage at flying before his Subjects.— A Long Ride ; Charles Weary and Hungry.—Battle of Saint-Denis, November, 1567.—Death of Montmorency.

THE Christmas of 1565 and the New Year, 1st of January, 1566, were celebrated by Charles IX., Catherine de' Medici, and the French Court, at the splendid Château de Moulins.* There, forty-four years before, the celebrated but unfortunate constable, Duc Charles de Bourbon, first prince of the blood, so magnifi-

* It had been customary hitherto to begin the year at Easter, which being a movable feast, had frequently occasioned much confusion and inconvenience. The chancellor therefore proposed, and the suggestion, generally adopted, was also approved by the Parliament of Paris, that 'henceforth in all judicial acts the year should begin on the 1st of January, as was formerly the custom of the Romans.'

cently entertained Francis I. and his Court, that the jealousy of that monarch and the cupidity of his mother, Louise of Savoy, were greatly excited—the grandeur of the duke's abode, and the royal state in which he lived, far surpassing that of the sovereign. At this princely château (confiscated after the duke's revolt) the Guises, the Châtillons, the Montmorencys, and the greater part of the princes and grand seigneurs of the kingdom were commanded to attend. The three years to which the decision respecting Coligny's imputed complicity in the assassination of Duc François de Guise was deferred had not yet quite elapsed. But in view of what was in her mind, with reference to the Huguenots, Catherine thought it well to settle that question at once.

During the period that royalty was making the tour of France, the Protestants lost their spiritual chief, John Calvin (24th of May, 1564)—a loss which Catherine imagined would occasion a large falling off in the number of adherents to the doctrines of the austere 'Pope of Geneva,' as Calvin was frequently called. The more zealous Catholics rejoiced extravagantly at his death, while Protestants mourned him deeply. Still they were not left as sheep without a shepherd. The learned and pious Théodore de Bèze worthily succeeded

Calvin, maintaining his doctrines with equal firmness, while less repellently stern in his manners. Calvin was in his fifty-sixth year, and had long been a great sufferer from a complication of painful maladies—so much so, that death would seem to have been an almost welcome release from a living martyrdom. 'To be united in Christ and inflexible towards the enemies of Christ' was his dying injunction to his followers.

Besides the accusation against Coligny, another question had been deferred for settlement by the council of grandees assembled at Moulins. A conflict—at that time threatening great disturbance in the capital—had taken place in Paris in the preceding year, between Marshal François de Montmorency, the constable's eldest son, who was Governor of Paris, and the Cardinal de Lorraine. The cardinal, always terribly alarmed at the possibility of harm befalling his sacred person, had become, since his brother's assassination, more nervously timid than ever. Consequently, he sought from Catherine authority to surround himself, when travelling, with an armed escort ; but haughtily refused to exhibit the document granting this permission, when required to do so by the governor. The latter therefore determined not to allow an open infringement of the recent royal order prohibiting any of his majesty's subjects from passing through the kingdom armed.

The cardinal, disregarding the marshal's announcement, proposed not merely to secure himself from danger, but, accompanied by his nephew and a numerous armed *cortége*, to make a sort of public entry into Paris, after his rather prolonged absence from the kingdom. At the gate of Saint-Denis the provost was stationed with a company of gendarmes, who required the cardinal's pass. He deigned no reply, and his escort, equally indifferent to the provost's command to lay down their pikes and arquebuses, passed after my lord cardinal through the gate. A body of cavalry, headed by Montmorency, was drawn up near the Marché des Innocents. The cardinal and his escort were again commanded to halt; but as they were not disposed to obey, the marshal's troops, armed with heavy horse-pistols, fired on the 'Lorrainers.' Probably this was intended only to frighten the rebel cardinal, as no one was killed or wounded.

That timorous prelate was, indeed, very much frightened. The sound of the first pistol-shot made him leap from his horse and rush into the nearest house, dragging his nephew after him; the youth indignantly resisting. In this hiding-place he remained until nightfall. His escort wisely dispersed, with as little delay as possible, and the cardinal, with the young duke and but two or three attendants, entered Paris quietly, shunning observation, instead, as he had proposed, with colours flying and beat of drum. He had expected to create a great sensation in Paris, and to revive the excitement caused by the late duke's death. Also to rekindle enthusiasm for the House of Guise by parading the young Duke Henry (a handsome youth of fifteen) before the admiring eyes of the Parisian people. Finally, as Marshal Montmorency favoured the cause of Reform, the cardinal hoped to make his duty, as governor, of maintaining peace in Paris, more arduous than it already was, by the additional strife and hatred he expected to stir up between Catholics and Protestants.

Full of gall and wormwood, having just returned from anathematizing at the Council of Trent, the cardinal addressed a memorial to the king, complaining of the outrage and indignity put upon him by the Governor of Paris. His brother, the Duc d'Aumale, also wrote to the most violent of the Catholic chiefs, asking their assistance in avenging the much-insulted cardinal. Montmorency, on his part, called in the aid of Coligny and his partizans. But when this affair came to the queen-mother's knowledge, she immediately forbade both the Guises and the Châtillons to enter Paris, and required that no further steps should be taken in this dispute until the assembling of the Grand Council at Moulins.

All who were summoned to attend were now assembled. The 'flying squadron' was there in full force; while to put everybody in good temper, and, with the assistance of the squadron, to inspire all present with the inclination to assent to whatever she proposed, Catherine opened the proceedings by giving a splendid fête. It does not appear to have greatly subdued the hearts of the Catholics, or seduced the Calvinists, who were thus compelled to attend a reunion which the austerity of their doctrines led them to regard as a species of temptation of the devil.

The reconciliation of the marshal and the cardinal was not readily brought about. The former was obstinately bent on refusing to utter words of peace. Catherine was compelled to persuade the constable—though he was rarely in a conciliatory mood, and far from it on the present occasion—to undertake the bringing of his son to listen to reason, which was to assure the cardinal that 'in what he had done there was no intention on his part of offering any personal offence. He had acted solely from the sense of a necessity of doing his duty.' This was all that the constable by threatening to disinherit his son could extract from him. The cardinal was more amenable to Catherine's persuasion. He professed himself satisfied, being anxious to secure the queen-mother's favour now she was independent of him.

The council having pronounced this quarrel amicably settled, judgment was next to be given in the Guise and Coligny affair. The admiral now ' solemnly swore that he had been neither the author of the assassination of the Duc de Guise, nor an accomplice in it, and that he challenged to single combat whoever sustained the contrary.' The council, after a short consultation, were unanimously of opinion that no grounds existed for the charges brought against the admiral. The king forthwith declared him innocent, and enjoined both parties to live henceforth in peace and amity.

The duke's widow had married again, and was now Duchesse de Nemours. She and the cardinal promised to obey the king's injunction, and gave the admiral the kiss of peace. The young duke, however, was absent, and the Duc d'Aumale purposely delayed his arrival that he might not be present at the reconciliaton. He openly protested against the decision of the council, and displayed such violent animosity towards the Châtillons, even in the presence of the king and Court, that both parties were requested to leave Moulins. The duke was accused of having authorized an attempt to assassinate Coligny and D'Andelot; and the young Duc de Guise, who had just completed his sixteenth year, afterwards declared that as he was not present he did not consider the promises of his mother and uncle binding on him. Thus ended the Grand Council of Moulins. Peace and goodwill were proclaimed, but hatred and resentment rankled in every heart.

Jeanne d'Albret and her children had accompanied the Court from Bayonne to Moulins. But finding that the queen-mother's new orders, strictly prohibiting within the residence of the Court the singing of psalms in French, or any other practices of the Calvinist form of worship, extended even to her, she speedily withdrew from the royal residence and returned, with her son and daughter, to Gascony and Béarn.

Charles and his mother did not greatly prolong their stay at Moulins after the departure of the dissatisfied disputants. Catherine brought their sojourn to an end, as she began it, with a very grand and very expensive fête. That it should be expensive was always to her the chief attraction of any Court festivity; but how the expense was to be provided for she cared not at all.

On the 1st of May, 1566, Charles IX., after an absence of two years and two months, returned to Paris, and, with his mother, dined in the Faubourg Saint-Honoré at Madame du Perrin's (Pierre de L'Estoile). Charles was now within a few weeks of completing his sixteenth year; he had grown considerably during his tour, and in general appearance was much improved. But his irascibility of temper had become more noticeable than before, and there was a restlessness in his manner, a sort of ill-suppressed exasperation, that noisy amusements and violent exercise alone relieved. But in his milder moods he displayed a fondness for music, and poetical talent that did not fall below Ronsard's; while later on he developed some skill in metal-chasing.

But a new element of discord was introduced about this time into unhappy France. The Jesuits, through the intervention of some influential chiefs of the Catholic faction, succeeded, against the strenuous efforts of the chancellor, the opposition of the University, the ancient religious orders and the municipal body, in obtaining from the Parliament—itself opposed to them—'provisional authority' for continuing their course of teaching in Paris. For as a community of teachers only, not as a new religious order, were they recognised by the ecclesiastical synod of Poissy.

What was provisional, of course, soon became perpetual. They established themselves in all the great towns of France, and as they were more learned and more dignified than the clergy of that period were generally, their success was rapid, and their importance daily increased throughout Europe. As preachers, their earnestness and eloquence were employed to arouse the bad feeling of the Catholic people against the Huguenots, teaching that 'faith need not be kept with them, and that to put them to death was an act agreeable to God.' One of their famous orators, Edmond Auger, was the instigator of many sanguinary attacks on the Protestants. Very singularly, after one of these conflicts in which several of their number were slain, Auger, who had fallen into their hands, was saved from being hanged, by a Protestant minister who, deeply moved by his eloquence, interceded for him.*

Horrible cruelties were then being perpetrated by order of Philip II. on the people of the

* The 'Preachers of the League,' C. Labitte.'

Netherlands, and, as if to abet and encourage the monstrous horrors which suggested themselves to that demon's mind, a pope of congenially demoniacal spirit had succeeded (December, 1565) to the papal throne—vacant by the death of Paul IV. Pius V., or Saint Pius—for he was afterwards canonized—was a man into whose soul not one single feeble ray of pity or human feeling of any kind had ever entered. Michel Ghislieri, the exterminating genius of the Inquisition, had passed from the office of Grand Inquisitor to fill the chair of Saint Peter. His pontificate of six and a half years was one long reign of terror, one long *auto-da-fé*, in which many of Italy's greatest men perished by his order.

This saintly pontiff was desirous of uniting with that zealous Christian, the Catholic king, in urging on Catherine de' Medici the adoption of a more vigorous course for purging France from heresy than that slow and ineffectual system she habitually followed, of alternate delay, concession, and dissimulation. He is said to have trembled with rage when referring to it, and especially to her endeavours to keep on terms with the 'apostate cardinal,' Odet de Châtillon. To remedy in some degree the woes of the kingdom, he would have thrust the Inquisition on France;

but Catholics as well as Protestants were resolutely determined not to submit to it. Its introduction at this time into the Netherlands, by order of Philip II., occasioned the rising *en masse* of the Protestant population, who, following the example of their French co-religionists, desecrated the churches, broke the statues, defaced the pictures of saints, and established their own form of worship in the greater part of the cities. But their triumph was of short duration, and terrible vengeance was soon to follow.

The 'Christian prince and avenger of God,' as Philip dared to call himself, delayed not to despatch the merciless Duke of Alva with a body of troops to 'exterminate' the Flemings and the Dutch. 'The extermination of the people and the laying waste of the country he preferred, he said, to allowing any obstacle to his absolute will henceforth to exist in that rebel State.' His wishes were carried out *con amore* by his able lieutenant and his myrmidons. Horrors unspeakable were perpetrated ; tortures inflicted that make the blood curdle but to think of, and which must surely have been suggested to these monsters in human shape by the satanic influence of the very spirit of evil.

If not exactly through France, yet close as

possible to its frontiers, marched the exterminating hosts of the 'Demon of the South.' The French Protestants were greatly agitated, and their alarm was shared by the Reformers throughout Europe. They no longer doubted that Catherine, conjointly with Philip and the pope, had concocted a similar plan for the extinction of the Huguenots in France. So widespread was this opinion that several of the German princes sent a united embassy to France to entreat the king, in the name of the long-existing friendship between the two countries, to extend tolerance towards his Huguenot subjects, and to enforce the observance of the edict of pacification.

Charles received the German envoys very discourteously. Scarcely restraining his passionate anger, he replied that he was 'fully disposed to respect the ancient friendly feeling between France and Germany, if the princes would not in future intermeddle in his affairs, as he certainly would not in theirs.' Equally harsh in tone, and disrespectful in manner, was his conversation with the admiral, when complaining to him of the ill-treatment and many unprovoked attacks the Protestants were receiving at the hands of some Catholic fanatics, urged on by their priests.

Charles was now seventeen, yet without his

mother's approval he dared not exercise any act of sovereignty. Appeals to him were futile, as he keenly felt—expending his rancour in the irritability of his replies. He yearned for freedom, and seemed to incline towards the counsels of the chancellor; but courage failed him to break the chain with which his hated and hating mother held him in bondage. Her strong will completely dominated his weak one, while his rage was vented in impotent acts of fury. Shortly before the arrival of the German embassy, Catherine, in the king's name, had asked the hand of a daughter of the German Emperor, Maximilian II. She desired his alliance as a counterpoise to the pressure put upon her by Philip II. and Pius V. respecting the Protestants, whom she would have preferred to exterminate after her own more subtle system, and without *autos-da-fé*.

Maximilian II. was a prince of a very tolerant spirit and estimable character. He greatly favoured his Lutheran subjects, and political reasons alone are said to have deterred him from declaring himself of their faith. He declined, however, to entertain the king's proposal, unless restitution was made to the empire of Metz, Toul and Verdun. Catherine had previously—disregarding the disparity of their years—suggested to Elizabeth of England a marriage with Charles, or with his brother, the Duc d'Anjou; for the latter she was exceedingly anxious to secure a throne, with or without a wife to share it, and had promised the fanatical Philip to co-operate zealously with him in 'avenging God,' if he would cede the Duchy of Milan to her second son.

Meanwhile it transpired that Catherine was secretly making great efforts to borrow money and to raise troops. Six thousand Swiss had already entered France, and were advancing by forced marches to the centre of the kingdom—it being given out that these six thousand Swiss were to form a corps of observation on the frontier of Picardy. As these preparations were not directed against Spain, they indicated some sinister intentions on Catherine's part towards the Reformers. Urged by Philip and the pope, she had resolved on aiming a blow at heresy that should strike terror into the hearts of the Huguenots. She was, in fact, about to follow the example of the Duke of Alva, who, in the Netherlands, as his first act of authority, had arrested Count Egmont and Count Horn, and brought them before his 'tribunal of blood.'

The two chiefs of the French Protestant party were secretly informed of this design by De

L'Hôpital, as supposed. Condé was to be condemned to perpetual imprisonment, Coligny to death. Hitherto they had restrained the Huguenots, though with difficulty, from again taking up arms. All France was, indeed, in a state of ferment. Murders and dastardly attacks by night on the Protestants were committed with impunity, while similar offences on their part, whatever the provocation, were punished with cruel rigour.

Now, however, it had become evident that action in self-defence was a necessity. Coligny therefore proposed the bold plan of calling on the Protestants to rise *en masse*; to attack and destroy the Swiss before they could join the royal troops; to arrest the Cardinal de Lorraine; to seize the person of the king, his mother and brothers, and to govern in the name of Charles IX. The Protestant nobility of the northern provinces were to assemble at Rosay, in Brie, and to begin the attack on the 29th of September.

The queen-mother, the king, and the Court were amusing themselves at the queen's Château of Monceaux, while awaiting the news of the surprise and capture of the Protestant prey. But when, instead of that welcome intelligence, Catherine's messengers informed her that large bodies of armed Huguenot cavaliers were arriving in Brie from various parts, she took alarm, and with the king and the Court fled in all haste to Meaux. Thence, courier after courier was despatched requiring the Swiss to hasten on to Meaux. Opinions were divided as to the best course to pursue. Should the queen-mother and the king remain at Meaux and negotiate, or, with their escort—eight or nine hundred unarmed gentlemen—and surrounded by the 6,000 Swiss, endeavour to reach Paris as quickly as possible?

The constable and the chancellor were for remaining; the cardinal and Duc de Nemours for departure. Catherine took the advice of the latter, and the Swiss having arrived late in the evening of the 26th, at four on the following morning the royal party, escort and guards, set out on their journey, Charles—in a very irritable mood at the idea of flying before his subjects—taking command of the Swiss, sword in hand. As the full force of the Huguenots had not yet assembled, Condé and Coligny, at the head of only 500 armed cavaliers, could not hope to break through a body of troops 6,000 strong. Some skirmishing, however, occurred with the royal troops, which induced the constable to recommend a change of route—in case Protestant reinforcements should arrive and endanger the king's safety—leaving the Swiss with him to oppose the pursuit of the Huguenots.

The king and the queen-mother assented. It was nightfall ere they arrived in Paris, Charles as usual in a rage ; his ride of fifteen hours was a longer one than even he cared to take. 'He was exceedingly weary,' we are told, ' also very hungry ' (Pierre de L'Estoile). Catherine had energy enough for anything ; but how the ladies generally, on their mules or in their litters, bore the fatigue and necessarily the attendant terror of flying before an enemy, the chroniclers do not say.

The cardinal was less fortunate than the royal party. He had recommended to them the more dangerous course ; but it was not in his nature to adopt it himself. He quietly trotted off to Rheims, expecting to reach his archbishopric without molestation or adventures. He, however, narrowly escaped falling into the hands of a party of Huguenots on their march to join the prince and the admiral. His Spanish mule bore him swiftly out of danger ; his attendants as swiftly followed, and there was no attempt at pursuit. For he left his baggage behind him, containing a costly service of plate, with which the Huguenots went on their way perfectly satisfied, and probably rejoicing.

Arrived at Rheims, his eminence lost no time in laying a statement of his trials and his losses before the King of Spain. He prayed him to send the Duke of Alva and his troops into France, and craved his powerful protection for himself and the House of Guise. The members of that house he assured him were all devoted to him, and 'when Catherine de' Medici's sickly sons had died off— of which there seemed a not distant prospect— would aid him in setting at naught the Salic law, and, in the name of his wife Elizabeth, claiming the throne of France.'

But the Protestant chiefs, being reinforced, speedily followed the royalists; and, with the intention of blockading Paris, directed their partizans to rendezvous under the walls of the city. Their headquarters were at Saint-Denis—the prince taking the precaution of closing the abbey to prevent its desecration. Several towns were occupied with the view of interrupting the arrival of supplies by the Upper and Lower Seine, the Marne, and the Yonne. Great was the outcry of the Parisians at the prospect of a dearth of provisions, while Catherine, amazed at the energy and audacity of the Protestant chiefs, was induced, at the suggestion of the chancellor, in which the constable concurred, to attempt negotiation.

It was rather a short truce than a peace that Catherine desired, to last until she could obtain the aid she sought from Spain. But the Protestants demanded liberty of worship throughout the kingdom, and, equally with the Catholics, admission to offices in the Government. Catherine refused. A stormy scene appears to have occurred in the Huguenot camp between the constable and his nephew Odet, the 'apostate cardinal,' whom, for the first time, he then saw in cuirasse and helmet, armed *cap-à-pie*.

War being inevitable, the queen-mother urgently demanded of the Duke of Alva, of the pope, of the city of Paris, and of the clergy, aid and support in troops and money. Forced loans were raised, and the Crown diamonds and rubies pledged to Italian bankers for 200,000 gold crowns. The Protestants applied for similar assistance to the Germans. On the 10th of November, the constable, commanding-in-chief, attacked the Huguenot army late in the day. Both sides fought with savage valour. Five times the constable was wounded, when a Scotchman, said to have been Robert Stuart, rode up and shot him in the loins, piercing his cuirasse. He was borne from the field of battle by his sons, who commanded under him.

Fighting was then resumed with greater energy by the Protestants, and intenser fury by the Catholics. Condé's horse being wounded, the prince determined to retreat on Saint-Denis, and darkness coming on put an end to the carnage. The victory was not a decisive one, but both sides claimed it as such. The Huguenots, being reinforced, offered battle to their adversaries on the following day. The Catholic chiefs did not accept the challenge. They were assembled round the deathbed of the constable, who died the next day (12th of November).* His funeral was of royal grandeur, and as a grand spectacle the Parisians flocked to gaze on it. But the constable, harsh in manners, brutal in character, had never, while living, awakened any sympathy in the people, and none regretted him now dead.

Catherine affected to grieve while inwardly rejoicing at the removal out of her path of the last of the 'Triumvirate;' the last of those powerful subjects who had contested her right to the supreme authority she sought to usurp, and had allowed her but a small share of it. Now, she was

---

* Anne de Montmorency was seventy-five years of age. He had been unfortunate as a commander, having lost more battles than he had won. His reputation, both as a statesman and a general, is said to have been greater than his merits.

wholly free—the uncontrolled sovereign of France. Henceforth, she was determined that only men—men chiefly of her own nation—who owed wealth and power to her alone should participate in the government with her.

As her last mark of respect to the constable, Catherine caused his heart to be enclosed in the urn containing that of Henry II. This urn—borne by the Graces, and, as already observed, one of Germain Pilon's finest groups—was originally designed by her to contain her own heart in the vacant place now ceded to that of Anne de Montmorency.

CHAPTER XVI.

Anjou Lieutenant-General.—Siege of Chartres.—Jean Casimer and the German troops.—Catherine's Treachery.—Warned by Tavannes.—Fording the Loire.—Jeanne d'Albret and her Son.—Odet de Châtillon and Elizabeth of England.—De L'Hôpital's Retirement.—Don Carlos and Elizabeth of France.

CATHERINE DE' MEDICI was fond of vaunting the fancied virtues of her second son, Henry, Duc d'Anjou. His youthful courage, martial ardour, great ambition, intense devotion, and remarkable docility of character, were habitually set forth as if to mark the strong contrast between him and the impetuous, irascible Charles and his uncertain moods of temper. Her training and her treatment of her children do indeed give warrant to the generally accredited statement that she had no affection for any of them, except this son; and that, so far as she was capable of any tenderness of feeling, 'she loved him—as the viper loves the most venomous of her brood' (Henri Martin).

Catherine had great hopes of Anjou. In him she looked forward to giving France a true Italian prince—a despotic tyrant—after the model depicted by Machiavelli, as understood by her, and such as the Borgia and Medici families had sometimes inflicted on Italy. The constable's death furnished her with an opportunity she hastened to seize of placing Henry, then sixteen, at the head of the armies of France. The vacant post of constable was not to be filled up. 'It put into the hands of a subject,' as she duly impressed on Charles, 'too large a share of power in the government.' But the Lieutenant-Generalship of the Kingdom—an office that involved the command-in-chief of the armies—was to be revived and conferred on Anjou.

The young king was disposed to head his army himself. But his mother and the Italians she was continually introducing to prominent posts in the government, urged on him that it was inconsistent with his dignity as sovereign to conduct in person an army to chastise rebels. Charles abhorred his brother, and this feeling Henry fully reciprocated. But he yielded to the advice, or rather the commands of the queen-mother, though not with a very good grace. Instantly he set off for Chambord to expend his rage in hunting—pursuing the wild boar with a sort of mad energy almost realizing the fury of the wild huntsman, who, according to the legend, hunted nightly in those forests, with 'a pack of demon hounds in full cry.' Charles would blow his hunting-horn with such force that his eyes would seem ready to start from their sockets, and would slay whatever animals he came across with a ferocious eagerness and savage joy.

To Chambord Catherine pursued this wayward, excitable son, who occasioned her so much disquietude, and inspired her with so much antipathy. She was always in dread of his eluding her grasp and acting in direct opposition to her. But her clutch on him was so firm that, however he may have desired to shake himself free, he was incapable of sustained effort long enough to accomplish it.

The Huguenot army was not sufficiently strong to subdue Paris by famine; it therefore decamped, hoping to join a detachment of 11,000 cavalry and infantry sent by the Calvinist Elector Palatine, under the command of his son, Jean Casimer. The weather was terrible in its severity, and the march of the Huguenots through Champagne was no less dangerous than laborious. They were without resources, without stores, or strongholds, and were compelled to levy contributions on the villages and small towns they passed through. An army double their number, well provided and equipped, was following them but at a few leagues' distance; an army, reinforced by Philip, the pope, and the Swiss, which might well have overwhelmed them and accomplished its mission of extermination. Its commander-in-chief was the Duc d'Anjou, with the able and experienced general, Marshal Tavannes, as his guide and counsellor. Notwithstanding, a want of discipline prevailed in the ranks of this motley assemblage of nations.

Marshal Tavannes could not certainly be accused of such weakness as a leaning towards mercy's side, or too large a share of humane feeling be imputed to Marshal de Cossé-Gonnor, who commanded the French division. Yet it appears that the latter, joined by other French officers, expressed some repugnance to slaughtering his countrymen—'in arms only for the defence of liberty and life.' As the French troops and their officers were alike generally influenced throughout this struggle by fanatic zeal rather than by humanity and a spirit of tolerance, it may be that the slaughter of their countrymen was objected to on this occasion because not wholly confided to them.

The presence of Spanish troops in France was an abomination to the French, and the interference of the pope and his Italian troop was no less so, however Catherine and her Court might have sought or desired their aid. But whatever the cause, dissension reigned in the royal camp, and the authority of the young lieutenant-general was too little respected to restore discipline. The Huguenots, meanwhile, were plodding on their weary way—effecting their junction with Jean Casimer in Lorraine before the royalist armies could overtake them. While besieging Chartres, they received the gratifying intelligence that the important maritime city of La Rochelle had declared for the cause of Reform—thus assuring them, in the west, a stronghold of the first order.

Catherine now divided her time, to the admiration of the Venetian ambassadors, between the Court and the camp. She had her scouts abroad, who diligently kept her informed of the proceedings of both armies.* As soon as she heard that harmony did not prevail in the councils of the lieutenant-general, and that Fortune was favouring the Huguenots, she set out immediately for the

* Gironamo Lippomano, 'Reports of Venetian Ambassadors.'

royalist headquarters. A suspension of arms was agreed on, while an envoy with proposals of peace was despatched to the Protestant camp. This was her usual proceeding when any success attended the Protestant arms. She now offered to abolish all restrictions on their freedom of worship enacted since the Treaty of Amboise, and to advance the sum due to their German auxiliaries.

After some hesitation—knowing how worthless were these treaties of peace—the Huguenots authorized Odet de Châtillon, the diplomatist of their party, to accept her proposals. They wanted to re-organize their army, to give it some needed rest; and they wanted money also. Silver shrines and silver statues, as well as the gold plate and other treasures of the despoiled churches, had been melted down and converted into coin. But the needs of the army, and the stern demands of their mercenary allies for prompt payment of their claims, soon emptied the military coffers. An edict of peace was therefore published on the 23rd of March, at Longjumeau. It was a temporary relief to the much-harassed army, but was regarded with fear and distrust by the Huguenot people.

This peace, however, excited the highest indignation of the Catholic king and the pope. The latter had sent a corps of Italians, equipped and paid by himself, and, further, on the strength of Catherine's promises to outvie in zeal even the Spanish king, had contributed 10,000 ounces of gold towards an exterminating war against the heretics of France. To Philip a peace apparently so advantageous to the Huguenots was exceedingly inopportune. It seemed as though Catherine had really designed by it to join with other nations in holding up both king and pope to universal execration.

The infamous Inquisition had just declared the whole population—'peoples, orders, and estates'—of the Netherlands guilty of heresy, apostasy, and *lèse-majesté*, and condemned them to death—the one part for having 'openly rebelled against God and the king;' the other, 'for not having repressed the rebellion.' This murder on a grand scale was then being carried out by the sanguinary Duke of Alva. All who could make their escape fled from the blood-stained territory of the 'Demon of the South.' Some to Germany to prepare for vengeance; others—chiefly merchants and manufacturers—to England.

Catherine had some difficulty in appeasing her allies. Her confidential agents were despatched with assurances that her plans were unchanged, but had been unexpectedly deferred by some necessary changes in the command of the army. That she was anxious to follow the counsels and example of Alva was soon made evident. The forced peace of Longjumeau was really nothing more than the cessation of open war for a secret one of murder, robbery, and assassination. France was in a more disastrous condition than ever. The kingdom was ravaged from one end to the other, and neither Catholic nor Protestant, priest nor merchant, artisan nor peasant, could rest in safety beneath his own roof. The land was left untilled, or where any attempt was made at cultivation, it was done with arms ready to hand.

'When the vintage is finished,' said the peasantry of the wine-growing districts, 'we will fall on these heretics in such force, that in a short time there will be an end of them.' 'But if the king should interfere to prevent it, what then?' 'He shall go into a convent,' was the reply, 'and another be put in his place.' This other was Anjou, who had gained amongst the populace a high reputation for sanctity. He was to be seen walking barefoot in all the religious processions, mumbling prayers and counting his beads, while privately, though so young, his life was of exceeding depravity.

In the midst of all the strife and turmoil of civil war, and the desperate condition of the finances, Catherine yet found both time and—thanks to the pope's gold ounces—means to devote to the building of a new palace. The Tuileries, for some unexplained reason—though a handsome structure and nearly completed—did not find favour in her eyes as a residence. The new palace, of which the façade was designed by herself, was somewhat smaller than the Tuileries. It was constructed by Jean Bullant, and had an elegant chapel attached to it; also a stone column of the Doric Order, eighty-five feet in height, designed and erected by Bullant in 1571.*

There Catherine with her mathematicians and astrologers nightly studied the course of the stars—her appeals to the heavenly bodies at that stormy sanguinary period being even more frequent than usual. For she sought to learn from their movements the most favourable moment for the accomplishment of that stupendous crime on which

---

* Catherine's magnificent hôtel—whose site was that of the present Halle au Blé and the surrounding streets which branch from it—was taken down in 1749. The stone column alone was left standing. The palace was then called the Hôtel de Soissons, from having belonged to Charles de Bourbon, Vicomte de Soissons, the romantic lover of Catherine de Bourbon, sister of Henry of Navarre.

she had long pondered, and which was probably first suggested by Philip's deeds of blood in the Netherlands and the satanic counsels of Pius V. Sometimes she wavered; not from repugnance to the deed, but from dread of failure, should the stars not be propitious. Then she made treaties and truces to gain time, to allay any suspicions, and to invite the confidence of her intended victims.

The two inhuman monsters of Spain and Rome could not understand her hesitation, and never wholly trusted her, notwithstanding her asseverations that she would prove herself their worthy colleague. Yet they urged her on—so piously anxious were they to free France from heresy—and incited her to keep in the strait path of Christian duty, and kill and slay for the honour of God and the holy Catholic Church.

In spite, however, of the efforts of the Chancellor de L'Hôpital, who addressed a memorial to the king—explaining in eloquent and forcible terms the necessity of maintaining peace for the welfare of his people and for securing returning prosperity to France—the third religious war was resolved on, and at the instigation of Pius V. He had consented to an application of the Court for permission to alienate certain Church property to the extent of 50,000 gold crowns of revenue, 'on condition that the amount raised should be expended on the extermination of heretics.' The chancellor energetically opposed the publication of an Act couched in such terms, and several members of the council joining him, the holy Father was requested to modify the wording of his Bull. To this Catherine also consented, while freely availing herself of the permission to raise the money and of employing it, or such small portion as she thought fit to spare, in the manner indicated. She merely desired to allay any fears the terms of the Bull might excite in the Huguenots; lest their alarm might prevent her from renewing the attempt she had concerted with her favourite Italian, Birago, and the Cardinal de Lorraine, of surprising and arresting the prince and the admiral at the château of the former at Noyers.

Marshal Tavannes, who had formerly been one of Catherine's admirers, and on whom she thoroughly relied, was commissioned to do the deed. From no friendly feeling to the Huguenot chiefs, he, however, contrived that letters should fall into their hands giving them timely notice of their danger. He thought there was a chance of failure, and that he might become the victim of the plot, and did not choose to incur the risk, even for Catherine, of being made responsible for violating the peace supposed to be still unbroken.

As soon as the news reached the château that troops were on their way to Noyers to arrest them, Condé, with his wife and children,* the admiral (then a widower) and his sons, with other Protestant chiefs and ministers, and a large party of their followers, immediately left Noyers. They were hotly pursued by the royalists, but reached the banks of the Loire before them. The river from recent heavy rains was already much swollen. But a friend from the adjacent Protestant town of Sancerre pointed out a spot where it was still easily fordable. Condé led the way, carrying his youngest son before him, and singing the 114th Psalm, 'When Israel came out of Egypt,' in which all joined as they waded across, and before nightfall safely reached the opposite bank. The whole party then knelt down and solemnly thanked God for their rescue.

A miracle similar to that of which they sang seemed to them to have been wrought in their favour. For at daylight on the following morning, when the royalist troops reached the Loire,

* He had married recently his second wife, a daughter of the House of Orléans Longueville.

the banks of the river were flooded, and the swollen stream was rushing impetuously onward in a foaming torrent. To ford it was impossible. Tavannes' mission was therefore brought to an end. He and his troops had but to retrace their steps, while the Huguenots, uninterrupted, moved onward to La Rochelle, the general rendezvous.

Not expecting the sudden attack devised by Catherine and her counsellors, the chiefs of the Protestant party were then rather widely dispersed. D'Andelot was in Brittany, but soon after appeared at La Rochelle with a corps of 4,000 men; his wife remaining at Noyers. Mdme. d'Andelot was a *grande dame* of Lorraine, who had fallen in love with her husband for his heroism; and, proud to share with him the dangers and hardships of civil war, had married him in defiance of all the attempts of her family to prevent her. The 'apostate cardinal,' who had also married a wife, was looking after the vintage on his estate at Beauvoisis. Not being able to reach La Rochelle, he contrived to pass over to England. As diplomacy was more his forte than fighting, he is said to have done his party far greater service in his interviews with Queen Elizabeth than he would have done in the camp.

She showed him much more consideration than

she was accustomed generally to do towards the foreign Protestants who sought refuge in England. She had frequent and long conversations with him, and although she rather preferred to discourse on *belles lettres* than on public affairs, yet she often yielded to his arguments and adopted his opinions.

When war was resumed she sent money, cannon, and ammunition to the French Protestants, and supported them much more effectually while he remained with her as their envoy than she had done before, or did afterwards. She liked to read his despatches, and greatly admired the clearness, the elegance, the smoothness and fluency of his style.*

The intrepid Jeanne of Navarre, who, with her son, was also to have been entrapped, left Nérac with a corps of four or five thousand Gascons and Béarnais, and succeeded in evading the pitiless Blaise de Montluc and his murderous band, who had orders to waylay the queen, and send her and the young Prince of Béarn to the Court; but Jeanne, with the prince and her troops, reached La Rochelle in safety. Having made up her mind to be saved or to perish with the 'cause of Reform,' she, on arrival, presented young Henry to the Rochellois, and having armed him herself

* Varillas, 'Vie de Charles IX.'

(he was then but fifteen), gave him to his uncle, the Prince de Condé, as his companion-in-arms.

Catherine de' Medici and her counsellors were disappointed and enraged beyond measure at the failure of their deep-laid scheme. The desired prey had not been entrapped, or person of any importance seized. 'There had been treachery somewhere.' To which remark the Cardinal de Lorraine suggestively murmured 'The chancellor.' He also called the queen-mother's attention to the king's growing regard for De L'Hôpital; the deference he had observed him lately evince in the council to any advice or opinions that came from him, and his apparent regret that they were not adopted. His eminence ventured to recommend precaution.

But Catherine had already determined on the chancellor's dismissal. She had used his integrity and uprightness of character to veil her own deceitful and tortuous policy. She now needed him no longer, for she had adopted the sanguinary counsels of Philip and the pope, and was resolved to follow Alva in his blood-stained path. The chancellor, with his unceasing arguments for mercy, tolerance, and peace, did but importune her. But they might yet have their effect on Charles, in whom there still lingered some traces of a natural feeling towards a less evil course than that in which she had assiduously striven to train him. She dreaded, therefore, that in one of those sudden impulses to which he was prone, the young king, influenced by the chancellor's precepts, might openly resist her and effectually free himself from her oppressive domination.

She resolved to ward off this threatened blow; first coming to an open rupture with the chancellor. The first effect of this step on the king was angry surprise. But Catherine insinuated that she had discovered him to be a Huguenot in disguise; a friend and abettor of rebels, whom he had warned to escape, and thus saved for a time from their well-merited doom. Catherine appears never to have suspected treachery in her former lover Tavannes. It is his son who tells the story, as editor of his father's memoirs.

On this occasion Charles certainly displayed less of the great intelligence many writers have credited him with than excessive weakness. He is said to have received the chancellor at his next interview with haughty coldness, and to have listened to the counsels he gave him on the then lamentable state of affairs, not as hitherto, with a willing ear, but in a resentful, disdainful manner, that seemed to bid him trouble him no further. Perceiving that

LE CHANCELIER DE L'HOPITAL.

Paris Richard Bentley and Son 1887

his efforts to serve unhappy France and her king must henceforth be unavailing, De L'Hôpital, without waiting for a formal dismissal, voluntarily retired to his modest home near Epernay, with his wife and family.* He had not enriched himself, as was the custom of the time, by inroads on the public purse, but was in such straitened circumstances that, when on his deathbed, Charles sent him word that he would provide for his family. 'Honour, patriotism and humanity,' writes the French historian, H. Martin, 'may be said to have been driven from the Court with him.'

Whilst Catherine was preparing to reveal herself in all the hideousness of her true character, and striving to convince both Pius and Philip that she was ready to dye her hands in heretic blood as deeply as their own had been, the death of her eldest daughter, the Queen of Spain, was announced. The young queen had just attained her twenty-third year, and was said to have died in childbirth on the 3rd of October—probably by foul means. For a terrible tragedy had doubtless taken place

---

* In the memorial written by De L'Hôpital shortly before his death (March 15, 1573), he says of the young king, 'He had no power whatever, and dared not speak his mind, or give utterance to his real thoughts.'

in Spain in the course of that year ; Don Carlos, Philip's son, having also died, according to the date given, towards the end of July, very mysteriously, in prison.

Philip was believed to have put both the queen and his son to death from jealousy. A very sad but romantic story was founded on that event ; and more reasons still exist for accepting it as true than for its rejection. That the ordinary feelings of humanity had ever stood between Philip II. and the perpetration of any crime, however terrible its nature, it would be difficult to credit. Don Carlos is represented, with evident exaggeration, to have been passionate, impetuous, unruly, and as he grew up, scarcely caring to conceal his contempt for the monkish rule that prevailed in Spain—declaring that, when he came to the throne, he would speedily change that—or to disguise his aversion to his fanatical bloodthirsty father. The cruelties inflicted on the Netherlanders he stigmatized as revolting, and strove to communicate with the envoys with a view of escaping to Flanders.

He is said to have been violent in temper even to ferocity ; but he may well have been maddened to fury, if detained against his will amidst such scenes as those with which Philip and the satanical tribunal of the Inquisition delighted to 'honour

God.' The suspected heretical views of the Spanish prince having developed into certainty as he attained manhood, Philip hesitated no longer. After conferring with the Supreme Tribunal of the Inquisition, he, one evening in January, accompanied by two or three of the Inquisitor's myrmidons, entered the prince's apartment, and with his own hand arrested him. Carlos was transferred to a prison, and Philip officially announced his son's arrest to the papal nuncio. He further stated that 'he had preferred the honour of God and the preservation of the Catholic religion to his own flesh and blood, and that, in order to obey God, he had sacrificed his only son.'

Nothing further is positively known concerning his fate—whether he was at once put to death in pursuance of a sentence of the Inquisition, or was allowed to linger on until the end of July, when it was announced that he had died of a malignant fever, the result of the excesses of a dissolute life. On the faith of some inexplicit and doubtful documents, it has been attempted to show that nature prevailed even in the breast of so unnatural a monster as Philip II. of Spain—that he did not actually with his own hand slay his son; but so far relented as to allow him to drag out a few months of grief and despair in a horrible dungeon..

The more generally accredited story is the more probable one—that he had formed an unfortunate attachment for the *fiancée* of his boyhood, whom political arrangements afterwards gave him for a step-mother. The attachment, unhappily, became mutual. That there was an eager desire on the part of this boy and girl of fifteen and fourteen to see each other on the arrival of the latter in Spain is evident from the letter of the Bishop of Limoges to Catherine de' Medici, giving the particulars of the young queen's first reception and her meeting with Don Carlos.* It was certainly ominous of what afterwards occurred, and seems at the time to have been so regarded. He appears then to have been gentle in manners, and rather delicate in health. That he should, as he advanced towards manhood, have become 'passionate, impetuous, unruly, subject to fits of anger, and have conceived an aversion for his father,' is thus easily explained.

But objection has been taken to there having been any reciprocity of affection on the part of the young queen, because of the energy with which, on her visit to Bayonne, she supported the views of Philip, as explained by the Duke of Alva

* See letter of Bishop of Limoges, pp. 42 and 43 of this volume.

to Catherine. Her 'energy' was described as 'feverish anxiety lest she should fail to play the part assigned her to the satisfaction of the duke, who watched her every word and action.' It was evident that this girl of eighteen had not become a fanatic, but that she was under the influence of fear. Philip himself, when writing to Granvelle concerning the Bayonne conference, says that 'Catherine proposed a marriage, but that the Queen of Spain replied evasively as he had commanded her.'

But whether she was poisoned, as at the time supposed, or died a natural death—death, doubtless, was welcomed, both by the unhappy young queen and the unfortunate Don Carlos, as a desirable release from the power of a despotic and unsympathizing tyrant.

CHAPTER XVII.

Battle of Jarnac.—Death of Condé.—Anjou's Delight; the Te Deum.—Henry of Navarre; the Oath and the Medal.—Death of D'Andelot; Poison suspected.—Fifty Thousand Crowns for Coligny, Dead or Alive.—Victory or Death; Money or Battle.—Battle of Moncontour.—Coligny wounded.—Peace of Saint-Germain, 8th of August, 1570.

CATHERINE DE' MEDICI never permitted useless grief to interfere with the pursuit of her projects. As on the death of her husband, and again when her eldest son died, so now, she indulged in no vain regrets on the death of her daughter—suddenly cut off in the bloom of youth, and under circumstances which she well knew to be more than suspicious. She was far more intent on fulfilling the promise she had given to Philip and the pope of exterminating a large part of her son's subjects. 'All edicts of tolerance,' she assured the Spanish tyrant, 'were to be immediately revoked. All ministers of the religion called Reformed were to quit the kingdom within fifteen days; also, within the same period, all persons holding any office in the Government who professed the same heretical opinions—the exercise of any religion but that of the Roman Catholic being henceforth punishable with death. An oath of fidelity to Catholicism was henceforth to be also required of all the members of the various Parliaments, the universities, and other public establishments in France.'

Philip and the saintly Pius were at last persuaded that they might now place some trust in the promises of this hitherto double-dealing intrigante. 'For nothing remained,' she told them, 'but to combine the military operations in France and the Netherlands.'

The edicts were duly published at the end of September, and in reply to them the Huguenots rose *en masse*. One long cry of fury and despair echoed through the land. The chiefs of the party were unable to restrain the rage of the soldiers. Onward they rushed in ever-increasing numbers and like a devouring torrent, ravaging and destroying all that lay in their way ; from province to province, from the Rhone to the Charente. For though the edicts were published, the Catholic army was not ready to march and enforce them. The Huguenots, who were always expecting to be attacked, may be said to have constantly lived with their arms ready to hand. They therefore were speedily prepared, and, for the three weeks during which they were unopposed, conquered all before them.

Unhappily, they committed terrible excesses—pillaging and devastating the churches; freely selling Church property, without asking leave of the pope, of course, in revenge for the pontiff's permission to Charles IX. to alienate Church revenues to raise funds for exterminating the Huguenots. But worse far than that, many lives were sacrificed to the blind fury of revenge. Certainly the Huguenots were sometimes the aggressors; but so persistently were they persecuted, that although it may be matter for regret, yet it can scarcely cause surprise that they did not always abstain from rendering evil for evil. Perhaps throughout the whole of the civil war, neither Catholic nor Protestant in his most maddening thirst for vengeance committed atrocities at all approaching in horror the deeds of the Duc de Montpensier and his brutal band. Inspired by the example of their savage leader, they seemed to glory in their career of blood and crime.*

* The Huguenots on their march towards Saumur took the Château de Champigny, the splendid residence of the Duc de

The two armies, however, met almost face to face on the 16th of November in the neighbourhood of Poitiers, but without coming to an engagement. The Catholic army was commanded by the able but brutal Marshal Tavannes, but nominally by the Duc d'Anjou; for whom Catherine was desirous of building up a great military reputation at the expense of the generals who were supposed to command under him. The winter of 1568 and 1569 was one of extremest severity; so much so, that the two armies were so thoroughly benumbed and unnerved by the intensity of the frost, that courage failed them to begin the attack. The hoar-frost (*verglas*) is said to have had so severe an effect on the soldiers' arms and legs, that they snapped and broke when a skirmish was attempted. Consequently, the generals on both sides determined to put their troops into winter quarters.

The interval was employed by the Huguenots in endeavouring to obtain additional resources for carrying on the ensuing campaign. Queen Elizabeth, at the solicitation of her 'good sister,' the

---

Montpensier. The duke was absent, but his confessor, a Cordelier monk, who shared in the infamous deeds of his penitent, was seized and hanged (Brantôme).

Queen of Navarre, sent 100,000 gold angelots,* and some ammunition. Jeanne herself authorized the sale of Church lands in those towns of her domains where the Huguenots were established. The privateers of La Rochelle, who pillaged all vessels of Roman Catholic nations, faithfully contributed the tithe of their booty—amounting to a large sum—in aid of the Protestant cause, while Protestant Germany promised to send a considerable force to its assistance.

Want of discipline in the Huguenot nobility appears to have greatly embarrassed the leader of the Protestant forces. He was therefore compelled, on the resumption of hostilities in the spring, to accept battle at a great disadvantage in the vicinity of Jarnac. On the morning of the 13th of March, as Condé was hastening to the admiral's assistance—though wounded in the arm on the previous evening—he was kicked on the leg by the Duc de Longueville's horse, and with such violence that it was broken. Rejecting all advice and persuasion to allow his troop to remove him to his tent, he exclaimed: 'Nobles of France! The long-desired moment has arrived.

---

* An ancient English gold coin of the value of about five shillings.

Remember in what a condition Louis de Bourbon enters the combat for Christ and his country!'*

He then charged the Catholics with so much impetuosity, that at first he overthrew all before him. But he was speedily surrounded by a mass of gendarmerie and thrown from his horse, which, wounded and dying, fell partly upon him. More than two-thirds of the small troop accompanying Condé were killed in the attempt to defend their prince; the rest, for the most part, were wounded or taken prisoners. Being released from the pressure of his horse, Condé, who was unable to rise, delivered his gauntlet to a gentleman of the royalist army. Scarcely, however, had he done so than the captain of Anjou's Swiss guards, recognising the prince, rushed up behind him, and committed the dastardly deed of shooting him in the back of his head. His death was instantaneous.

The Duc d'Anjou, it is asserted, suggested this act to several of his favourites in the camp, desiring them to be diligent in seeking the opportunity and availing themselves of it. It fell to the lot of the Swiss, Montesquiou, to gratify the great general's wish.† Anjou was returning from the

* The device on his standard was 'Doux le péril pour Christ et le pays.' † Brantôme.

performance of his morning devotions, and receiving the sacrament, before looking on the battle well out of harm's way, when the pious youth had the satisfaction of seeing the dead body of his heroic relative stretched on the ground before him, and of 'knowing from that event that God had favoured his arms.'

An ass was brought by his direction, and the body thrown across it, to be thus ignominiously carried into Jarnac for the amusement of the duke and his favourites, and for the derision of all good Catholics. The prince's brother-in-law, the Duc de Longueville, however, protested against this indignity, and, after some hesitation, Condé's remains were delivered to him to be sent to Vendôme for burial.

To celebrate this 'manifest interposition of heaven' on behalf of her gallant son, Catherine de' Medici, despite the king's anger at Anjou being thus honoured, ordered a Te Deum to be sung in every church in the kingdom. Madrid, Rome, and Brussels followed her example; and, as a further act of thanksgiving, the queen-mother gave one of her sumptuous *festins* at the Louvre, in the Hall of the Caryatides—then Salle des Gardes, or des cent Suisses—with scenic representations, in which the band of dissolute women, always in close attendance upon her, appeared in full force. So great was Anjou's joy at Condé's death that he was about to order the building of a chapel on the spot where the Swiss assassinated him; but an officer of his troop, Carnavalet, his former governor, dissuaded him from thus openly avowing himself the instigator of the deed.

The death of their leader naturally occasioned some confusion, as well as deep regret, in the ranks of the Protestant army. But the cavalry only had taken part in the combat of Jarnac, and were quickly rallied by D'Andelot and Coligny, who, two days after, effectually repulsed the attack of the royalists on Cognac. Jeanne d'Albret, who was at Saintes with her son and her nephew, hastened to Tonnay-Charente, where, after an affecting address to the troops—her own emotion causing a deep impression—she presented to them the two youths of sixteen and seventeen (Henry of Navarre and Henry of Condé) as the heirs and avengers of the assassinated prince. Before this army they took the solemn oath never to abandon the Huguenot cause. The men repeated it after them, and proclaimed with enthusiasm Henry of Navarre their chief; the effective command of the army devolving of course on Coligny.

To commemorate this event a gold medal was

struck by Jeanne's command. It bore her own effigy and her son's, with the noble motto, '*Pax certa, victoria integra, mors honesta.*' Her devotion to 'the cause' was testified by raising a loan for its service on the security of her jewels, and the alienation of a portion of her estates for the same object, 'preferring' (writes D'Aubigné) 'liberty of conscience to wealth, grandeur, or even life itself.'

Notwithstanding Tavannes' energy and military skill, and the reinforcements daily expected from the pope and the Duke of Alva, the royalist army —often repulsed with great vigour by the Protestants—achieved but very partial success.

They were unable to take any of the heretic towns on the Charente. But this appears to have been chiefly due to Court intrigues. Charles IX. was outrageously jealous of his brother. He exhibited also intense resentment towards the queen-mother, who was using every means to secure popularity for her favourite son amongst the more influential of the chiefs of the Catholic party. The king, in fact, refused to send the heavy cannon required for siege operations, thus preventing the royalist army from profiting by any advantages it had gained. Discord, as usual, reigned in the camp, and both officers and men were enraged at having to beat a retreat to avoid being enclosed between Coligny's army and the German troops marching to join him.

The king was secretly encouraged in his opposition to the queen-mother and Anjou by the intriguing Cardinal de Lorraine. The cardinal, while plotting with Catherine to carry out the views of Spain and Rome against heresy, was actuated by a feeling of jealousy similar to the king's towards Anjou, on account of the young Duc de Guise, whom the cardinal desired should take the late duke's place as the head of the Catholic party, but who, as he considered, did not hold a sufficiently prominent command in the army.

The saddening intelligence of the death of the valorous D'Andelot, at Saintes on the 27th of May, threw a heavy gloom over Coligny and his army. After the admiral, D'Andelot was the most eminent man of the Protestant party. He was much beloved by his troops, and was in every sense a great loss, both to them and the cause of Reform. Another misfortune befell them in the death of the commander of the German cavalry, the Duc de Deuxponts, on the 14th of June, the day following his junction with the Protestant army. Both these deaths were attributed to poison. But D'Andelot had been out of health for some time; while the sufferings and privations undergone by both generals during the extraordinary severity of the preceding winter, together with the fatigue of long marches harassed by their enemies, and the general anxiety occasioned by this prolonged civil war, have been thought reasons sufficient to account for their death without the aid of poison.

Yet Catherine had become very anxious to secure the chiefs of the party, whether by poison, pistol, sword, or imprisonment. A cowardly attempt to poison Coligny, by seducing one of his attendants to administer some potent potion to him, was discovered shortly after, and the miscreant hanged. On the 12th of September, on raising the siege of Poitiers, Coligny learned that a decree of the Parliament of Paris condemned him as 'chief of the rebellion against the king and State,' to be hanged on the Place de Grève, and his body afterwards exposed on a gibbet at Montfaucon. Against his brothers, their families, and the valiant Count Montgomery, and others, a similar decree was issued. The sentences were executed in effigy, and, at the king's or queen-mother's request, a reward of 50,000 gold crowns was offered for Coligny, dead or alive.

During the short period of repose that Coligny felt compelled to grant his weary troops, a reinforcement from the pope and the Duke of Florence of another 6,000 Italians **joined** the royalist army. Their commander, the Count **de** Santa Fiore, was especially charged by his holiness to 'kill on the spot every heretic who fell into his or his soldiers' hands; to give no quarter; to let not one escape.' Though barbarous enough, **it** appears that the **count** did not carry out the monstrous **orders he had** received, so literally as would have found favour with the holy pontiff; for he is said to have spared more than one of **the** Protestant leaders, and amongst **them the great** Huguenot captain, La **Noue.***

* At the same time Pius **wrote to the queen**-mother to stimulate her zeal in the **murderous work he had so** much at heart:

'In **no manner, and under** no pretence, must the enemies of God be **spared.** No considerations of human respect, either for persons or things, should lead you to entertain the thought of sparing the enemies **of God,** who have never spared **either** God or you. It is only by the utter extermination of these heretics that the king will be able to **restore the ancient** religion to that noble nation' **(France).** 'We **are informed that** some persons are striving **to get a certain number of** prisoners pardoned. But you must use every effort to prevent that, and to make sure that those flagitious scoundrels **are** given up to receive the punishment so justly their due.'

To the inhuman Duke of Alva—who, in 1568, beheaded

This reinforcement, together with 3,000 or 4,000 troops of various nations, sent by the Duke of Alva, enabled the royalists at once to take the field. The chief command was now divided between Marshals Tavannes and Biron, who, with 25,000 fresh troops, pitched their tents within a league of the Huguenots. Coligny, with a force but of 18,000 men, ill provided, worn and weary, would have willingly avoided the battle until joined by an expected corps of German cavalry, which the Prince of Orange had gone in disguise to conduct to him. But the impatience of the Huguenot nobility, weary of so much suffering and fatigue, would not allow him. 'Victory or death!' they exclaimed; while the mercenary German troops, dissatisfied that their arrears of pay were not yet forthcoming, replied with no less energy, 'Money or battle!'

The two young princes were also eager for the combat. But Coligny impressed on these youths that they were reserved for the support of 'the

---

Counts Egmont and Horn with twenty others of the chief nobility of Flanders, and condemned hundreds daily, at his 'tribunal of blood,' to tortures and deaths the most horrible he could devise—the saintly pope wrote (accompanying his letter with the present of a helmet and sword, blessed by himself): 'Continue, dear son, to pile up those praiseworthy deeds as steps which will conduct you to life eternal.'

cause' in the future ; then giving them an escort of 4,000 cavalry, he sent them to Parthenay, whence, from some hilly ground, they could see the battle. From the impetuosity of one part of his troops, and the indiscipline and mutinous disposition of the rest, Coligny was prevented from choosing the most advantageous spot for receiving the enemy's attack. After a long cannonade the battle began at three in the afternoon of the 3rd of October in the plain of Assay, near Moncontour. Desperate valour was displayed on both sides.

But when the Comte de Nassau repulsed the cavalry charge of the young Duc de Guise and dispersed his troops, Henry of Navarre, who from the heights of Parthenay perceived this, was with difficulty restrained from rushing down with his 4,000 cavalry, and attacking the *corps de bataille.* 'Ah!' he exclaimed, 'then we lose the battle, as we give the enemy time to reconnoitre and receive succour.' It appears he was right, and that the royalist army would have been beaten if the prince's corps had at that moment charged the enemy. Great expectations were founded on this circumstance of his military capacity (J. Servan, ' Guerres des Français ').

Coligny was aimed at and wounded in the cheek

by the Rhingrave in command of a corps of German Catholic cavalry. Coligny replied with more effect, for the Rhingrave was killed on the spot. But he was near being killed by the Rhingrave's troops, who were surrounding him, when Wolfrad de Mansfeld rode up and released him from his perilous position. Mansfeld was then attacked himself, and in the skirmish that followed the Margrave of Baden, commander of the royalist Germans, was killed. Coligny was conveyed to his tent for the dressing of his wound. The issue of the battle was, as he had foreseen, a defeat for the Huguenots. According to D'Aubigné, they lost near 15,000 men at the battle of Moncontour, the royalist army only 500. The disproportion is so great that there would seem to be some error in the statement. Coligny's whole army is said to have amounted but to about 18,000 men, of whom 4,000 were detached as an escort for the young princes.

This small detachment of cavalry excepted, the Huguenot army must have been annihilated. The queen-mother and the Court certainly believed the Protestant cause ruined, and again Te Deums, and pæans in honour of the young victor, resounded through the land. The blessing of Pius V., with the addition of a consecrated helmet and sword, was also conveyed to him, and he was admonished 'not to grow faint or weary in well-doing.' Charles could bear this triumph of his hated brother no longer. Secretly encouraged by the cardinal, he resolved to repair to the camp. Neither persuasion nor remonstrance availed to detain him. Thither he was speedily followed by Catherine, accompanied by the cardinal, who was playing a double part, caring neither for Catherine nor Charles, but anxious only that the prestige so lately attaching to the House of Guise should, with all its pretensions to military rule and its eye on the throne, revive in his nephew. The youthful valour of this brilliant young duke—then in his nineteenth year—he feared to see obscured by the false *éclat* bestowed on a worthless scion of the degenerate House of Valois.

Notwithstanding the defeat of Moncontour and the magnitude of the Huguenot losses, Coligny without delay assembled the wreck of his army, and revived the failing courage of his men by his firmness, hopefulness, and energy. On the morrow of the battle letters were already written, and trusted envoys despatched to their Protestant confederates of England, Scotland, Denmark, Germany, and Switzerland, to inform them that ' hope survived defeat,' and requesting aid as soon as possible. Garrisons were placed in the towns on the Charente, and Coligny and the young princes, leaving Jeanne d'Albret at Rochelle, took the route of Quercy to join Montgomery, who had beaten the Catholics of Gascony.

Neither these measures nor the diligence with which they were accomplished would, it appears, have saved the Huguenots, but for the dissension in the enemy's camp. 'Tavannes and his most experienced captains suggested that Coligny and the princes should immediately be pursued, even into Gascony, where, reduced to seek refuge in some fortress, they might be besieged, and the war terminated at one blow.' But the king had written to Anjou that nothing was to be attempted until he arrived. In the contemplated final dispersion of the Protestant army, Charles was resolved that his brother should not defraud him of a share of the laurels of victory, stained though they might be with the blood of his subjects.

Charles quickly made his appearance in the camp, and the council of war assembled. Tavannes' proposals were at once rejected. The marshal was known to have long been one of Catherine's devotees, and though his advice in a military sense might be good, yet if followed, the credit of it would redound on her favourite son;

so Charles immediately vetoed it. The Montmorencys had opposed Tavannes, which seemed to give sanction to the young king's act. Their motive, however, was sympathy with 'the cause,' as moderate Catholics, and a desire that the admiral, their near relative, should not be too hardly pressed. Tavannes, greatly offended, required to be relieved of his command, and returned to his estates in Burgundy.

The military council then decided that before pursuing Coligny and the princes, the fortresses on the Charente occupied by the Huguenots should be recovered, and their garrisons, of course, massacred. This, it was supposed, would be easily and speedily accomplished. The siege of Saint-Jean-d'Angely was the first attempted; but the small garrison, instead of surrendering at discretion, made so vigorous and determined a resistance that the royalist army was detained for upwards of six weeks under the walls of the town, and had lost between five and six thousand men before the garrison, exhausted by fatigue and suffering, and wanting ammunition, would listen to any terms of capitulation.

Winter had then set in with some rigour; an epidemic prevailed amongst the troops; many of the Germans deserted, and as no more laurels were likely to be gathered by seeking further conquests that year, the army separated, and the king, with the queen-mother and the Duc d'Anjou, returned to Blois. Attempts at negotiation were made in the month of January. But the king would not grant the demands of the Protestants, and the concessions he offered were rejected by Coligny and the Queen of Navarre, to whom Catherine sent an envoy.

Marshal Biron was also despatched in the spring by Charles IX. to Languedoc, where the admiral had arrived with the young princes and some small reinforcements to his army. The marshal was the bearer of letters from the king, the queen-mother and Anjou, couched in the most friendly and conciliatory terms. But Coligny was not then disposed to be ensnared by the protestations and fine promises of those who had so lately set a price on his head, had hanged him in effigy, and sought his death by poison and dagger. He courteously acknowledged the missives of that amiable trio, but did not suspend his march.

He was aware that the king and queen-mother were at the end of their resources; that the immense sums received as gifts from the clergy and the large towns, the loans Catherine had effected, and the considerable amount derived from the sale of **Church** property, which had been sold at a very high rate, had been spent, not only on the army, but to a great extent squandered by Catherine herself. For fêtes, balls, banquets, and bonfires went on unceasingly, in celebration of **some skirmish and** massacre **on** a small scale, in default of success in a regular battle to triumph over.

The Court then exhibited in its habits and manners a singular *mélange* of gallantry and bloodthirstiness, voluptuousness and ferocity; strange contradictions, which then threatened to become national characteristics. It was, indeed, one of the queen-mother's aims to seduce by this courtly depravity and licentious freedom of manners, those weaker brethren amongst the Huguenot nobility **to** whom the severe austerity of life enjoined by Calvin's doctrines rendered existence an almost cheerless **burden.**

There have been few such noble examples of Calvinism as that displayed in the character and acts of the Protestant martyr Coligny. He was without fanaticism, was humane, tolerant, **and** patriotic, yet firm in the faith he **had adopted.** Doubtless his influence was generally felt by the Calvinists, and served to restrain **many** from abandoning 'the cause.' The small army he commanded at the period now in question was kept together only by their confidence in him. Yet many fell away from him when early in April he halted at Nîmes, and there communicated to his companions-in-arms the project he had formed of carrying the war into the neighbourhood of Paris, to disquiet the Parisians, and compel the Court to make peace. A wild and hazardous scheme it appeared to them, and few were found to approve it.

But Coligny explained that their numbers would be increased by rallying the Reformers in every province they passed through, and the facility of joining the troops promised by the German princes become greater the nearer they approached the North. But it seemed to the Reformers of the South too adventurous an expedition, and not more than 5,000 were inspired by his heroism to share its perils with him; but naturally they were those whose audacity would be likely to contribute to its success. The Huguenots had no artillery, but all were mounted, and set out on their daring and hazardous campaign in high spirits.

Catherine, informed by some of her emissaries of Coligny's project, despatched, as it would seem, on her own authority, a corps of 12,000 men under Marshal Cossé-Gonnor to exterminate Coligny and his troop, even to the last man ('Guerres des Français,' J. Servan). On arriving at Saint-Etienne, Coligny was taken suddenly and dangerously ill. Consternation spread amongst his followers; but fortunately for them (if not for him, considering what a fate he was reserved for) that famous remedy for all maladies at that period —bleeding—was in his case efficacious. Weak and weary, he was scarcely able to do more than give the young commanders the necessary instructions for repulsing the royalists encountered at Arnay-le-Duc.

The nature of the ground was favourable for the advantageous disposal of his small force, and here occurred Henry of Navarre's first exploit of arms. As it was a successful one, it was regarded as of fortunate augury.* Having completely repulsed their assailants, Coligny with his troop passed on so rapidly that Cossé, encumbered with heavy artillery, could not keep up with him. On reaching the Protestant town of Sancerre, the admiral despatched a messenger to the king with proposals of peace. The moment was well chosen; for the Protestants had beaten the Catholics in several provinces. All the towns between Les

* Henry was fond of referring to it when in after years he succeeded to the throne.

Sables-d'Olonne and the Gironde had fallen into their power, and La Noue had taken Sainte-Gemme and Fontenay. At the siege of the latter town his arm was shattered by a ball from an arquebuse. Jeanne d'Albret is said to have held it during its amputation.

Catherine was perplexed and disquieted by the change in the prospects of the heretics. She suspected Cossé of having purposely allowed Coligny to escape. The king was less docile of late, and in his hatred of Anjou continued to thwart all her projects for the great successes of her favourite son. The zealous Catholics, whose chief she intended he should be, rejected him for the young Duc de Guise. The Montmorencys sought the recall of De L'Hôpital; the Protestants expressed a similar wish. But that she resolved should never be; and Charles was also unwilling to make that concession, so thoroughly had the queen-mother imbued him with the idea that the chancellor was a Huguenot in disguise and a friend of the rebels.

With that exception he had no objection to peace, and as Catherine needed time more effectually to reconstruct her plots for heretic extermination, peace was signed at Saint-Germain on the 8th of August, on terms very favourable to the

Protestants. Some few days after, the effigy of the admiral, which had dangled for several months on Montfaucon, was quietly removed in the night, and the gibbet taken down. It was Coligny's hope that this treaty would be honourably carried out, and that the country would have rest to recover from the ravages inflicted on it by civil war. 'But Catherine's sentiments were of an entirely opposite character, and treason was already in her heart at the moment when, with her full concurrence in all its stipulations, her son signed the treaty of peace' (H. Martin).

CHAPTER XVIII.

Peace disapproved by Philip and Pius V.—Marguerite and Duc de Guise.—Anjou refuses to marry Queen Elizabeth. —Philip's Fourth Wife.—Charles marries Elizabeth of Austria. — Marguerite's Hand refused by Sebastian of Portugal.— The Bourbon Marriage resolved on. — Biron sent to Queen of Navarre to offer Marguerite to Henry. —Coligny invited by Charles IX. to Château de Blois.— Sets out from La Rochelle, against Advice of Friends.

WHEN rumours reached Rome and Madrid that projects for the renewal of peace were again entertained by the Court of France, the righteous spirits of Philip II. and Pius V. were exasperated exceedingly. Again the Florentine intrigante had deceived and disappointed them, and at the very moment, too, that his holiness thought so favourable for launching his anathemas and bulls of excommunication against the heretic Queen of England. But a few months previously he had issued his harmless bull of deposition in favour of Mary Stuart—harmless to Elizabeth, but doubtless tending to increase the rigour of the unfortunate Scottish queen's captivity.

But for the perversity of the queen-mother in giving her sanction to this 'infamous proposal of peace,' Pius had intended to incite the Catholics to further acts of rebellion both in Scotland and Ireland. In the hope, however, that the calamitous peace might yet perchance be averted, Pius, in virulent language, addressed letters to the queen-mother and her two sons: 'Know ye not,' he wrote, 'that between Satan and the sons of light there can be no fellowship? It should therefore be held as certain that between Catholics and heretics there can be no agreement or composition, unless it be one of dissimulation and pretence.'

This rebuke was accompanied by an offer from Philip of nine thousand troops, if reinforcements were needed to put down those 'scoundrels.' (Philip and the pope were both fond of applying the epithet scoundrels (*scélérats*) to the Huguenots. Yet surely no two individuals ever deserved it more than themselves.) Philip's offer was declined. 'Articles of peace were signed before its arrival;' but Catherine could console the Spanish tyrant and the persecuting pope with the promise that the consummation which they, and no less she, so devoutly desired was but deferred, and was even almost assured by this peace. She is said to have insinuated at Rome and Madrid that the peace of Saint-Germain would prove more murderous to 'those of the religion' than a war. The Huguenots generally put little faith in its possible duration, though it was guaranteed by assigning to them for two years the four strong places they held on the Charente.

Coligny, however, was more hopeful, and with the two young Bourbon princes and the principal Huguenot nobility—after conducting their German allies to the frontier—rapidly crossed the kingdom to join Jeanne d'Albret and the little Princess Catherine at La Rochelle, to await there in security the conclusion of the peace negotiations. The cessation of the long-continued state of anarchy in France gratified most of the moderate Catholics; but the fanatical zealots of Rouen and Orange, at the suggestion of their priests—taking 'the rise and overflowing of some of the rivers of France at that time as an expression of the anger of God at this peace'—fell suddenly on the Protestants and savagely massacred them.

Hitherto such murderous attacks, though frequent, were never inquired into, or anyone concerned in them arrested. On the present occasion a different course was pursued, and the perpetrators of these outrages severely punished. This inspired confidence in the more sanguine of the Huguenot party. The Court, too, was said to be peacefully occupied with matrimonial negotiations, which, however, seemed likely to end in revenge and resentment. Even before the peace was signed, the Montmorencys, in the interests of tolerance, suggested the marriage of Madame Marguerite, Catherine's youngest daughter, with Prince Henry of Navarre.

Twelve years before, when Henry, a bright little boy of five, was taken to Amiens by his father, King Antony, Henry II. was much pleased with him, and asked him if he would be his son. To which, in the Gascon patois, he replied:

'Quet es lo seigne pay.'

'Will you then be my son-in-law?' said the king.

'O bé,' he answered.

No betrothal had ever taken place, yet, until events arose that seemed to put their marriage out of the question, Henry and Marguerite were regarded as destined for each other. Jeanne was said rather to incline to the idea of marrying her son to Elizabeth of England, notwithstanding the disparity of age.

It had been for some months understood that Marguerite was to marry the young Duc de Guise, the handsomest and most brilliant cavalier of the French Court. 'She had given him her heart.' Such, at least, was the joke of 'the squadron;' and Marguerite, then eighteen, beautiful, accomplished, and *spirituelle*, had inspired the duke, they laughingly said, with love as ardent as her own. He was probably the first of her rather long list of lovers. To the dismay of the brilliant young couple, the audacity of Guise in pretending to the hand of the princess suddenly put Charles IX. into one of his fits of rage. He ordered that Guise should be shot when attending the royal hunt; but, warned by a friend, the young duke escaped. Catherine also expressed her deep indignation at the conduct of both Marguerite and Guise, though she had hitherto made her daughter the lure by which she sought to gain the duke over to her interests.

Anjou, however, was the most violent of the three. Guise so entirely eclipsed him in military capacity, in popularity, and personal advantages, that, in the excitement of jealousy and hate, he vowed he would 'put a dagger in his heart.' The prudent young duke, following the counsels of his worthy uncle, the Cardinal of Lorraine, at once smoothed the ruffled feelings of the royal trio by assenting to a marriage **with** Catherine de Clèves, **the** young widow of the Prince de Portien. Guise was at once restored to favour. The ambitious projects attributed to him were, in a measure, disavowed **by this** alliance voluntarily contracted; while there was the further advantage that, sheltered **by it,** Marguerite, without any shock to **the courtly morality of that day,** could still **retain her lover.**

She, however, decidedly expressed her **aversion** to a marriage with Henry of Navarre. **It was** not yet formally decided to propose **it to Queen** Jeanne. Catherine was awaiting the result **of the** offer she had made of Marguerite's **hand to** Sebastian, the young King **of Portugal. He** declined the proffered honour; **such a** marriage being **highly displeasing to Philip** II., Catherine having **some vague** pretensions to the Crown of Portugal, **which** she thought by its means **to** strengthen.

Charles, too, was seeking a matrimonial alliance, being for the second time a suitor for the hand of the Archduchess Elizabeth, younger daughter of the Emperor Maximilian II. The emperor, after a lengthened negotiation, consented to give his daughter to Charles, and without again demanding, as one of its conditions, the restitution of the three bishoprics to the empire. To the fact of Charles and Catherine having this marriage in view may be ascribed the unusual steps taken to punish the perpetrators of the outrages of Rouen and Orange. To have allowed such murderous attacks to pass unnoticed would have been unfavourable to Charles's suit, in the eyes of so humane a prince as Maximilian II., whose alliance Catherine hoped to turn to political account by using it as a means of securing that of the Protestant princes in the event of new wars against the '*seditious* Calvinist chiefs.' For that difference of religious belief or persecution for heresy was the cause of them, Catherine, at all events, affected to ignore.

The marriage of Philip II. to his niece, and fourth wife, the Archduchess Eléonore, the elder sister of the Archduchess Elizabeth, took place a month or two earlier than that of Charles and his bride. The queen-mother had been careful to inform herself of the character of this young princess, who was of a very gentle amiable temper, and compared with the effrontery of the women who chiefly composed the Court of Catherine de' Medici, her manners were pronounced 'very retiring.' A second Mary Stuart, ruling her husband, interfering in public affairs, and assuming to lead the Court, would not have suited the queen-mother. Charles, too, was not so likely to be transformed into a doting husband as poor Francis II. He had already his mistress, Marie Touchet, to whom he was much attached, and 'le petit Charles,' who in later years proved himself worthy to have been a legitimate scion, instead of a bastard offshoot, of the degenerate race of Valois, had already come into the world.

The marriage of Charles IX. and the Archduchess Elizabeth was celebrated with great magnificence on the 26th of November, at Mezières, whither the bride was conducted by the archbishop, Elector of Trèves, Chancellor of the Empire. The winter was setting in with its accustomed severity; great distress prevailed throughout the country. The people complained of the ever-increasing burden of taxes, and the treasury was said to be empty. Yet all sorts of expedients—and chiefly the old ones of creating titles of nobility, inventing new offices, and selling them to the highest bidder—were resorted to for funds to defray the expense of the unprecedented pomp of this royal wedding. The princes and the most distinguished of the Huguenot nobility were invited to share in the marriage festivities; but they begged respectfully to decline, thinking themselves safer in the stronghold of La Rochelle. Coligny, however, wrote to assure the queen-mother that 'the past was entirely forgotten, and to place his services at the king's disposal.'

Once more the recall of De L'Hôpital was suggested; but Catherine was inflexible, and the chancellor himself did not greatly desire it. At one time he had hopes that Charles might be saved from the domination of his mother. But that vain hope was ended. Since the chancellor's departure, she had surrounded her son with Italians —Birago, who succeeded De L'Hôpital; Gondi (created by Charles Comte de Retz); Davila, her secretary; and others of similar character—men who owed everything to her, and faithfully carried out her views, while availing themselves to the full of the opportunities she gave them of enriching themselves at the expense of the State. The chancellor would have found Charles more excitable and violent than ever, yet occasionally sinking for hours and even days into a state of languor or deep melancholy. He had a worn, weary appearance, too, unusual in so young a man. The name of God was always on his lips; but only to give more emphasis to the frightful oaths with which he was accustomed, in common with the young nobility of the period, to preface almost every sentence he uttered. It was the fashion thus to proclaim their orthodoxy—profane swearing being forbidden to the Calvinists.

An embassy from the German Protestant princes met Charles, on his return from the frontier, to congratulate him on his marriage and the re-establishment of religious peace in France. An address, in the name of the princes represented, was read to the king, earnestly recommending the continuance of tolerance. Charles responded more courteously than was his custom, and took immediate steps for entering into a defensive treaty with the Protestant States of Germany.

Another negotiation was also on foot, in the success of which Charles, in his desire to get rid of the presence of his brother, was greatly interested, and Catherine also, from anxiety to find a crown for her favourite Anjou—this was the young duke's proposal for the hand of Queen Elizabeth. But the proposal was Catherine's rather than Anjou's; for while the agents of the Court of France were urging for a favourable reply, Anjou, announced to his mother that he would not marry Elizabeth on any conditions whatever. This perversity on the part of the usually docile Anjou perplexed the queen-mother. La Mothe-Fénelon was then French ambassador in England. He had but just before informed the English queen how greatly this alliance was desired by the Court of France, when a private letter from Catherine made known to him the young duke's resolve to reject the position of 'husband of a queen who conferred on him neither title nor power.'

But Anjou, urged by his favourite Lignerolles, gave as his chief objection, the 'reports he had frequently heard to her dishonour.'* 'She was very sorry,' Catherine said, 'but trusted that means might be found of making the younger brother, the Duc d'Alençon, acceptable to the queen. This was a rather delicate commission for the ambassador, as, respecting Anjou, the initiative was said to have indirectly been taken by Elizabeth herself, at the suggestion, in the previous year, of Odet de Châtillon, the 'apostate cardinal,' and the Vidame de Chartres, who had sought refuge in England in 1568, both of whom were well received by the queen.

De Châtillon 'was returning to France in February, 1571, after an absence of three years in England—charged by the queen to confer with Coligny on the subject—while letters respecting this matrimonial negotiation were passing between

* This refers to her supposed relations with Dudley, Earl of Leicester.

Catherine de' Medici and the French ambassador. At Southampton, when about to embark, Odet de Châtillon was taken suddenly ill, and died almost immediately. He was poisoned by his servant, who, being afterwards arrested as a spy, confessed the deed, and declared that he was instigated to it by the queen-mother. Lignerolles, of whom she had said 'he should repent of the advice he had given Anjou,' was also assassinated shortly after in open day, by five or six men wearing masks. No one doubted by whom they were employed. Such assassinations were frequent in Paris, the victims being, for the most part, those who had opposed, or were in some way obstacles to, the carrying out of the queen-mother's schemes.

The pope and Philip II. were decidedly averse to the marriage with the excommunicated heretic queen. To tempt Anjou to reject it they offered him either the command of the fleet which the pope, conjointly with Spain and Venice, had armed against the Turks, or the direction of the descent on Ireland, with the hand of Mary Stuart, who was to be divorced by Pius V. if they succeeded in effecting her release. But Charles, in a great rage, forbade his brother to accept either command, and Catherine immediately wrote to the French ambassador that the Duc d'Anjou, notwithstanding some religious scruples, yet was exceedingly desirous of securing the honour of Elizabeth's hand.

The ambassador probably refrained from informing the queen of her young suitor's change of mind. It, however, effected none in hers, and no further negotiation on the subject seems to have taken place as regarded Anjou, with whom she had refused to enter into any public engagement respecting 'the free exercise of the Catholic religion in his chapel.' The Bourbon alliance was now formally proposed by the Court; the hand of the Princess Marguerite being offered by the king to the Queen of Navarre for her son Prince Henry, and Marshal Biron sent to La Rochelle as the negotiator.

Count Louis of Nassau, who was then with the Huguenots, was at the same time desired to repair to the Court, secretly and in disguise, to confer privately with the king and queen-mother. He had solicited the aid of Charles IX. for the unhappy Netherlanders, 18,000 of whom the Duke of Alva had already put to death, and was still adding to their number; still 'piling up,' as Pius V. had urged, to make of their bodies a ladder by which to reach heaven. Nothing could exceed the misery which the wretched Philip and his worthy lieutenant had inflicted on the people, the desolation and ruin they had brought on the country.

After a twelvemonth of carnage he at length deigned to grant to the remnant of the population an amnesty, from the benefit of which all were excluded who had ever acted or spoken in favour of public rights or liberties. The publication of this gracious edict, which was to be proclaimed in the name of the pope and the Spanish king by Alva, seated on a lofty throne in the centre of the great square of Antwerp—was still deferred. Blood enough had not yet been shed to satisfy these sanguinary monsters. The commerce of the country was also to be ruined by a tax of the tenth part of the price of every object sold. This impost on the various manufactures and products of the country could not be supported. A cry of alarm and despair arose among the people, and all who were able fled to France or England, but chiefly to the latter country, because of their religion. The historian, De Thou, names several partly abandoned English cities—Norwich, Colchester, Sandwich, Southampton, etc.—that were repeopled by the Flemings and Dutch, and owed their future prosperity to the manufactories of various kinds they then established there.

To stay the stream of emigration Alva racked his satanic brain for new and even more terrible tortures, and crueller modes of death. To serve perhaps as a warning to the more timid, he set up in the citadel a statue of himself 'crushing the demon Rebellion under his feet.' It was cast from the cannon he had taken from 'the rebels' at Gemmingen.

It was scarcely sympathy that Louis of Nassau expected from Charles IX. and Catherine de' Medici, who were little less cruel and sanguinary than the agent of Philip II. and Pius V., whose infamy and crime they were waiting but for a favourable opportunity of rivalling. Yet Charles appears to have listened with deep attention to the sad tale of the people's wrongs and sufferings. It was, however, to his ambitious views that the appeal was especially addressed—the great advantages that would ensue to France should she decide on protecting the unfortunate Netherlanders, and aiding them to throw off the yoke of Spain. Charles seemed to be vividly impressed in favour of this project—so much so that he bade the prince be 'of good hope,' adding that he desired to hear the opinion and have the advice of Admiral de Coligny on the subject.

A letter inviting him to repair to the Court for

that purpose was sent off to La Rochelle, where it occasioned considerable agitation, and was regarded by most of the Huguenots as a mere device of the queen-mother to ensnare their leader. The perfidy of her character forbade any confidence being placed in her, while she had trained her sons, they said, to 'heed neither law nor gospel.' Madame de Coligny also expressed great fear lest by complying with the king's command the admiral's life should be endangered.* Charles, however, authorized him to surround himself with an armed escort for his personal safety. He therefore ceded, hoping to prevent the renewal of civil war, which in the highest degree was repugnant to him.

He might, he knew, be risking his life in the attempt to avert it, but, at all events, he would make the attempt. He believed that further intestine strife could only be averted by a foreign war, which would give employment to those

* Coligny had lately remarried, under circumstances as romantic as the marriage of D'Andelot. A noble lady of Savoy had fallen in love with the admiral's great renown, and 'desired,' as she said, 'to become the Martia of this new Cato.' The Duke of Savoy, the suzerain of the 'Dame d'Entremonts'—such was her title—forbade her to leave her domains. She, however, escaped from Savoy, and married Coligny at La Rochelle, March, 1571 (H. Martin).

restless, turbulent spirits, both Catholic and Protestant, to whom the warfare of the last ten years had made war a need. Coligny, though not too sanguine of success, yet trusted that he might be able to bring the king to consent to this war, by showing him that his true interests were involved in it; thus—such, at least, was Coligny's noble wish—would their fellow-Protestants of the Low Countries be released from the tyranny they now groaned under, and France be indemnified for the troubles of the past by the increase of her territory and her power.

CHAPTER XIX.

Coligny's Reception at Blois by Charles IX.—Catherine jealous of Coligny's Influence.—Jeanne d'Albret visits the French Court.—Jeanne's Letter to her Son, Henry of Navarre.—The Court of Catherine de' Medici.—The Pope refuses the Dispensation for the Marriage.—Catherine's Proposals to Queen Elizabeth.—Warlike Preparations: Coligny's Plans. —The Court leaves Blois for Paris.—Death of Jeanne d'Albret.—Poison suspected.

CHARLES and the queen-mother, on learning that Coligny was about to leave La Rochelle, at once announced the departure of the Court for Blois. Their new attitude towards the Reformers was made evident to all by the courteous information forwarded to the admiral that the king would advance thus far to meet him and spare him the fatigue of half his journey. Coligny arrived at Blois on the 19th of September. On approaching the king, in the humble attitude customary at that period, his majesty graciously raised him, pressed his hand, embraced him three times, and kissed him on both cheeks. 'My father,' he said laughingly, 'now we have got you, you will not escape from us again' (D'Aubigné).

Though no sinister interpretation was put on the words at the time, yet the manner of the admiral's reception seemed to those chiefs of 'the Reform' who remained with the Bourbons at La Rochelle, to be an exaggerated affectation of friendliness on the part of the king, which increased rather than allayed their fears and suspicions. They, however, thought that the fact of his having avengers at hand, should any treachery be attempted, might serve to lessen his danger. But as no signs of any danger appeared, they were gradually lulled into confidence.

Charles appeared thoroughly fascinated by Coligny's grand designs, the desire to realize them increasing as they were more and more fully explained to him. 'France,' the admiral told him, 'should have the Scheldt for her frontier; Flanders and the Walloon and Belgian provinces, speaking the French language, be reunited to the Crown. Independence given to Brabant and Holland under the protectorate of the princes of Nassau, a portion of Zealand being reserved for England. The French navy should be, he proposed, powerfully organized, and Spain attacked not only in the Netherlands but in America, where the possession of the new world should be disputed with her.'*

No schemes on foot in the French Court, however secretly carried on, were unknown to Philip II. He had his emissaries even in the king's council chamber and the queen-mother's private cabinet. Therefore, not long after Coligny's arrival, the Spanish ambassador Alava, in Philip's name, threatened Charles IX. with war if the Huguenot intrigue was not brought to an end. The king replied that 'Spain might do what she pleased ; for he feared her not.' Catherine, more prudent, complained to Philip of his ambassador, who, she said, 'invented false rumours, and generally, by his officiousness, gave much annoyance at Court.' Philip knew better. But he recalled his

* This latter part of his scheme was a favourite one with the admiral. In 1555 he endeavoured to found a colony in Brazil. 'Five or six years later three or four small vessels were sent by his direction to discover a fitting spot for a French settlement. They sailed along the coast and ascended some of the rivers of Florida, Georgia, and Carolina, then unoccupied by Europeans. As soon as the Peace of Saint-Germain was signed, Coligny again turned his thoughts towards colonization, and but a few weeks before leaving La Rochelle he despatched from that port a small squadron to reconnoitre the Antilles and prepare for an attack on that archipelago' (H. Martin).

ambassador, replacing him by one no less intriguing and officious.

Coligny was much gratified by the ardour with which the king appeared to enter into his views. It exceeded his expectations. The Montmorency or 'politique' party also approved them, and even Catherine was almost persuaded by her relative Strozzi—who looked for a prominent command in the Flanders expedition—to give them more than a tacit assent by an open expression of her approbation. But it was not the scheme for the aggrandizement of France—though she desired not war with Spain—that displeased her, but the growing influence which the man who proposed it appeared to be gaining over the king.

Charles IX. at this time was probably playing no dissembling part under his fiendish mother's directions. As he had formerly shown respect for the Chancellor de L'Hôpital and deference to his advice and opinions, so now the honest, upright, and sensible counsels of an honourable man like Coligny produced the same effect on him. For Charles was not, like his brother the Duc d'Anjou, naturally vicious. His mother was his evil genius. Yet his better nature was not wholly extinct. Some flickering gleams of it did at rare intervals still appear, and under judicious and friendly guidance he might possibly even then have triumphed over that perversion of his moral senses by which the queen-mother had gained the mastery over him.

That the Parisian people might be witnesses of the honour now paid to the admiral, Charles entered his capital on December the 16th, with a numerous retinue, the new favourite riding on his right. This distinction conferred on the 'chief of the heretics' was far from meeting with general approval. The exasperation of feeling that existed in both factions was as yet very slightly toned down, and much distrust prevailed. Coligny was then about to return to his domain of Châtillon-sur-Loing. His château had been sacked and pillaged during the civil war; the king therefore, as some compensation for the loss sustained, made him a present of 100,000 livres, for (as Brantôme says) 'M. l'Amiral was poor for a man of his rank and station, having valued honour more than riches.'

The negotiation respecting the Bourbon marriage was continued through the winter. Coligny had been charged to present to the king the Queen of Navarre's letter of thanks for the honour he had done her by the offer of his sister's hand to her son. But so strong was her repugnance to the match, so great her fears that Henry might be led to renounce his religious profession, that Jeanne, though six months had elapsed, had not yet been persuaded by the assurances of the king's sincerity in his advances towards the Reformers, and the triumph which, through this marriage, the Huguenot gentlemen believed would accrue to 'the cause,' to visit the Court with her son. She foresaw in this alliance the destruction of those plans of conduct she had formed for the young prince, the evil influence of the queen-mother, and the seductions of her surroundings.

At last, after much hesitation, she yielded to Coligny's entreaties, and, with the ladies and gentlemen of her Court, left the Château of Pau early in February, 1572. The Princess Catherine, then in her twelfth year, accompanied the queen; but the young prince, to whom his mother revealed all her anxieties, remained at Béarn. They were received at Tours on the 4th of March by Charles and the queen-mother with every appearance and expression of friendship and welcome. Jeanne was sumptuously lodged at Blois, and the next day the Princess Catherine writes to her brother:

'Monsieu—— j'ay veu Madame (Marguerite) que j'ay troué fort belle et eussé bien désiré que vous l'eussié veue, ie luy ai bien parlé pour vous qu'elle vous tinst en sa bonne grace ce qu'elle m'a promis et m'a fait bien bon chère et m'a donné un bau petit chien que jeme bien.'

The young princess was much admired at the Valois Court, and was pronounced charming. At all events, she charmed as a novelty by the quaint plainness of her Huguenot style of dress, so different from the voluminous finery in which young girls of high station were then usually arrayed, even at Catherine's age. There was much *naïveté*, too, in her manners and mode of speech, and she had a graceful bearing, a bright, lively countenance, a joyous temper like her brother, and already was almost as quick at repartee as he. It may have been found judicious to admire the queen's interesting young daughter. It was a sort of mild flattery wherewith to smooth over the many proposals and concessions that were to be laid before the Queen of Navarre relating to the marriage of her son, and to which, against her better judgment, consent at last was wrung from her.

On the 8th of March, she writes to Henry from Blois, complaining of the obstacles she has to surmount ; of the intrigues to which she is exposed ; of the trickery she has to baffle.

'I have to negotiate this matter,' she says, ' in a quite different manner from that I had expected and was promised, no opportunity being given me of speaking to the king or madame, but to the queen-mother only, who treats me with treachery and deceit. Madame, indeed, I never see, except in that very improper place, the queen-mother's apartments, whence she stirs not, and where, without being heard by some of the ladies in attendance, who never think of withdrawing, I cannot speak to her.'

'Seeing then, my son, that no advance was made, that there was no desire to conduct matters in due order, but simply a design to force me to precipitate them, I several times spoke on the subject to the queen-mother. She did but jest, and laugh at me, and immediately told everyone something altogether contrary to what I had said to her, so that my friends blamed me. And when I said, "Madame, such and such things were not spoken by me, but by yourself," she contradicted, and said, "There's a fine tale," and laughed in my face, so that it may truly be said my patience passes that of the Griseldas.'

Jeanne's character being honest, open, and confiding, she could not comprehend the machiavelian genius of Catherine de' Medici. She at last succeeded in having some conversation with Marguerite, whom she describes as

'handsome, discreet, and docile, but brought up amidst the most cursed (*maudite*) and corrupt society that ever existed;' and she makes no exceptions. "I meet with none," she says, "who are free from its influence. Your cousin, the marquise (the recently married wife of the young Prince de Condé) is so much changed by it that there is no longer any appearance of religion in her, except that she goes not to mass; but, idolatry excepted, she does as the papists do."'

Marguerite acknowledged to the Queen of Navarre that 'she had but little mind towards the match, but on the ground of her religion'—to which, contrary to what Jeanne had been assured, she declared she was greatly attached. In another letter to Henry, the queen says:

'As I write privately the bearer will tell you what kind of life the king leads, putting no restraint on himself whatever. It is a great pity. I would not for all the world that you should come here to reside; for you could never escape the contagion except through the great Grace of God. My wish, should you be married, is that you and your wife should retire from this scene of corruption, which, indeed, I had believed to be great, but find it far worse than I had imagined. It is not the men who make love here to the women, but the women to the men.'

The hideous fashions of the period, both those of the men and the women, were also displeasing to the Queen of Navarre. She would have persuaded Marguerite to give up the habit of excessive patching and painting, then in vogue, which spoiled her complexion, and instead of heightening, as she considered, diminished her beauty. Nor could she see grace or elegance in increasing the size of that part of the body naturally larger than the rest, by spreading the dress over the 'vertugadin' eight or ten feet in a circle around her. Reform in the fashions of the day was certainly needed. But the preaching of Jeanne d'Albret as a reformer of Court costume, though it may have afforded amusement to the belles of Catherine's squadron, certainly made no converts.

At length, after much hesitation, and less of her own free will than to satisfy the urgent entreaties of her Huguenot advisers—amongst whom was Coligny, so fully assured was he of the king's sincerity—Jeanne gave her consent to this inauspicious marriage. It was her wish that it should be celebrated at Blois, and according to the rites of the reformed religion. To the proposal of mass and the Catholic ceremony she would not listen. But the queen-mother was bent on its performance in Paris. Charles was also of her opinion that the capital of France was the proper place for the marriage of its kings' daughters. On that point Jeanne then ceded, though she knew that the Parisians cherished the deepest hate towards the Huguenots. Catherine also knew that well, and hence, it was afterwards believed, she determined that the marriage should take place there. Doubtless also, the compromise respecting the ceremonial was acceded to because of the exasperation it would cause amongst the Catholics of the capital.

But although the marriage treaty was signed on the 11th of April, no dispensation from the pope had arrived. Pius V. had already sent his nephew, the Cardinal Alessandrino, to Paris to induce the king to abandon the idea of marrying his sister to a heretic; at the same time absolutely refusing to grant the dispensation required on account of their relationship as cousins.

The king, replying to the Queen of Navarre's remark, which probably expressed her wish, that 'it would be very long indeed, she believed, before it was obtained, because of the religious difference,' said, 'Not so, dear aunt, for I honour you more than the pope, and fear him less than I love my sister. I am not a Huguenot, neither am I a blockhead; but if M. le Pape plays the fool too long (*fait trop la bête*), I will take Margot by the hand, and will publicly lead her to the Huguenot temple to marry Henry.'

Pius continued inflexible, though Charles is said to have sent him word that 'this marriage afforded him the only means he had of revenging himself on his enemies.' If he did so, the pope of course understood that the wholesale murder he had so long recommended was about to be perpetrated. 'Heaven, however, as he would have said, did not permit him to see and rejoice over the accomplishment of this good deed. For on the 1st of May the persecuting Pius V. departed this life; whether for a better or more congenial one, who shall declare. Pius was succeeded, to the great disappointment of the Cardinal de Lorraine, by Cardinal Buoncompagno, who took the name of Gregory XIII. The new pope was less absolute than his predecessor in his refusal of the dispensation. Certain conditions were proposed by him, which, being agreed to, he was willing to yield. Negotiation on the subject then commenced.

On the 29th of April a defensive alliance was concluded between France and England. The queen-mother apparently thought this a favourable opportunity for renewing proposals of marriage to Elizabeth—no longer on the part of Anjou, but of her youngest son, the Duc d'Alençon, a boy of sixteen—Elizabeth being then thirty-eight. This royal youth raised no scruples on the score of religion. He required no private chapel or staff of priests. On the contrary, his religious sympathies inclined towards heresy. Nothing came of this proposal at that time, for it was accompanied by a preposterous request from Catherine, in the interests of her favourite son, 'that Elizabeth should consent to the marriage of Anjou with her captive, the Scottish Queen Mary, whom she should also declare her heir.*

* Yet at the time of his death Pius V. and Philip II. were plotting to put Mary on the English throne, after marrying

But Elizabeth did not wholly reject this third boy-husband offered by Catherine de' Medici to the English queen during the last three or four years. She was then somewhat incensed at the ungallant conduct of Anjou. Later on, however, she amused herself at the expense of this gay-tempered, valiant, and adventurous prince, now partly accepting his proffered hand—now declining it—and again raising his hopes but to damp them. His interests did not allow him to be deterred by her years from playing the lover, and Elizabeth, herself so open to flattery, probably saw little to object to in that respect. Her ambassador had insinuated that she looked scarcely older than the prince, and that there was 'more beauty in her majesty's little finger than in the whole body of any lady he had seen at the French Court.'*

The Papal Court was slow in its decision concerning the heretic marriage, for Gregory's proposals were not well received by Jeanne ; but meanwhile, great preparations, military and naval, were making at Bordeaux, Brouage, and Normandy, and a numerous corps of Protestants was

---

her to the Duke of Norfolk, and imprisoning Elizabeth, or, better still, putting her to death.

* 'Foreign State Papers'—'Correspondence of English Ambassadors,' 1572.

forming at Poitiers at the king's expense. Coligny had retired during the king's *grandes chasses* to Châtillon to spend some time with his family, who urged him not to return to the Court. Not only his wife and children on their knees entreated him, but friends and partizans of 'the cause' warned him not to put faith in Charles IX. They reminded him of the Catholic maxim that 'faith ought not to be kept with heretics,' of the perversity of the queen-mother, the detestable education she had given her sons, of Charles's horrible cruelty and mad delight in slaughtering beasts and bathing his hands in their blood—a fitting preparation for the slaughter of human beings.

But Coligny declared that 'he would rather be dragged dead through the streets of Paris than witness the renewal of the horrors of civil war.' He departed then for the Court. Charles had urged his speedy return; he could not live without his 'good father.' He would have, he said, Margot's marriage no longer delayed, and the Court, in consequence, towards the end of May repaired to Paris.

The bridegroom was still at Béarn. Jeanne so feared the evil influence which the depraved morals and manners of the Court might probably have on her son, that she was anxious he should defer his arrival until the date was fixed for the ceremony actually to take place. She expressed a fear of falling ill, so much had the anxiety and annoyance she had undergone affected her. To add to her troubles, her daughter Catherine had been attacked by pleurisy, and reduced to a state of such extreme weakness by the copious bleedings then in vogue, that months of repose would be needed, she said, for her restoration. (Catherine's constitution, it appears, was permanently affected by this weakening system.) They, however, decided on following the Court to Paris, and on the 4th of June, in solemn silence, the Queen of Navarre, her friends, and a small escort entered the capital. The secret influence of the Guises was already felt, and the people received the ally —as they were told—of the heretic Elizabeth of England, and the Protestants of Germany, with a sort of hostile curiosity. She preferred instead of the Louvre, as a residence, the Hôtel de Condé, offered to her by her relative. Her anxiety respecting the marriage had produced a feverish energy, to which great languor now succeeded, and a depressed state of feeling she was unable to surmount. Preparations were making for the marriage, and by a great effort she strove to appear the gracious, eloquent, brilliant, and enlightened person she naturally was (Mademoiselle Vauvilliers).

Accompanied by Marshal Montmorency, the queen visited the ateliers of the artists and the armourers of renown, and made many purchases of jewels and other presents for the bride, her friends, and her children; deeming it right not to be sparing of expense on this occasion, for her son's sake. Seeing the magnificence of the preparations then making by the Court, she sent orders to Béarn for the due equipment of the numerous *cortége* destined to attend the prince. The high-spirited Jeanne d'Albret, notwithstanding her general adherence to Huguenot ideas of simplicity, would not allow Prince Henry of Navarre to be wholly eclipsed by the splendour of his bride.

It was while visiting the various establishments of Paris that the queen entered the laboratory of Catherine de' Medici's perfumer, and purchased a pair of perfumed gloves, said to have been prepared with some subtle but odorous poison. On the morrow she was attacked by violent pains in the head. The king's physicians were instantly sent to her, but on the following morning, the 9th of June, she died—but five days after her arrival in Paris.

THE FIRST THUNDER-PEAL.

It was long generally believed that Jeanne d'Albret was the victim of one of the poisoning secrets of the Borgia and Medici. But although it has been urged that she suffered from an affection of the chest, the symptoms of which were aggravated by the fatigue and mental anxiety she had undergone respecting her son's marriage—to which she had been urged by Huguenot partizans to consent, though she could not give it her approval—it has never been clearly proved that the unscrupulous Catherine de' Medici, through her no less unscrupulous agents, had not some hand in the Queen of Navarre's death. Her body was opened and (according to Palma-Cayet) her head also, and no trace of poison, of course, was discovered. The Court physicians declared that her death was caused by an abscess on the lungs. But Catherine's Italian secretary, Davila, who has been at such pains to exalt her crimes into traits of the great genius and elevation of mind with which he credits her, says of Jeanne d'Albret's death, ' it was the first thunder-peal announcing the tempest then preparing against the Huguenots.'

The unexpected death of the Huguenot queen did certainly spread consternation as of the fall of a thunderbolt amongst the Reformers. ' Sublime in the hour of death as in the many perils that already had menaced her life, her only regret was leaving her children ; the destiny of her daughter especially occupying her thoughts. She entreated Coligny and the Cardinal de Bourbon, who with the Prince of Nassau were hastily summoned to receive her last wishes, to supply the place of parents to both Henry and Catherine—the pledges of her dearest affections and of her bitterest regrets.*

Jeanne d'Albret was buried with as much of the ceremonial customary at royal funerals as the austere simplicity of the religion she had adopted would permit. She lay in state for five days in a room draped with black. Her dress was of white satin embroidered in silver, and a royal mantle of violet velvet was thrown over her. 'The bed she lay on,' writes Marguerite de Valois, 'was her ordinary one, and the curtains were open ; but there were no wax lights, no priests, no cross, and no holy water.' The public walked slowly through the gloomy apartment, bowing reverently as they passed the body.' A sentiment of profound pity arose in the hearts of all who could momentarily contemplate the now rigid features of the valiant and noble lady, whose counsels had so often troubled the projects of her adversaries.

* Mademoiselle Vauvilliers.

CHAPTER XX.

Marriage of Marguerite and Henry deferred.—Catherine seeks to thwart Coligny's Plans.—Charles flies from his Counsellors.—Catherine opposed to War with Spain.—Elizabeth again pressed to marry D'Alençon.—Arrival in Paris of Henry of Navarre.—The Betrothal.—The Dispensation dispensed with.—'Les Noces Vermeilles.'—Marguerite declares she never accepted Henry.—The Admiral's fatal Confidence in Charles IX.—A Saturnalia.

THE marriage of Marguerite and Henry of Béarn—now King of Navarre—was delayed for two months by the death of Jeanne d'Albret. It was even supposed by the more zealous of the Huguenot party that it would not take place at all, and that Coligny's relations with Charles IX. would either come to an end, or be greatly modified by the suspicious circumstances that surrounded Jeanne's sudden and mysterious death. But this did not appear to be the admiral's view of the subject. Suspecting no foul play, he accepted undoubtingly the declaration of the physicians as to the true cause of death, just as he believed, as a man of honour, that the king was acting towards him in good faith respecting the projected war against Spain. He rejected, therefore, the suggestions pressed upon him to refrain from following up the plans agreed on between Charles IX. and himself.

It was, indeed, too late to draw back. Louis de Nassau and the valiant La Noue—'the Bayard of the Huguenots'—had taken Valenciennes and Mons, entering those cities to the cry of 'France and Liberty!' It was now for Charles to keep his word, and ready enough he was, it appears, to draw the sword. But Catherine, opposed to war with Spain and jealous of Coligny, would not let him. She succeeded also in preventing orders being sent for the sailing of the fleet from La Rochelle. At the same time she and Anjou informed the Duke of Alva of the object of these warlike preparations, and the Cardinal de Lorrain conveyed similar intelligence to Philip II.

France at this period has been compared to a vessel buffeted by contrary winds. The helm of the State was certainly in very unskilful hands. But having proceeded thus far on a hazardous course, a council was held to determine what further steps should be taken.* Anjou and the queen-mother attended this council, with their sworn allies, the Italian chancellor, Birago, and the ferocious Marshal Tavannes. But while opinions for and against this Spanish war were being debated, news arrived that Alva, reinforced, had retaken Valenciennes and was besieging Mons, the 'military operations being supplemented by the enchantments and divinations of soothsayers and astrologers' ('Lettres de Morillon à Granvelle'); and further, that the second corps of Catholic and Protestant volunteers from Picardy, which the Huguenot captain, Genlis, was marching with to relieve Mons, had been surprised *en route* and defeated. The greater part of this corps had been put to death as heretics, and Genlis, their captain, taken prisoner, thrown into a dungeon, and strangled.

Catherine and Anjou rejoiced in this result of their treachery. This check had also, for their purpose, the further advantage of inducing those who were before undecided to protest against the

* The memorial presented to the king by Coligny on this occasion was prepared by a young Huguenot gentleman, Du Plessis-Mornay, who afterwards became famous as the diplomatist and friend of Henry of Navarre and the Huguenot party.

war. Coligny remained firm, and Charles seemed still to cling to his view of the question, giving him authority to raise another corps of volunteers, notwithstanding that further news from Flanders reported that in Genlis' baggage a letter from Charles IX. was found, fully proving that the King of France had aided and connived at the rebellion of the princes of Nassau.

The king was pressed to disavow his complicity with the Nassaus by some striking act that should appease the resentment of Philip II. He, however, did not, and to free himself from the distracting importunity of both parties, he fled to Brie for some days of violent hunting. But the queen-mother would not let him escape so easily. She followed him with all haste to reproach him with his ingratitude to a mother who had sacrificed herself for him, and whose enemies he now preferred to her. She therefore humbly requested permission to retire, with her son Anjou, to her own country and family. A torrent of tears followed the request of the heartbroken mother. But Charles had seen this torrent flow so often and so readily that it affected him not. If she and Anjou had really decamped without troubling him, he would have been only too glad. Such scenes, however, put him into a frenzy of passion,

CATHERINE DE MÉDICIS.

Paris Richard Bentley and Son 1887

and to be **free** from them he promised anything she asked of him. ' He would follow **her** counsels, **he** now told her, after his rage **at being pursued had** spent itself ; and Catherine, but partly con**soled and** scarcely assured that she had regained her authority over him, **returned** to Paris with murderous thoughts **in her heart towards Coligny.**

But when **Charles, after an absence of some** days, again met the **admiral in** Paris, his influence **once more seemed** likely to supersede that **of the** queen-mother. **After his** promises to her, Charles dared not declare **war** openly ; **but his anti-**Spanish policy revived ; the armaments **were** continued, and all that now **was wanting to** engage in war against Spain was that **the German** princes and the Queen of England **should** come to **a** decision **on the proposal of France to** make their alliance with **her offensive as** well defensive. Several **months had elapsed** since the proposal was made ; **but distrust of** Charles and the queen-mother had **occasioned this** hesitancy in acceding to it. Elizabeth also **was** scarcely willing **to take** the initiative, as Charles desired, and declare **war** against Philip.

But Catherine was far more **anxious that** Elizabeth should decide **to** accept the Duc d'Alençon for her husband. This marriage was continually forced on her attention. The good qualities of the young gentleman's head and heart were lauded in glowing terms; but, alas! little could be said in favour of his personal advantages, on which Elizabeth seems to have laid some stress. In that respect, he was the least favoured of Catherine's children. He was short, and inclined, like his mother, to obesity, and unfortunately the ravages of that fearful disease, the smallpox, had made him (not to say hideous; it is an unpleasant term) sublimely ugly. He, however, bore his misfortune gracefully, and as the disease had at that period many victims, the disfigurement was not so remarkable.

The queen-mother had hoped to celebrate this marriage with the excommunicated heretic queen at the same time as Marguerite's with the King of Navarre. But Elizabeth had decided neither on the political nor matrimonial alliance when, on the 12th or 13th of August, Marguerite's heretic bridegroom made his entry into Paris with his cousin, Prince Henry of Condé, and attended by eight hundred Huguenot gentlemen. All were in deep mourning. Amongst the spectators the same ominous silence prevailed as when, but two months past, Queen Jeanne and her modest *cortége* arrived in the capital. But the young king had a jovial air; he rode well, and bore himself gallantly, the few Huguenots who greeted him gazing on him with pride and pleasure.

Certainly he was not handsome, but the expression of his countenance was pleasing. His eyes were lively and penetrating, and shaded by thick black eyebrows. His hair was black and wavy; his nose aquiline and rather too long for beauty; while of beard he, as yet, had little to speak of, being then but in his nineteenth year. But he was 'altogether a goodly prince,' and as 'at the French Court all who were not lame or humpbacked were accounted handsome,' Henry of Navarre, who was neither, though he could not contest the palm of manly beauty with Duke Henry of Guise, might have advantageously been compared with many of the beaux chevaliers of the Court of Charles IX.

The betrothal of Marguerite and Henry took place at the Louvre on the 17th in the presence of the Court and a brilliant assemblage of the principal Catholic and Huguenot nobility. The Duc de Guise and his brothers were present, and Charles, considering the occasion favourable for a reconciliation, insisted on the duke giving his hand to the admiral, who, on his part, repeated his denial of any complicity in the assassination of the late duke, and proposed to sign a solemn declaration to that effect. The duke, in deference to the king probably, appeared satisfied, but his feeling towards Coligny and burning desire for vengeance, as the event proved, remained unchanged.

No dispensation had been sent from Rome. The four conditions: 1st, that Henry should make profession of the Catholic faith before the king; 2nd, that he should re-establish the Catholic faith in his own domains; 3rd, that he should himself make the request to his holiness for the necessary dispensation for his marriage; and 4th, that the marriage should be solemnized in the church, without any variation from the customary ceremonial, were not agreed to. Charles urgently pressed the pope to renounce these four conditions, assuring him, rather suspiciously, that he asked it 'in the interests of religion,' and praying him to take it in good part should he be constrained, notwithstanding his refusal to yield, at once to celebrate the marriage.*

The Cardinal de Bourbon was to officiate at this ceremony, but was not prepared to do so without the authority of Rome. 'The cardinal,' according to Geronimo Lippomano, 'was one of the most zealous Catholics in France,' yet withal it appears

* 'Histoire des Ducs de Guise,' par M. de Bouillé.

a man of narrow views and little intelligence—
rather a simpleton, in fact. It seemed then likely
that after all the grand preparations were made
for it, there was to be no marriage at all. The
king, however, undertook to convince the cardinal
that his objections were not valid. The dispensation truly had not yet arrived, but 'it was granted,'
he told him, 'and on its way to Paris.' Putting
faith in the king's word, the cardinal promised
compliance with his wish, and on the 18th these
strange nuptials, these 'Noces Vermeilles,' destined
to be sealed with blood, took place. 'They were
celebrated,' as Marguerite herself informs us, 'with
a triumph and magnificence that none other had
hitherto been.'

The King of Navarre, the princes of his house
and his eight hundred gentlemen, had discarded
their mourning for the occasion, and appeared in
the glittering gala costume in vogue at that extravagant period. The royal bridegroom wore a
State mantle of black velvet, embroidered in gold ;
doublet and trunk-hose of light brown and white
silk, with jets and trimmings in gold ; pantalon of
white silk with gold embroidery, and black velvet
hat with a white plume. His sword-belt and
sheath were black ; the hilt of the sword gold.
His shoes, and gold-fringed gloves also, were white,

much ornamented with seed-pearls and gold. The Order of Saint-Michel, surrounded with precious stones, completed the young king's costume. Charles IX. and his courtiers were similarly attired, but surpassed the Huguenots in the number and magnificence of their jewels.

The bride herself was 'arrayed,' as she says, 'à la royale,' wearing a 'circlet, stomacher, and corset of spotted ermine, or minever. The dress itself was of cloth of silver embroidered with pearls, and opening over a richly jewelled satin petticoat—pearls and diamonds also bordering the long Venetian sleeves of the under robe. The Crown jewels of France were worn by her for this occasion. Her mantle was of blue velvet embroidered in gold, the train four ells in length, and borne by three princesses.' But this train of four ells was but a small affair compared with that worn by Elizabeth of Austria on her marriage with Charles IX. 'Its length,' says Marguerite, 'was twenty ells, and, being heavily embroidered in gold, required eight ladies of the Court to assist the four princesses who were selected to bear it.'

From the residence of the Archbishop of Paris to the great portal of the 'Temple of Notre Dame' (D'Aubigné), a high platform was erected, from which descending by a lower one, the nave of the temple was entered. These platforms were protected from the pressure of the crowd by barricades covered, like the platforms, with cloth of gold. The bride was conducted from the archbishop's house by Charles IX., the queen-mother, the princes of the blood, also those of Lorraine and the great officers of the Crown. On the opposite side walked the King of Navarre with his two cousins, the admiral, the Comte de la Rochefoucauld, and other nobles and gentlemen. The two processions arrived together at the entrance of 'the Temple,' where the Cardinal de Bourbon was waiting to receive them, and where, according to a ceremonial and form of words already supplied to him, and which satisfied neither party, Marguerite and Henry were married. The bride with her relatives and their retinue then entered 'the Temple' to hear Mass, the bridegroom meanwhile retiring to the courtyard of the bishop's house, while the rest of the Reformers promenaded the cloisters and nave (D'Aubigné). Mass being ended, Marshal de Montmorency reassembled the party, and the cardinal then gave the nuptial benediction. It was remarked by several persons of the company (according to Davila), that when the cardinal asked Marguerite if she would take the King of Navarre for her husband, she gave no reply. Charles, noticing this, laid his hand on her head, and compelled her to bend it in assent. 'But,' continues Davila, 'both before and after the ceremony, she declared—whenever she could venture to speak freely—that she never would consent or had consented to renounce the Duc de Guise, to whom her faith was previously engaged, or to take as her husband one of the duke's chief enemies.'

The pledge of alliance between Catholic and Protestant was now supposed to be solemnly given to the Reformers. Coligny, therefore, lost no time in urging on the king no further delay in taking those steps already resolved on against Spain. But Charles laughingly excused himself for setting aside all thoughts of war at a time when the propitious nuptials, now happily concluded, called for a brief space of mirthful rejoicing. Though about to share in the pastimes and festive doings prepared to celebrate the auspicious event, 'the admiral might rest assured,' he said, 'that he would not leave Paris before he had fully satisfied him.' The admiral, under a sort of infatuation, as it would seem, continued to place full confidence in Charles, a flattering mark of which he gave him in the surrender, some months before the time had expired, of the four strong cities assigned for two years to the Huguenots, as guarantees, on the signing of the Treaty of Saint-Germain.

Some festivity on the occasion of a royal marriage was certainly expected by the Court, if not by the more rigid Huguenots. The admiral accordingly reconciled himself to the delay of a few days of gaiety. In the interval Elizabeth might make up her mind. She had asked for the restitution of Calais as the price of her alliance; but Coligny resisted that demand. Flushing, he said, was more advantageous to her, and the suggestion was not unfavourably received.

The festivities prepared under the direction of the Duc d'Anjou in honour of his sister's marriage were of a kind that fully exemplify the excessive depravity of the Court of France under Catherine de' Medici and the last of the Valois kings. They were no less singular than revolting. Strange scenes of debauchery, masquerades, and divertissements which one shrinks from describing, and in which the Court 'squadron' of dissolute women figured prominently. 'In one of the allegorical divertissements, paradise and the infernal regions were represented, with a party of knights-errant defending the entry of the former against another party who, finally defeated, were drawn away by devils and cast into the flames of the latter place.' This was understood to be the fate reserved for the heretics at the hands of the faithful.

Charles IX., his brothers, and the Guises, the young King of Navarre, the Bourbon princes, and some of the younger Huguenot nobility, were the principal performers, together with 'the squadron,' in this saturnalia. The elder and more austere Reformers were both grieved and disgusted. It was well, perhaps, that poor Jeanne d'Albret was spared the pain of witnessing how easily her cherished son was led astray, as she feared he would be, in the midst of the gross seductions of the dissolute Court of France. The queen-mother observed him narrowly, and clearly perceived that he had inherited much of the weakness of his father's character. But that he had other qualities which in some measure counterbalanced that weakness, she apparently did not then suspect, as she for some time thought but contemptibly of her heretic son-in-law.

CHAPTER XXI.

Anjou a Candidate for the Crown of Poland.—The Kiss of Peace twice given.—Attack on the Admiral instigated by the Guises.—The King in a Rage when informed of it.—Charles visits the Admiral, but cannot free himself from his Mother's and Brother's Company.—The Admiral's Private Advice to Charles.—The Massacre arranged.—A Band of Demons.—Charles long withstands his Infamous Mother's Arguments.—' Par la Mort Dieu ! give your orders. Let them die ! Let none remain to reproach me.'

THE boisterous joyousness with which Charles had taken part in those strange festivities, though consistent with the fitful moods of his violent and impulsive character, was yet partly due to the hope he then had of being quickly freed from the hated presence of Anjou. Sigismund Augustus, King of Poland, had lately died, and Catherine, ever on the watch to secure a throne for her best beloved, despatched, on the 17th of August, Montluc, Bishop of Valence, to Cracow to support, conjointly with another of her secret agents, Gaspard de Schomberg, the candidature of the Duc d'Anjou; to secure whose election they were to be 'sparing neither of flattery, promises, nor bribes.'

The bishop had formerly favoured the cause of Reform when, like Catherine, he thought it likely to gain the upper hand in France. He had since returned to his allegiance to Rome—in outward seeming at least. He, however, still retained a certain interest in the success of 'the cause,' which induced him before setting out on his Polish mission to warn the Comte de la Rochefoucauld, and some other Huguenot gentlemen, that they would do well to return to their homes, or to seek refuge in their strong cities, for mischief was plotting, and great danger menacing them. Little attention was given to this warning, or to other secret intimations to be on their guard, for the admiral's confidence in the king acted as a check to any doubts his partizans might otherwise have entertained.

But the four days' saturnalia being ended, Catherine, to her intense consternation, perceived that the king's inclination towards Coligny was not only not abated, but that the private conferences concerning the war in Flanders were to be renewed. Her terrible anxiety was shared by Anjou, who saw that his brother's aversion to him was increasing daily. He relates that, 'on one occasion when he entered his apartment, so furiously was Charles pacing to and fro, and so fiercely did he glare on him, at the same time placing his hand on his dagger, that he quickly slipped out of the room while Charles's back was turned, fearing that he meant to kill him.'*

Further intrigue appeared to the queen-mother to be useless. She had not regained her influence by the weeping scene at the Château de Montpipeau, and of the disgrace of the admiral by any act emanating from the king, there was now apparently no hope. She would hesitate no longer to free herself from this hated rival; and the course suggested to her by Alva during the visit to Bayonne in 1564, in the remark that 'one salmon's head was worth more than the heads of twenty thousand frogs,' probably arose in her mind. During the eight years that had elapsed the same suggestion, in other words, had been often urged on her. Twice she had tried to put it into effect, and had failed. But just as the fortunes of the Huguenots during that interval had fluctuated between success and defeat, so had Alva's suggestion to deprive them of their leaders recurred to her, been rejected, and again recalled.

* 'Discours de Henri III.'—Mathieu's 'Histoire de France.'

It was now to be put into practice with a better chance of success ; for the victims were caged, and in former attempts they had first to be caught. But now, as before, though Catherine was to profit by the '*crimes utiles*' she incited or hired others to commit, she would not take on herself the responsibility and the odium of them. In this instance she determined to lay them on the shoulders of the Guises. The Duchesse de Nemours accordingly was secretly sent for by Catherine and Anjou. They knew that her hatred of Coligny was implacable ; that notwithstanding that the farce of reconciliation had twice taken place before the king, and the 'kiss of peace' twice given, her belief that the admiral had assassinated her former husband, and her desire for revenge, remained strong as ever.

With her usual calmness, Catherine told the duchess that she placed in her hands the vengeance she had so long and so earnestly desired. It was believed that she had a double motive in selecting the Guises to do this deed of blood for her. 'The Huguenots, she doubted not, would rise in arms to avenge the murder of their chief, and would attack the Guises even in their hôtel. The duke's partizans and the Catholic Parisian populace would hasten to defend him, and Huguenot and Politique in the heat of this savage conflict would slay each other. The former would be overpowered by numbers; the Lorrainers exhausted by their victory—the butchery ending in the massacre also of the Guises by the royal guards—leaving Catherine mistress of the field.'

Such was the sanguinary programme attributed to her and accepted as true by contemporary writers—De Thou and others.* But whether or not, events did not follow exactly in the order proposed or expected. The young Duc de Guise, in the prospect of vengeance, exhibited a sort of furious joy, a mad paroxysm of delight worthy of Charles IX. Under its influence he would have had his mother take up the arquebuse, and with her own hand, 'in, as he said, the very midst of the Court,' fire the shot intended to pierce the admiral's heart, and kill him on the spot. But she suggested less publicity, and that a surer hand than a woman's, though strengthened by revenge, should be employed to assassinate the assassin. Maurevert was then summoned—a man whose business it was to do such deeds for hire, and who shrank from no atrocity. He had already been

* De Thou was the director of the commission appointed by Charles IX. to inquire into the attack on Coligny, and to discover and punish its authors.

charged by the Court to take the admiral's life, failing which, with unusual brutality even for those bloodthirsty times, he had murdered one of his officers.

This wretch was put into a house belonging to the duchess, to watch from behind a curtain for the admiral, who was accustomed to pass that way on returning from the Louvre to his own residence. The assassin took his aim from the window, his practised hand rarely failing to strike a vital part. But the admiral happened to be reading as he slowly passed along, and the position of his hands prevented the shot taking the direction intended. The ball struck the forefinger of the right hand and entered the lower part of the left arm. Thus disabled, the admiral was assisted to his hôtel, whence he sent to inform the king of what had happened, that he might judge of the manner in which the Guises kept their promises of peace and amity.

Meanwhile, the admiral's people had forced the door of the house whence the attack proceeded. The arquebuse they found, but the arquebusier had fled. A swift horse from the stables of the Duc de Guise had been waiting for him at the back of the building. He was pursued; but having had considerably the start of his pursuers, and all trace of him being soon lost, the pursuit was given up.

Charles was playing at tennis with the Duc de Guise and the admiral's son-in-law, Teligny, when news of the attempted assassination reached him. He heard it at first with a sort of stupor; then, changing to violent anger, he dashed his racket on the ground with such force that it was broken, and exclaiming, 'Am I then never to know peace?' went hastily to his apartment, while Guise slunk off in silence. The King of Navarre and his cousin of Condé were quickly at Coligny's bedside. He was attended by the famous surgeon Ambroise Paré, who amputated his finger, and afterwards extracted the ball from his arm. 'With quietude and a little patience,' he told the princes, 'the admiral would do very well'—the ball not being poisoned, as at first supposed.

Believing that their lives were not safe in Paris, they sought the king's permission to leave the capital. He begged them not to stir, and with one of his customary oaths, emphasized by a violent blow on the table, swore that he would make such an example of the assassin and his accomplices that should not be soon forgotten in France. He then sent a detachment of his guards to protect Coligny's house, and seemed even more angry and more grieved than were the princes themselves. 'It is I who am wounded!' he continually exclaimed; to which Catherine, who never allowed him to be a minute alone, rejoined, 'It is all France!' artfully adding, 'Soon we shall have these desperadoes attacking the king in his bed.' A message from Coligny was soon after received, praying the king to come to him, as he had many things of importance to tell him. Charles at once complied, but could not escape from the companionship of his mother and brother.

Arrived at the admiral's bedside, the king was profuse in expressions of concern for the injuries he had received. 'To you, my father,' he said, 'the pain of the wounds—to me the insult and outrage.' Catherine affected to be greatly moved, and vehemently inveighed against the 'dastardly assassins.' But Coligny, as though on his deathbed, appealed to Heaven in witness of the sincerity of his attachment and fidelity to the king and the State. He blamed Charles for neglecting the great opportunity Providence had given him of extending his dominions, and protested against the treason of those persons who betrayed the secrets of the king's private council to the Duke of Alva. He then requested to speak to the king alone.

Charles signified to his mother, his brother, and the courtiers, his wish that they should withdraw. This was agony to Catherine and Anjou; but the former, though she could not prevent this secret conference, determined that it should be but of short duration. Affecting anxiety for Coligny, she rose, and approaching the king, said aloud that it was 'unkind and even dangerous to make M. l'Amiral talk so much. Such exertion might produce fever, which should be particularly guarded against.' The king hesitated, and glanced furiously at her and his brother; but Catherine did not flinch. She succeeded in leading him away.

On returning to the Louvre, the queen-mother and Anjou pressed the king to tell them what Coligny had said to him. At first he gave no reply to their repeated inquiries, but in an angry tone muttered his usual oaths. As they ceased not to torment him with questions, he at last burst forth: '*Par le sang Dieu!* what the admiral told me is true! You two,' he raved at them, 'have artfully drawn into your own hands all power, and the whole management of the affairs of State. Your power and your authority may some day become very prejudicial to me as well as to my kingdom. I should beware of it, he said, and keep a watchful eye on you! As you wish to know, that is what the admiral told me, as my faithful servant, which he is; for, *par le sang Dieu!* what he said is true!' Catherine and her son listened to Charles's words with so much consternation that Anjou says ('Discours de Henri III.') 'they were unable to decide that day what course it would be best to pursue, so put off its consideration until the morrow.'

The reports of the commission respecting the attack on the admiral greatly compromised the Guises. The king, in consequence, ordered the arrest of some members of their household, and threatened the duke himself, at the same time conferring many marks of his favour on the Protestants. In the afternoon the duke and his uncle D'Aumale sought an interview with the king to request permission to retire from the Court, as their presence there appeared to be no longer agreeable to his majesty. Charles replied abruptly, 'they might go wherever they pleased; but that he should be able to find them if it were proved that they had any hand in the attempt on the admiral.' But the Guises retired from the Court no further than their own hôtel.

The night of the 22nd passed off quietly. The Huguenots had taken some precautions against an attack, but on the following one they failed to do so, relying on the protection of the king's guards and the Swiss guards of the **King of Navarre.** Charles had desired the two Bourbon princes **to bring their** friends to the Louvre, where he also offered **to lodge** the Huguenot nobility in **the** suite of the admiral.

Meanwhile, the **Florentine Jezebel assembled** her trusty **counsellors** at the Tuileries—Birago, the Piedmontese chancellor ; **Gondi**, the Florentine, employed **by Catherine to** corrupt her **son ; the** Duc de Nevers, **of the** Mantuan family **Gonzaga ;** and the ferocious Tavannes, a Frenchman **and** marshal of France ; the **rest, Italian assassins.** Amongst them they arranged **the plan for** the massacre—to begin, of course, **with the admiral.** But Catherine dared not **strike Coligny unless the king was** implicated in **the act.** The council therefore **adjourned, to re-assemble at the Louvre,** in order to bring over the half-mad king to their views, **by working on his fears by false reports of the designs of Coligny and the principal Huguenots then in Paris.** 'It was she,' Catherine tells her son, 'who sought the admiral's life ; but it was that she might save his. She has begun the work ; it remains with him to finish it.'

'Surrounded **by this band of demons, of** whom the worst was his mother,' Charles (as stated by

Anjou) resisted their murderous arguments for more than an hour and a half. 'The Huguenots were arming,' the queen-mother told him, 'but not in his service; rather to deprive him of all authority and to obtain complete mastery over him. The loyal Catholics were determined to put an end to these traitorous projects, and, if the king was not on their side, to elect a captain-general, and under him to attack the pretended Reformers.' Charles scowled fiercely at his brother. He quite understood that he was the threatened captain-general, and Catherine well knew the exciting effect it would have on him. 'Paris is already under arms,' she said. The king, with a sudden start, inquired, 'How is that? I forbade them to arm in the *quartiers*.' 'But they are armed,' she replied curtly. 'One man only,' she continued, 'is the cause of all these troubles. He deceives the king, and, under the pretence of extending his dominions, urges on the State to its ruin. Let the king remember the conspiracy of Amboise; let him recall to mind Meaux, when he fled before his revolted subjects to Paris.' That long and rapid ride from Meaux to Paris in 1569, to escape falling into the hands of the Huguenot troops, was always a vexatious subject to touch upon with Charles.

'The Huguenots,' Catherine went on, ' will cry for vengeance on the Guises, who, to exonerate themselves, will denounce your mother and brother as the authors of the attack ; and if the king does not finish the work, both he and we are lost.' Charles, pacing the room in a frenzy, declared, with many oaths, that ' he would not have a hand laid on the admiral.' Then, sinking into gloom and despondency, he prayed his mother and her agents ' to find some other mode of ensuring safety. ' There was no other way,' they told him ; ' the death of the admiral and his chief captains alone could ensure it.' Strangely enough, the Comte de Retz (Gondi)—who had taken a principal part in the arrangement for the massacre— declared, to the great surprise of his associates in crime, that ' what was proposed was dishonourable both to the king and the nation, and would lead to a series of calamities of which neither they nor their children would see the end.'

' Too late !—too late !' was the vehement response. ' The Guises will denounce the king as well as his mother and brother, and war will be inevitable. Better far to gain a certain battle in the streets of Paris than to risk one in the open field.' De Retz made no reply, and Charles, reclining in a chair, exhausted and panting for breath (he was then suffering from incipient consumption), had given no heed to his governor's remarks. Had he noticed and supported them, he might have been saved from his fearful crime by the very man who had been specially engaged to work his moral ruin.

Catherine, however, had not spoken her last word. 'Sire,' she asked, 'do you refuse?' No answer. 'Grant me and your brother, then, permission to take leave of you—to depart.' Charles trembled with suppressed rage, but uttered no word. Again she spoke, 'Sire, is it fear of the Huguenots that makes you refuse?' Starting up in a fury, he exclaimed, ' *Par la mort Dieu!* since you are resolved that the admiral shall die, let it be so; but also every Huguenot in France, that none may remain to reproach me afterwards with his death. *Par la mort Dieu!* give your orders promptly;' and he rushed like a madman from the room.

All, then, were to be murdered. So Catherine and her assassins had already determined, the two young Bourbons excepted. They were to be spared, lest by their death the Guises should become too powerful.

CHAPTER XXII.

Arranging for the Success of the Massacre.—The Provost of Paris, Le Charron.—Catherine regardless even of her Daughter's Safety.—To the Guises the Honour of beginning the Massacre.—Alert before Dawn.—Guilty Consciences.—The Admiral's Death countermanded : Too late.—Already slain.—His Head sent to Catherine.—Charles like a Madman : 'Kill ! kill !' — Catherine and her 'Filles d'Honneur.'—Rejoicings in Rome and Madrid.—Bells, Bonfires, Te Deums and Cannon.—Medals, Pictures and Compliments.

IN the evening, Anjou and his mother were joined by the Ducs de Guise and D'Aumale, Tavannes and the rest, for the purpose of assigning the murderers their *quartiers*, and arranging for the full and successful execution of their plot. Le Charron, provost of the merchants and chief of the municipality of Paris, was sent for, and the king—who apparently had now reconciled himself to the commission of the crime which, as M. Henri Martin says, 'was to be his damnation in history'—gave him orders to have the city artillery ready that night to be moved to any part of the town that might be directed, and to station detachments of the militia, armed, in all the squares and open parts of the capital. When at last Le Charron comprehended what was required of him, he protested against it as horrible, and declared that his conscience forbade him to take part in such a crime. He was threatened with hanging, but was allowed to go his way. The orders he received he detained, so that the regular authorities of the Hôtel de Ville did not participate in the slaughter.

That Le Charron would not obey appears to have been expected, and measures were therefore taken to secure the aid of some less fastidious agent, to rouse as many 'good Catholics' as possible in those parts of the capital to which the municipal authority did not extend. They were to be informed that the king had resolved to exterminate, in Paris and throughout the kingdom, the seditious faction which had already taken up arms against him, and had now reassembled in Paris to organize a fresh conspiracy. The bell of the clock-tower of the Palais de Justice, at break of day, would give the signal for these 'good Catholics' to come forth and slay; each one having, as a sign of recognition, a white cross in his hat, that the faithful might not perchance be slain with the heretics. Towards midnight the king's regiment of guards, 1,200 strong, and a corps of Swiss Catholics were placed under arms, inside and around the Louvre, also round the admiral's hôtel, and in some parts of the neighbouring streets.

The Queen of Navarre, who has given so graphic a description of the occurrences in her apartment, and her participation in the dangers of that night of horrors, was unaware of what was about to take place. Solely intent on the success of her sanguinary plot, Catherine cared not to save her daughter from the probable vengeance of any Huguenot who might escape from the general slaughter. Some hints of the tragedy in preparation had been given to the Duchess of Lorraine, who therefore endeavoured that night to detain her sister in her own or the queen-mother's apartment. Catherine angrily forbade it. 'You are deliberately sacrificing her,' remonstrated the duchess. 'Whatever may happen,' replied this anxious mother, 'she must go, lest any suspicions should arise'—amongst the Bourbons, of course, and their friends in the Louvre.

To the Guises was accorded the gratifying honour of beginning the massacre at dawn of day, August the 24th, the festival of Saint-

Bartholomew. How great then their exultation, inspired by the fact that the first victim was to be the man in whose blood they had so long ardently yearned to slake their thirst for vengeance. In their eagerness to begin the carnival of murder, they were probably on the alert before dawn. For a few minutes before the first faint flush of day appeared in the east, those three great criminals, the king, his mother and brother, repaired to the upper part of the grand gate of the Louvre, thence to witness the beginning of the general slaughter, when, suddenly, the report of a pistol startled them. But for the stillness of the hour, and the deed of blood that had brought them there, it would have passed unnoticed. It now struck terror, as of a solemn warning, into the guilty consciences of those three associates in crime. Trembling with fear lest their plot was discovered, and dreading the consequences that might ensue from it to themselves, a messenger was instantly despatched in the king's name to the Duc de Guise, prohibiting him from making any hostile attack on the admiral. This order obeyed, would have put an end, it appears, to the whole of the sanguinary proceedings of that terrible day. But the messenger returned with the announcement that the order had arrived too late, and the queen and her sons, having recovered from their fright, 'resolved to let matters take their course.'*

Guise, with his uncle D'Aumale and the bastard of Angoulême—natural son of Henry II.—together with a whole band of assassins, led by a man named Bœsme, was already in the courtyard of the admiral's hôtel. At first the noise was attributed to some encounter between the Huguenots and Guise's partizans. But when the admiral became aware that it was an attack on him, 'he requested the Calvinist minister, who was with him, to say a prayer.' 'He had long been quite disposed to die,' he said, 'and now commended his soul to his Saviour.' Bœsme, at that moment, rushed into the room. The French guards closed round him. 'Are you the admiral?' asked Bœsme. 'I am, young man,' he replied. 'Do whatever you choose, for you have no power of yourself to make my life shorter than God has ordained.'

* 'Discours de Henri III.' This discourse, or recital, was dictated by the Duc d'Anjou, when King of Poland, to his principal physician, Miron, while suffering from sleeplessness and anxiety of mind occasioned by the vexation he felt at the affronts he met with from the German princes, who, because of the part he had played in the Saint-Bartholomew massacre, received him with extreme coldness on his journey to Cracow. It is generally regarded as authentic by French writers. It differs on several points from other narratives, which indeed one would expect it to do.

Muttering one of the horrid oaths of that period, Bœsme thrust his spear into the admiral's breast. The rest of the band then advanced, and also plunged their spears into him, aided in their murderous work by the guards, whom the king but two days before had placed there for the admiral's protection. He now fell at their feet covered with wounds.*

'Bœsme,' called the duke from the courtyard (he had not dared to face Coligny himself)— 'Bœsme, have not you finished?' 'The deed is done, and well done,' answered Bœsme. 'Then throw him out, that we may look at him.' Out of the window the dying man was instantly thrown. He fell on his face; but the vile bastard kicked him over, and wiped away the blood that hid his features, 'that he might recognise him,' he said. Guise, equally vile, also stooped and peered into his face, then spurned him with a kick. An Italian servant of the Guises cut off his head and sent it to the queen-mother, who ordered it to be embalmed and forwarded to the pope. (It was

---

* Some accounts relate that the admiral defended himself with his sword, and afterwards with the bed-clothes, which must be an error, as on the previous day he had undergone two operations which would prevent him from using his sword with either hand.

never known whether this present safely reached his holiness.) The populace, who with yells of frantic joy assisted at this scene of blood, took up the headless corpse and dragged it through the streets, finally hanging it by the feet on a gibbet at Montfaucon.

Teligny, the admiral's son-in-law, and some other Huguenot nobles and gentlemen, thinking to escape by the roof of the admiral's hôtel, were hunted down and shot by the king's guards, who also fired on the Swiss Protestant troops who escorted the King of Navarre. All those whom the king had lodged in the Louvre were surprised in their beds, and killed before they could, in their bewilderment, attempt defence. The streets were now full of infuriate people, who were told that the Huguenots had risen in the night and attacked the king in the Louvre; that they had killed several of his guards and refused quarter. To avenge this attack, as they fancied, cruelties the most barbarous were inflicted on the helpless and unoffending. Passionate rage, vengeance, frenzy, fanaticism, presided at the horrible scenes that at every step met the eye on that fatal day. Maddened by excitement the people rushed through the city, breathing only murder. Doors were forced in, houses pillaged, and the inhabitants killed—private hate availing itself of this opportunity of taking vengeance. The dead and the dying lay together in the streets; old men, women and children—some of them the victims of a barbarous zeal, others of the cupidity of those who slew only the more effectually to rob. The robberies on the 24th and following days produced a large sum in money, besides jewellery and plate; the king, it was asserted, not disdaining to take his share of the booty.

Catherine and Anjou continually drew the king to the window, that there might be no doubt of his approval of the massacre. He, indeed, seemed to glory in the butchery that was going on around him; to be jealous of being deprived of the merit of so magnanimous a deed. 'Kill! kill!' he cried as he leaned from the window, and raved that 'all was done by his order.' Yet sometimes he seemed stupefied by this excess of carnage; again he was furious, levelling his carbine at every Huguenot he recognised. But the range of this weapon appears to have been too limited, happily, to do much mischief.

The King of Navarre and Prince de Condé were, by his order, brought before him, with the gentlemen of their suite. The latter he presently disposed of. 'Send those scoundrels below!' he cried. No sooner had they left the room than the king's guards fell upon them, one or two only escaping with life. To the young princes he declared that, henceforth, he would tolerate in France no religion but his own, offering them the choice of '*Messe, mort, ou la Bastille.*' Henry of Navarre prayed the king 'not to force his conscience.' The Prince de Condé rejected the Mass, but left death or the Bastille to the king's decision. Charles, however, gave them three days to consider the matter; but with the threat of death hanging over them should they refuse to abjure.

Although the greater part of the leaders and the chief men of the Huguenot cause were slain, yet a remnant escaped the ' net of death,' and lived for vengeance. They were those who either had not accepted the ' king's proffered hospitality,' or, for want of room at the admiral's hôtel, were lodged on the opposite bank of the river, in the Faubourg Saint-Germain-les-Prés. Awakened by the strange uproar and confusion of sounds that burst forth in Paris on the signal for the massacre being given— the howls, the yells, and hootings of the frenzied mob, mingled with the frequent reports of the arquebuse and pistol—they imagined that some serious riot had occurred, probably between Huguenot and Catholic. Hastily assembling, to aid, if needed, their own and the king's party, they proposed to cross the river, but found all the boats removed. Two or three bleeding corpses floated by them, and descending the Seine were several boats filled with the king's guards and led by Guise and his party, who fired on them as they advanced.

Comprehending from these acts and previous warnings that serious danger threatened them, they mounted their horses and fled. Guise and other massacrers prepared to follow ; but the precautions taken to enclose in their net as many victims as possible, served others to effect their escape. The city gates had been locked, and for the Porte de Bussy, opening on the faubourg, the wrong keys were sent to Guise, causing a delay, which, though every exertion was used, rendered his and 'the bastard's' pursuit useless. Charles, from the window of his apartment, was a witness of this scene. Stamping with rage and uttering a series of curses and horrible oaths, he cried in accents of agony, ' *Ah ! mort Dieu !* they fly, they escape !' But a scene then passing under his eyes in the front of the Louvre just below him, must have soothed him in his then insane state of mind. Hundreds of his subjects who could not escape their doom—bleeding corpses of whom it was necessary to clear the streets—were being thrown into the Seine, leaving, as the stream carried them away, long streaks of blood behind them.*

On the morning of the 25th, Catherine and her 'maids of honour,' with the courtiers in attendance, went down to the entrance of the Louvre to examine the pile of dead and yet bleeding bodies, raised up as a trophy before the grand portail. 'The maids,' with their dishevelled hair and scanty attire, as they jested and gibed, and laughed at the revolting jokes of the queen-mother and courtiers, on the nakedness of some of the bodies and the clothing of others, seemed to represent the Furies, or Bacchanals drunk with the vapour of blood, instead of the juice of the grape.

The number of victims on the 24th and two following days in Paris has been variously estimated from two thousand to four or five thousand, and with the slaughter in the several provinces from twenty to thirty thousand. The anniversary of the Saint-Bartholomew was ordered by Charles to be 'celebrated in perpetuity by a procession in Paris, and thanksgiving to God for saving the king and the State.' A 'jubilee extraordinary' took place on the 28th, at which Charles would have had the King of Navarre and Prince de Condé

* Brantôme says, 'Charles y prit grand plaisir.'

attend. But neither by persuasion nor menaces could he prevail on them to appear, or to follow afterwards in the procession. On the same day the king's declaration was issued, professing 'to make known the real cause and occasion of the death of the admiral and his accomplices.'

A few days after, the chief officer of the Mint presented the king with two medals 'commemorative of his victory.' On one Charles was represented seated on his throne; beneath his feet was a heap of dead bodies. In one hand he bore the sceptre, in the other a sword and the palm of victory. The legend was *Virtus in rebelles*. On the reverse, laurel and olive branches surrounded the arms of France, with the device chosen for the king on his accession by De L'Hôpital, but accommodated to the occasion, *Pietas excitavit Justitiam*, instead of *Pietate et Justitiâ*. The other medal bore the king's effigy, with the legend in French, '*Charles IX., dompteur des rebelles*,' 24th August, 1572.

But while the massacre of the Huguenots was still going on in the provinces, and even in Paris, where it was found more difficult to stop it than Catherine expected, the news of that unparalleled crime spread through Europe. In the Protestant States it was received with one general cry of

horror. The humane and tolerant Emperor
Maximilian II. is said to have wept bitterly on
hearing of the savage brutality of his son-in-law
Italy and Spain, on the contrary, burst forth into
songs of joy and gladness, and the 'Demon of the
South' 'laughed for the first time in his life.' No
expressions could he find sufficiently strong, ardent,
and full of meaning, to convey to his 'most
Christian majesty' his profound admiration of so
holy a deed. The conduct of the queen-mother
also excited his high approval ; nor did he exclude
Anjou and the Guises from their share in his
commendations, but pronounced their efforts in
the service of God and the Church most praiseworthy. He then bade them all 'continue in
well-doing,' offering his aid to Catherine and her
son for the completion of their great work. He
feigned, too, to believe all that Catherine told
him of the king's pretended hostility to Spain in
order to more effectually deceive the Huguenots.

As regarded Rome, not even 'Saint-Pius' himself
could have displayed more enthusiasm than did
Gregory XIII. on receiving intelligence of this
deed of blood. Every street in Rome was ablaze
with bonfires ; bells rang out joyously ; the cannon
of Saint-Angelo thundered forth in the face of
heaven the infamous act that was called ' the good

news.' Gregory and his cardinals, with the ambassadors and a swarm of priests, went in procession from church to church, concluding with a Mass of thanksgiving to God for the double victory of the Church, over the Turks at Lepanto and the heretics in Paris. The Cardinal de Lorraine was beside himself with joy. As well may be imagined from the fact that in his enthusiasm, he—who so loved to put money in his purse, but so disliked to take any out of it—actually gave a thousand crowns to the messenger who brought him the news of that ' glorious work ' in which his nephew and brother had so greatly distinguished themselves. He overwhelmed the king, queen-mother, and Anjou with congratulatory compliments. ' They had achieved on that great day of extermination more than he had ever dared hope to see, or even pray for.'

' May it please Heaven to send the Poles a truly Catholic king,' prayed Gregory, ' for they are a nation proud and haughty rather than submissive.' This was a message for Anjou. Further, in celebration of the great event, the pontiff ordered of the painter Vasari that horrible picture of the massacre of the Huguenots, for the adornment of the Vatican, and from the inscription —*Pontifex Colignii necem probat*—one must infer for his own glorification also. A medal, too, was struck, having on one side the effigy of Gregory XIII. ; on the other, the exterminating angel slaying the Huguenots, and around it *Hugonotorum strages*. Venice was not behindhand in congratulatory addresses and the pope sent a legate expressly to offer his felicitations to the Court ; also to suggest the establishment in Paris, at this favourable moment, of the holy Inquisition, and to propose a marriage between the Duc d'Anjou and an infanta of Spain.

But the king and queen-mother began to be much embarrassed by these extravagant compliments and felicitations, and, in order to avoid receiving the congratulations of the legate, absented themselves from Paris on his arrival. So cold and distrustful was the attitude of the rest of Europe towards them, that they were compelled to request their admiring friends to be more moderate in their praises, and less demonstrative in their enthusiasm, as they were desirous of assigning to the events of 'that great day' a political rather than a religious motive.

END OF VOL. I.

www.ingramcontent.com/pod-product-compliance
Lightning Source LLC
Chambersburg PA
CBHW022108290426
44112CB00008B/595